Phyllis Horton
68 Lloydminster Cr.
Willowdale

221-8242

# A Splendid Harvest

# A Splendid Harvest

## Germanic Folk and Decorative Arts in Canada

### MICHAEL BIRD & TERRY KOBAYASHI

VAN NOSTRAND REINHOLD LTD., TORONTO
New York, Cincinnati, London, Melbourne

Published simultaneously in the United States of America by Van
Nostrand Reinhold Company, New York.

Library of Congress Catalogue Number 80-50576

Canadian Cataloguing in Publication Data
Bird, Michael S., 1941-
A splendid harvest
ISBN 0-442-29620-7
1. Art, German — Canada. 2. Art, Decorative — Canada. 3. Folk art
— Canada. 4. German Canadians.* I. Kobayashi, Teruko, 1939-
II. Title.

NK841.B57      745'.0971      C81-094631-9

Design: Howard Pain
Editorial Consultant: James T. Wills
Jacket Photograph: Peter Paterson
Typesetting: Fleet Typographers Limited
Printed and bound in Canada by The Bryant Press Limited
81 82 83 84 85 86 87 7 6 5 4 3 2 1

# Contents

*To Leslie, Tacey, Tom and Kristen*

# Foreword

The fascinating volume you are about to examine gathers together evidence of the decorative objects produced by the Germanic settlers who arrived in Canada from its earliest days until this century. These settlers included healthy segments of Pennsylvania Germans (or Pennsylvania Dutch as they are sometimes called), of Continental Germans and of Russian-German Mennonites and Hutterites. Before they found their way to Canada, each of these groups had continued to practise traditional Germanic arts in both their first and second *Heimat* or homeland. In Canada, whether in the Maritimes, Ontario or the western provinces, these arts continued to a surprisingly strong degree.

A thread of commonality is visible throughout all of the folk-art examples found in this book. It betrays origins in the striving of peasant and small craftsman levels of society for a sense of identity in the Germanic lands of central Europe from the end of the Thirty Years' War to the onset of industrialization. Once the dust of the Thirty Years' War had begun to settle, people in the small villages of Germany — then, as now, more a cultural than a political unity — began to dream of the good life as exemplified in the monied classes of the society around them. The townsmen, especially those who practised a craft, began to have the capital for luxuries, and bit by bit the tastes of the elite filtered down to the countryman and were copied and adapted by him.

The range of objects called folk art and the decorations upon them do not represent ancient motifs, quietly passed from generations of antiquity to modern man, as they have sometimes been represented. Rather, they are the things and designs that were once the mode among the taste-setters of the world and were then aped by the poorer classes. The silver beaker of one man became the pewter or redware beaker of the next. Such exchanges among levels of society became less personalized, perhaps, once mass production filled the homes of the urban men industrialization created, but they are still obvious, even today.

The relative cultural isolation of various Germanic groups allowed them to continue to produce objects with the decorative styles current a century or more earlier. The Germans in Pennsylvania, Russia and later in Canada were cut off from the parent culture, and they are good examples of how *retardataire* designs survive. The textiles produced by all these groups demonstrate this point.

At the same time, of course, isolation from the parent culture meant fraternization with a new host. The isolation that language imposes does not necessarily restrict the range of what the eye can see. In spite of the relatively closed nature of German communities in Canada, there is evidence before you that copying went on in the new environment. The clearest example of this phenomenon may well be Pennsylvania-German folk architecture in Canada. The ancient three-room floor plan had originally developed around a central hearth that heated all the rooms. The basic plan survived in Canada, but the central hearth did not. As in England, fireplaces at each gable heated the house.

There may be a subtle message in the folk designs shown in this volume. Most of Canada's Germans were Protestants, some of them from the far-left wing of the Reformation churches, and therefore iconoclastic in the extreme. Even today, Old Order Mennonite meeting houses and cemeteries are totally bare of Christian symbolism. There is not even a cross to be seen. Can we expect, as a result, to find meanings of a religious nature in the objects these people decorated? Perhaps — perhaps, in fact, even more than the producers realized. Crowns often appear on Germanic show towels, possibly because a favourite text of these people was from the Revelation of St. John, "Be faithful unto death and I will give you the crown of life." A motif frequently occurs made up of the initials OEHBDDE or OEDHBDDE: *O edel Herz bedenk dein End* (O noble heart, ponder thy demise). At the centre of the motif is a heart. But did the girl who stitched such a towel in Waterloo County in the last quarter of the nineteenth century necessarily know the meaning of the initials and their relationship to the design? Was she merely copying what she had seen?

A book such as this must be a springboard to continued study in Canada, the United States and Europe. Every facet of human experience merits the examination of each generation's scholars. The text and illustrations here for you to see will have achieved a grand purpose if, through the study of them, men and women long dead still speak of their values, of their labours, or of their dreams. The yearnings of peoples all about the globe today may be more understandable if we recognize them as nothing new.

Pastor Frederick S. Weiser
Editor
Pennsylvania German Society
Saint Paul's Church
Biglerville, Pennsylvania

# Preface

We are privileged to have the opportunity to share a story of people in the act of creating things of beauty. On the one hand, much effort has been expended in gathering impersonal information — dates, statistics, names, events, geographic backgrounds, materials, and artifacts — but on the other we recognize that all of this is important only insofar as it pertains to people transforming their environment. Alongside an accumulation of factual information are the many tales, recollections and accounts which taken together comprise a totality, in effect, a story. This totality is distinctively Canadian, revealing the full range of experiences from tragic to joyful, serious to humorous, predictable to surprising.

The precise beginning of our involvement in this project is somewhat difficult to isolate. In part it grows directly out of earlier studies on woodcarving and *Fraktur* (manuscript illumination) — two aspects of the Pennsylvania-German folk-art tradition in Canada. But it also represents a significant shift in interest toward a broader field which incorporates not only Pennsylvania Germans but also Continental Germans, not only Ontario, but also the Maritime and Prairie Provinces, not only Mennonites but also Lutherans, Roman Catholics, Amish, Hutterites and others among that great diversity of Germanic settlers who came to Canada in search of new opportunity.

Several specific events in recent years greatly intensified our own interest in the subject of Germanic folk and decorative arts in Canada. One of these events was the 1977 publication of Charles van Ravenswaay's *The Arts and Architecture of German Settlements in Missouri.* The other was an invitation by the Heritage

Center of Lancaster County, Pennsylvania, to serve as co-curators, along with Patricia Herr, of a half-year exhibition entitled "Pennsylvania-German Parallels: Decorative Arts of Lancaster and Ontario." Many interested persons travelled from Waterloo County and other parts of Ontario to Pennsylvania in order to view the first comparative display of Pennsylvania and Ontario-German furniture, *Fraktur,* woodcarving, pottery, textiles, ironwork and other artifacts. The enthusiastic response to this exhibition and inquiries about further studies were a much appreciated stimulus for A *Splendid Harvest.*

It would be nearly impossible to outline adequately the full number of unexpectedly delightful events along the road toward completion of this project. It always seemed that when one detail was finished, another lay just around the corner. Friends have frequently remarked that trips for interviewing, recording and photographing seem to be peculiar ways to spend evenings, weekends and holidays. The countless hours spent in archives or in the darkroom provided excellent opportunity for weeds to achieve record heights in the garden, untended as it was for long periods of time. There were vicissitudes, to be certain — dropped cameras, missed dinners, car stuck in muddy ruts — but such frustrations were overwhelmed by the stimulating times — interviewing the Mayor of Lunenburg, alternating visits with South Shore fishermen with eating lobster obtained at Risser's Beach, being surrounded by thirty young, curious Hutterite girls during a photographing session in Manitoba, invitations to stay for dinner at countless farm homes in Ontario, crouching on the ground during driving rainstorms to photograph gravemarkers, risking notorious Buffalo blizzards on repeated trips to Pennsylvania.

We cannot overlook the important role played in the study of artifacts by the first-hand tours of major collections, restorations and research facilities in the United States and in Canada. Among these were the Henry Ford Museum and Dearborn Village, the Pennsylvania-German Farm Museum of Landis Valley, the Ephrata Cloisters, the Schwenkfelder Historical Library, the Free Library of Philadelphia, the various county historical societies, the Heritage Center of Lancaster County and other institutions. Perhaps the most important and memorable experience was our four-day stay at the Henry Francis du Pont Winterthur Museum, where we were given every access to its files and superb collection, and the extensive personal assistance of Mary Hammond Sullivan. It was on this same trip that we had the happy experience of being house guests of Pastor Frederick S. Weiser in Hanover, Pennsylvania. He and Larry Neff provided us with sumptuous banquets of Pennsylvania-German food, a dramatic and blessed change from the pizzas on which we had been surviving previously.

The happy memories of persons who have become not so much purveyors of information as extenders of friendship could provide the basis for a book. But that story will have to be told at another time and place. For the present, our story concerns the artisans and artifacts that are at the centre of a decorative tradition which is rich in continuity and stunning in diversity.

# Introduction

My boyhood trips to the farmers' market in Kitchener were such remarkable events that they have been remembered for a lifetime. They were my personal introduction to German pioneer roots in Canada and became the stimulus for an interest in Germanic culture that spread to similar communities in many parts of the country. These occasional shopping expeditions during the 1920s had a flavour of visits to some distant land, for there one mixed with people who had an aura of something "different" about them; their ways suggested the romance of the unknown.

The wares of these Germanic farmers were displayed in a drafty old building, where crowds passed slowly up and down to inspect tables laden with produce. Much in these displays was strange to a native of one of the country's older Scottish communities, who lived only a few miles away. The whole interior of the market was filled with the spicy smell from a variety of herbs. There was the smell of garlic sausage and salami and the equally pervasive, but more pungent smell of sauerkraut, a food then unknown in many Canadian kitchens. Vegetables piled high on the tables were crisp and fresh. One saw jars of apple butter, loaves of rye with caraway and a variety of prepared foods.

The real fascination for me was in mixing with the local German farm people who stood waiting for customers. Mennonite women were dressed in conservative garb of sombre grays and blacks as they placidly tended their stalls. About them was such a quiet shyness that it seemed immodestly rude to stare at their dress and faces. But when one dared to steal a glance, it was possible to read there a combination of gentle ways complemented by great strength of character; this firmness was echoed in the solidity of their menfolk. They were a people to be remembered.

It was the earnest task of the authors of A Splendid Harvest to document the life patterns of these and other peoples in similar German-Canadian communities before the past becomes too remote and old traditions cease to be remembered. Their searches have laid before us a tale of humble riches which probes behind the superficiality of contacts in the marketplace. In this humanist study, these Germanic pioneers and their descendants emerge as a people seeking freedom and toleration. Some pioneer immigrants, notably Mennonite, Amish and Hutterites who sought to practise their religious beliefs on strictly pacifist principles, showed profound honesty in their simplicity and demonstrated a deep respect for their fellow men.

The lives of these settlers were austere, as reflected in the articles of daily use they fashioned with an eye for practicality. Yet, in the very frugality of these objects is an almost imperceptible but very real overtone of quiet beauty, whether in furniture fashioned for the home, weaving, painted inscriptions or embroidery. One senses the pleasure to the eye on many sides. It strikes most forcibly in the brilliant colours and strange harmonies of *Fraktur* paintings, where flowers and birds combine with medieval Gothic inscriptions. This same beauty manifests itself more subtly in the gentle curves or quietly rich glazes of jugs and bowls thrown on local potters' wheels. The same mood pervades both weavers' patterns or utilitarian articles decorated with tulips, flowers known to these people centuries before their ancestors came to America.

Varied and rich truths are contained in this book. On

the one hand is a toughness of moral and physical fibre in men and women who carved their homes out of rough wilderness. But this toughness is delicately balanced by the contentment in the melodious touches and sparkling accents of colour with which they have overlaid their surroundings. It is as if the numbing drudgery of endless toil, from ploughing the first furrows in the newly felled forest, to gathering the first harvest, were compensated for by the decorative, non-utilitarian aspect of their lives that speaks to the soul. These objects portray a satisfying expression of beauty and simple pleasure which cancels bodily fatigue — a major component in a rationally ordered existence.

Respect for elders and forefathers is a long-standing tradition in German communities which has characterized them since the first newcomers arrived in Nova Scotia during the eighteenth century. It is found equally among the settlers who reached the Canadian Prairies within the past century, after wanderings had already taken them to Prussia and the Ukraine in search of an environment attuned to their needs and beliefs.

Both as a reminder of the past and as a token of their origins, furniture was painted in yellows, greens, browns and oranges, perhaps with an overlay of decoration, all in the distinctive Germanic tradition which is so different from that of their neighbours. In the same way, a Lutheran church was erected in Williamsburg Township, eastern Ontario, in 1784. On its spire the congregation erected a weathervane fashioned in the shape of a swan, symbolizing Luther, the Swan-Knight, who had been the adopted patron of their home town in Germany. This kind of respect for origins pervades *A Splendid Harvest.* It portrays the little-known history, humble foundations, quiet simplicity and unhurried continuity of Germanic tradition in rural Canada.

J. Russell Harper
South Lancaster, Ontario

# 1 A Germanic Plenitude

For some years the history of Canada's fine and decorative arts has been conveniently divided between the English and the French. No one would argue that these are the dominant influences, but we should not overlook the very real fact that the Germans who originally came from the Continent and Pennsylvania form Canada's third largest cultural group. Over nearly two centuries these Germanic settlers have contributed an impressive and important body of folk art. It has been overlooked too often and too long.

Canada's Germanic folk art was produced by trained and untrained craftsmen, by teachers and pupils, men and women. This book is their document. It seeks to draw attention to the small but always spontaneous expressions of beauty that grow out of a strong sense of community, spiritual harmony and historical place.

Folk-art motifs common to many ethnic European groups are shared by the Germanic peoples. The heart, tulip, pointed star, compass star, whorl, swastika, birds and geometric designs embellish almost every conceivable object, whether registered by knife, pen, brush or chisel. The appeal of this decorative work is not the element of innovation, but rather that of convention. This kind of art attains individuality not so much from a conscious effort toward self-expression, but from the varied perceptions and naïvete of people attempting to emulate things already familiar to them.

Germanic decorative arts are at times boisterous, at times subtly refined. The material legacy of Canada's Germanic settlements provides a colourful, even fanciful vision of the world, a vision no less evident in pioneer circumstances than in more prosperous periods. The objects these settlers adorned, whether joyous cradle or austere gravemarker, whether imposing architecture or lowly gamesboard, reveal the basic truth that the difference between mere survival and purposeful existence is the phenomenon of creativity. To create enjoyment through pattern, shape and colour is to actualize the inherent desire to decorate, to complete, to perfect. This, in the end, becomes a type of aesthetic fulfilment.

One of the joys of delving into Canada's multicultural past is the realization of possibilities not easily understood in an earlier age. The idea that the Germans of Canada (or any other non-English group for that matter) had a strong tradition of artistic excellence and competent craftsmanship was not immediately evident to early observers. Lord Durham, Governor General and High Commissioner of British North America in 1838, once said that the French in Canada had no language or culture worth preserving.[1] How much less appreciation would he have been able to muster for the German settlers scattered in insignificant communities isolated from the emerging cities of a young Canada?

Two views, one from Nova Scotia and a later one from Canada West, give some insight into early perceptions. In 1795, Reverend James Munro of Antigonish characterized German settlers at Lunenburg in this way:

> They in common seem to be a heavy sort of people or phlegmatic. Have not that liveliness as some others; nor do I think that they have so strong passions, or capable either of sensation of Mind whether pleasant or painful as some other people are.[2]

The assessment of Ontario's German settlers was perhaps still harsher. In a letter dated 1844 Bishop Strachan, the first bishop of Toronto, voiced his concern about an animal-like coarseness that extended even to their spiritual leaders:

> They seem to prefer Lutheran preachers from the States who appear as rude and uncultured as themselves.[3]

On the basis of these characterizations, it might seem surprising that from the ranks of German-Canadians there arose such distinguished figures as the printer, Anthon Henrich (1734-1800); the painter, Cornelius Krieghoff (1815-1872); the many-talented pioneer William von Moll Berczy (1744-1813); and such later individuals as the businessman and parliamentarian, Adam Beck (1857-1925); the statesman, William Hespeler; the piano manufacturer, Theodor August Heintzman (1817-1899); and the choirmaster and founder of the Mendelssohn Choir, Augustus Vogt.

However, this book does not deal with such widely acclaimed public figures. Here the concern is for the many craftsmen and artists who have for the most part been recognized only within the communities in which they worked. In most cases, these individuals practised their crafts on a part-time basis. They were farmers first, weavers second, or housewives and mothers first, quilters second.

There were "professionals," of course, who made products for the local market, but these cabinetmakers, potters and weavers normally pursued their trades during the winter months when the demands of farming were least heavy. Those who can be called "amateurs" made things for domestic use or enjoyment, quilting, whittling or embroidering in time left over from the day's work. Fraktur artists fall into both categories. There were professional scriveners who were often schoolmasters supplementing slim salaries by illuminating Bibles or handlettering family registers for a fee. Other Fraktur artists were persons who had more than average graphic skill and made their pieces for enjoyment or as gifts for family, friends or visitors. Taken together, all of these people probably would have been embarrassed at the title "craftsman" or "artist" and much surprised that their works would one day become the subject of articles and books.

A compelling motive for writing books such as this one is the hope that it will draw attention to the distinctive quality of Canadian folk art in an international context. A great deal of literature has focussed on the art and culture of Pennsylvania Germans in the United States, but it is only recently that serious thought has been given to the idea that Germanic Canada might have developed a decorative tradition worthy of the attention of artists, collectors, historians and cultural analysts.

Long ago, at least some individuals were aware of the quality of Canadian folk art. This is evident in the many sad accounts of Germanic artifacts being sent off from Nova Scotia and Ontario to be sold in the United States as "Pennsylvania German." To grasp the point, it is worth considering the 1930 American book on hooked rugs by William Winthrop Kent. In this detailed study, the author includes one revealing chapter entitled "A Hunt for Rugs in Canada." The introductory paragraph may shock those who have believed that the sale of Canadian artifacts in the United States was a modest activity involving few objects. Kent observes:

> The hunting of the rug is going on daily. Literally thousands of attics and farmhouses have been searched each year in New England and Canada and the supply in many places has given out. Nova Scotia, New Brunswick, Prince Edward Island and even Labrador have sold most of their early ones.[4]

Kent's report deals with the Maritime Provinces in relation to New England decorative arts, but an identical situation also existed between Ontario and Pennsylvania. It is well known that many pieces of Waterloo County and Niagara Peninsula furniture have been sold over the years into the American market, their origins usually obscured by silence or even alteration. During travels in Pennsylvania, we have come upon Fraktur, show towels and woodcarvings from Waterloo County. There are several hooked rugs by Maria Warning of Perth County, Ontario, in American collections, for example, in addition to pottery and other articles.

The intensity of interest in Ontario-German folk art among Pennsylvania collectors is evident in a 1944 comment by Earl Robacker. Speaking of the availability of hooked rugs in Canada, he reveals:

> Canada has also been a fruitful source of supply, and tourists have been able to purchase good rugs quite reasonably.[5]

A contemporary chapter in the story of the dispersion of Canadian artifacts concerns a situation we encountered while doing research in Manitoba. For several years much Manitoba-Mennonite furniture has been funnelled from around Winkler to collectors in the Minneapolis-Saint-Paul and Chicago areas of the American Midwest. In the summer of 1979, we saw a superb Manitoba primitive bench with an eagle incised on its backboard. Sadly, it had been sold to an American dealer and was awaiting shipment to North Dakota. In conversation with knowledgeable dealers, it was further learned that an important decorated cupboard had also been sold to a dealer and then to collectors in Minnesota.

This continual loss of indigenous artifacts makes it difficult to record decorative and folk-art expression in Canada. The problem is compounded by a general disbelief in the idea that a fully developed craft tradition could have evolved north of the border. For many years there has been a tendency to assume that superior examples of furniture, pottery, *Fraktur* and other artifacts found in Ontario-German households had been brought along from Pennsylvania. The eminent Canadian historian, G. Elmore Reaman, illustrates this point in a 1957 comment:

> Examples of 'Fraktur,' or pen-and-brush illumination of Gothic letters, are to be found in birth and marriage certificates, but it is difficult to know whether they were made in Upper Canada or Pennsylvania. One is inclined to think that in most cases they were made in the latter country.[6]

The overcoming of this bias has been a slow process, but it has been greatly aided by the gradual unearthing of evidence and the documenting of pieces of known provenance produced in the Germanic settlements of the Maritimes, Ontario and the western provinces.

The history of the Germans in Canada begins in the late seventeenth century. In 1664, the earliest known German settler, Hans Bernhardt from the Mosel Valley, purchased two "arpents" of land near Quebec City.[7] But even though Bernhardt was followed in the waning years of the century by numerous German soldiers who found their way into the army of New France, no actual community existed until the arrival of German immigrants at Halifax in 1750 and the establishment of a settlement at Lunenburg in 1753. The Germans in Ontario, on the other hand, first arrived in the 1780s, originating in Pennsylvania and Continental Europe. In the western provinces, Germanic pioneers took up lands toward the end of the nineteenth century. These settlers were largely Mennonites and Hutterites.

The decorative and folk-art traditions of the Lunenburg- and the Ontario-Germans occasionally exhibit strong similarities; at other times there are striking differences. Although prairie settlements were relatively late in comparison, their inhabitants also retained some of the customs visible in the folk-art vocabularies of these earlier groups. Mass production eventually replaced hand work in all these areas, but the persistence of tradition is still evident today. Hutterite girls in Manitoba continued to cross-stitch samplers in the conventional manner, but by the late nineteenth century they were using commercial linen towelling obtained from mail-order catalogues. In Ontario's Old Order Mennonite homes it is not uncommon to find a modern refrigerator and stove sponge-painted or even grained in the manner of furniture decorated more than a century ago.

*A Splendid Harvest* centres on the artifacts themselves, and as such is a kind of "material history" of Canada's Germanic pioneers. But it is also possible at times to catch fleeting glimpses of the lives of the craftsmen who made them. Documenting makers' names is a difficult task which is impossible without the cooperation of descendants, owners, dealers, collectors and historians. All of us should be grateful for their willingness to share their knowledge. From such diverse sources as documents, wills, letters, diaries, church records, photographs, deeds and verbal information have come a surprising number and variety of human insights.

Often, these insights fall into illuminating or even humorous categories. In the will of the cabinetmaker Samuel Bowers (died April 17, 1855) is the peculiar turn of phrase: "I give and bequeath to my beloved wife my whole household and kitchen furniture, my buggy and harness, one cow and two pigs, to have and to hold...."[8] Religious divisions sometimes figured in the division of property. When, for example, the Berlin chair-maker Jacob Hailer drew up his will (he died March 6, 1882), he stipulated that, "Another sixth portion thereof I bequeath to my daughter Caroline provided she do not marry a Roman Catholic husband...."[9]

The careers of some craftsmen were occasionally unplanned, as in the story of *Fraktur* artist Christian L. Hoover (1835-1918). According to descendants, virtually all his work was accomplished during a one-year confinement due to serious illness. Still other careers began late in life. Not until after a crippling stroke did David B. Horst (1873-1965) become a productive woodcarver. He created beautifully carved and painted animals for relatives, friends and visitors.

Some artifacts were made to mark special occasions.

When each of his four daughters married, the immigrant cabinetmaker John Gemeinhardt (1826-1912) presented the bride with a specially made piece of furniture. The styles of some of these pieces were more than a half-century out of date.

The distribution of articles among family members occasionally became a "problem for Solomon." The embroidered hand towel made by Barbara Horst during the winter of 1864 was much admired by each of three grandchildren. The only solution found was to cut it into three sections. They survive today as individually framed samplers.

Not every craftsman could sustain himself at one profession or within the confines of the local community. Some *Fraktur* artists were itinerant, travelling from community to community performing their work at modest rates for whatever customers could be found. Some, like Joseph Lochbaum, trekked far and wide across Upper Canada, Pennsylvania and Maryland.

Whether amusing or informative, these episodes and observations reveal a fascinating interplay between objects and their makers. The artifacts themselves are vigorous and creative expressions of a vitality somehow missed by James Munro and Bishop Strachan. Far from being "a heavy sort of people" who were "rude and uncultured," Germanic pioneers from Nova Scotia to Alberta have left us a legacy of excellence, joy in creation and respect for tradition.

# 2 Nova Scotia and the East

The historical beginnings of Germanic settlement in Nova Scotia were marked by the political and economic considerations expressed by the young British governor of the colony, Colonel Edward Cornwallis. Inspired in part by knowledge of the successful settling of Pennsylvania by Germans, as well as by the programme initiated the previous year to bring Palatines to New York State, on July 24, 1749 he requested that an effort be made to recruit "foreign Protestants" from Switzerland and Germany to settle Nova Scotia. A large block of reliable settlers under the English flag would mean political ascendancy for the British in the struggle between the English and the French to gain absolute control of the region.

Cornwallis knew that potential European settlers could be induced to leave difficult conditions at home and start anew in the North American wilderness. He was supported by the English Board of Trade, which contracted the merchant John Dick to provide transportation for prospective settlers.[1] Given the English-French conflict, there were also religious factors to be considered. These were indicated in correspondence between the governor and the Lords of Trade: "A proposal was sent me when at Spithead which might perhaps answer the purpose to make known through Germany that all husbandmen, tradesmen or soldiers *being Protestants* should have the same rights and privileges in this province as were promised on His Majesty's Proclamation to his natural born subjects. . . . "[2]

The earliest recorded arrivals of German immigrants at the port of Halifax occurred on August 24 and September 2, 1750. On the first date, the ship *Alderney* docked with some Germans among its 353 passengers, while on the second, more than 300 "Germans" disembarked from the ship *Ann*.[3] Shiplists in the Public Archives of Nova Scotia indicate that these "foreign Protestants" originated in the central and south German states of the Palatinate, the Duchy of Württemberg, the Landgravates of Hesse (particularly Hesse-Darmstadt and Hesse-Kassel) and several small states just north of the River Main. Still other settlers came from Switzerland, and one sizable group migrated from Montbéliard. This region had escaped the French annexation of the nearby states of Alsace and Lorraine, because it was situated between Switzerland and France. Montbéliard, "French in language, but Protestant in religion,"[4] provided the South Shore of Nova Scotia with many of its first settlers.

Shortly after their arrival in Halifax, many of these immigrant Europeans were re-established about sixty miles down the coast near present-day Lunenburg. The origin of the name of the town has been a matter of some dispute. Earlier writers frequently suggested that it was named by settlers originating in the area of Lüneberg in the Electorate of Hanover. This notion is discounted, rather effectively, by historian Winthrop Bell on the grounds that the name had been determined by the British governor and his Council prior to the arrival of the first shiploads of immigrants.[5] Such a conclusion is further supported by the fact that almost all of these settlers came not from Lüneberg at all, but from German states considerably to the south and west.

Although the German population of Lunenburg County was to grow substantially during the decades following the settlement of 1753,[6] a small group had remained behind at Halifax. The size of this community was

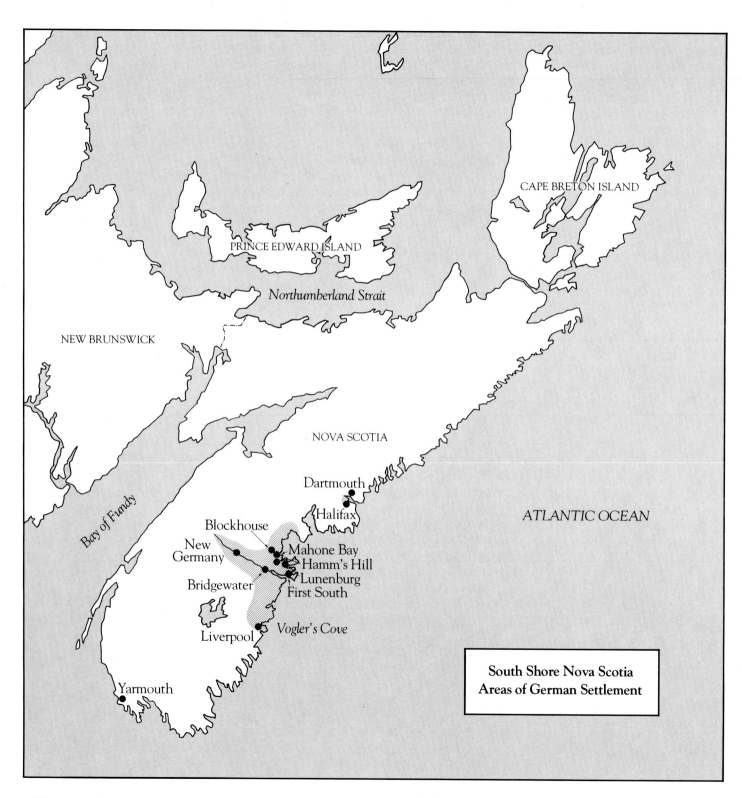

CAPE BRETON ISLAND

PRINCE EDWARD ISLAND

*Northumberland Strait*

NEW BRUNSWICK

NOVA SCOTIA

Dartmouth

Halifax

ATLANTIC OCEAN

*Bay of Fundy*

Blockhouse

New
Germany

Mahone Bay

Hamm's Hill

Lunenburg

Bridgewater

First South

*Vogler's Cove*

Liverpool

Yarmouth

**South Shore Nova Scotia
Areas of German Settlement**

never large; most individuals were eventually assimilated into the general population. They were able, however, to successfully petition that their north Halifax suburb be named Gottingen.[7] A German-speaking religious congregation was maintained, and the first church built for them was St. George's (erected in 1755 and consecrated in 1761). Called the "Little Dutch Church" (a corruption of *Deutsch* or German), a name by which it is still known today, it came under the agency of the Church of England at an early stage through complicated arrangements. Nevertheless, it was served for a considerable time by German-speaking clergymen, perhaps the best known of whom was the Reverend Bernard Michael Houseal, who is interred beneath the church floor. Houseal (1727-1799) was born at Heilbronn, Württemburg. Upon condition of receiving Anglican ordination, this Lutheran clergyman was appointed missionary to the Germans at Halifax from 1785 to 1799.[8] A plaque in the church indicates that he "held services in German using the Prayer Book of the Church of England."

The question invariably arises, why should the British governor seek "foreign [German] Protestants" as settlers in Nova Scotia, rather than fellow Englishmen? In part, the reasons have to do with the relative political and economic stability of England compared with the chaotic situation in central Europe during the eighteenth and nineteenth centuries. The Thirty Years' War (1618-1648) had left a disorganized array of small religious states under the dictate of princes. Centralization of economic life was, therefore, almost impossible in the eighteenth century. Religious and economic hardships were intensified by the revocation of the Edict of Nantes in 1685 and by the military conquests of Protestant populations by Louis XIV in the eighteenth century. All of these factors suggest the accuracy of Bell's observation that " 'foreign Protestants' were obviously available."[9] With refugees from the European mainland seeking asylum in North America, while England was actively discouraging emigration, these "foreign Protestants" were a natural choice for the settlement of non-French areas of the Eastern Seaboard. They responded to promises of free land and material aid once they had agreed to become loyal British subjects.

Among common names found in Lunenburg County, many are of Palatinate or southwest German origin. These include Eisenhaur, Gorckum (Corkum), Götz (Gaetz), Heckman, Kraus, Lippert, Reichert, Ramichen (Romkey), Rieser (Risser), Weihnacht (Whynot), Haas, Kuhn, Lässle (Leslie) and Schlagentweit (Slauenwhite), while from the states just north of the River Main are to be counted the names Jung, Schupp (Shupe), Hiltz, Meissner and Volker.[10]

A particularly interesting name that appears on the shiplists of 1751 is T. Schömacher, a candidate in theology from Hamburg,[11] who in 1754 moved to Pennsylvania and was a controversial figure in Lutheran ecclesiastical circles. He is perhaps best known as the prolific *Fraktur* artist, Daniel Schumacher, whose artistic activity extended to illuminated church books, records, his personal record of baptisms and confirmations, New Year's greetings, house-blessings and miscellaneous drawings.[12] No examples of Daniel Schumacher's work have been found in Canada. His stay of less than three years in Nova Scotia may simply have been too brief and too early in his life for him to have developed this artistic pursuit.

From the region of Montbéliard migrated numerous individuals with French language but Protestant faith, including such familiar Lunenburg County names as Langille, Mailliard and Vienot.[13]

These transplanted farmers and labourers, most of whom had probably never seen the ocean before they took ship, quickly developed the villages of Lunenburg (originally called Merligash), Mahone Bay (originally called Mushamush), Blockhouse, Hamm's Hill, First South, East and West LaHave, Riverport, Crousetown, Bridgewater, Petite Rivière, Voglers Cove, East and West Berlin and the inland settlements of New Germany.

While it is often difficult to isolate specifically Germanic design elements in the articles made by these settlers, certain features appear again and again in Germanic sections of Lunenburg County and nearby regions along Nova Scotia's South Shore. In these areas there is a preoccupation with the decorative possibilities of chip-carving and other folk-art ornamentation, emphasizing recurring motifs such as whorls, faceted stars, whirling swastikas, compass stars, hearts and stylized floral elements. These motifs are carved, incised, drawn or painted on architectural surfaces, furniture, gamesboards and utilitarian objects of all sorts.

## Architecture

In general, the architecture of the German settlements of Lunenburg County is a reflection of the dominant English taste as it came to be expressed in the British Colonies along the Eastern Seaboard. One cannot help but be impressed by the fine structures built by pioneers and successive generations in the picturesque villages and byways along the South Shore. For the most part, early Lunenburg architecture is derived from the English Georgian style of the late eighteenth century. This style is characterized by simple, harmonious lines, symmetrical fenestration, or window placement, central doorways and residual Neoclassical features, such as lintels, pilasters and returned roof eaves. Only occasionally is there a subtle indication of a German background, visible in the use of certain colours, ornamental trim or moulding, construction techniques or decorative refinements. It is in suggestiveness of detail, rather than statement of outline, that one perceives the distinctive character of the structures which housed a transplanted German culture in the English environment between Halifax and New England.

Among houses in the village of Lunenburg proper, a particularly fine example is the Romkey House (Plate 1). Believed to have been built by one Bernard Kreller as early as 1762, it is thought to be the oldest house in the community. Other imposing homes, such as that built about 1775 for Henry Koch, are of refined Georgian design. A striking building of late eighteenth-century construction is the Zwicker House in the centre of the town. Like many local houses, its original Georgian symmetry and chasteness of line were nearly obliterated during the Victorian period of whimsical modification, during which elaborate bay windows and porches were added to houses throughout the region. Entering the central hallway of this grand structure, one is treated to a magnificent expression of Lunenburg interior architecture. Inside the outer entrance is a superb arch and double door (possibly moved back somewhat at an earlier time). The side pilasters and arch have been finely adorned with meticulously detailed chevron reeding and marbleized painting and remain in completely original condition (Plate 2).

In the nearby countryside are numerous modest structures, including the Hamm House at nearby Hamm's Hill. This small house of typical Maritime design reveals Germanic nuances upon closer inspection of interior details. While the kitchen has an outstanding open dish dresser of the English-style "North Shore" type often found in Massachussetts, the living room has both a built-in cupboard and a mantel in which a Germanic design background is evident. Each of these units features elaborate architectural framing consisting of reeded sections interspersed with carved lozenge motifs (Plate 3).

In these and other structures of Lunenburg County are modest vestiges of a Germanic decorative arts vocabulary. Unlike German regions of Ontario and the Prairie Provinces, it is difficult to identify a Germanic architectural form in Nova Scotia. Rather, the architecture of the South Shore is strongly English in overall conception, but occasionally flavoured with Germanic accents.

## Furniture

The loose term "Lunenburg furniture" has been used for some time to describe a broad range of decorative pieces found in the South Shore areas of Lunenburg County and adjacent Queen s. They are frequently distinguished by bold colour schemes, strong turnings, painted motifs, chip-carving and other ornamental elements. Rarely does this furniture possess clearly Germanic form, rather its "Germanization" is likely to be found in individual parts rather than the whole. As in architecture, the furniture found here is essentially English in outline and is given Germanic interpretation in particular details.

The earliest furniture from Nova Scotia's South Shore reflects the Queen Anne style popular in New England at the middle of the eighteenth century. This form is particularly evident in the open pine dish dresser, usually given formal treatment in the shaped cornice and scalloped sides. Several examples of the built-in type are known, with sides shaped by means of alternating concave and convex semi-circles. A rare free-standing dresser of this type features an arrangement of such circles staggered in order to produce decorative "spurs" (Plate 6). This dresser is embellished with lavish chip-carving and a two-colour painted surface. Another characteristic English form found along the South Shore is the open, arched corner cupboard. Several cupboards of this variety from around Lunenburg are distinguished by traditional Germanic designs such as carved or painted stars, hearts and geometric elements.

Yet another "external" design to be given a peculiarly Lunenburg County interpretation is that of American Empire. Several chests of drawers have survived with strong features from this popular style: backboards with chimney-pot ends, pilasters, carved Neoclassical motifs and typical overhanging upper drawers. Lunenburg County examples of these "bonnet chests" are often rather whimsically painted in contrasting colours with sides grained or abstractly decorated in red and black, typical of painted furniture found also in Germanic areas of Ontario.

The table is perhaps the most boldly decorated type of furniture from this region. Early forms with tapered square legs, sometimes connected by a stretcher base, were given decorative painted finishes. More common in Lunenburg County are Sheraton-type tables with turned legs. Such painted decoration may take the form of graining or achieve more spontaneous effects with random black strokes over a red base. A more unusual interpretation is the table in Plate 8, where the painted and carved geometric decoration is within the Germanic folk-art vocabulary, but where the colour scheme and fanciful turnings seem to reflect the eccentricities of its maker.

Two pieces whose designs grow more out of personal idiosyncrasy than cultural tradition or current style are a desk and storage box (Plates 10 and 11). The colours on the surfaces of these two pieces are bold to the point of garishness, while the decorative embellishments are improvisations upon a theme of cyma-curve variations placed in symmetrical arrangement. Each features a heart motif, almost as if intended to offset these strange designs with a form more familiar in the immediate community.

Cabinetmakers and amateur craftsmen working in the Lunenburg County area produced a diverse range of furniture. Whether the external outline of these pieces is derived from various English period styles, or is of uniquely individual conception, there are elements of colour, carving and ornamentation which impart to them something of the Germanic decorative background of the region.

## Textiles

It is probable that large woven textiles found in the Germanic settlements of Nova Scotia, including blankets and coverlets, were made by Scottish weavers, not German craftsmen. "It seems unlikely that a Germanic tradition [in textiles] was brought to Lunenburg in Nova Scotia when this settlement was founded in 1753. It would most certainly have met with official discouragement, and if it ever existed, it appears to have vanished without a trace."[14] Indeed, few samplers, embroidered pieces or woven coverlets from the South Shore betray a distinctively German background in terms of construction technique, colour or motif.

For evidence of a Germanic folk-art tradition in the textile arts, one has to turn to such forms as painted sail mats, hooked rugs and quilts. Sailcloth, an important material with many uses in the Maritime economy, was ingeniously employed as an inexpensive yet attractive floor covering. Varying considerably in width and length, but usually taking the general shape of a "runner," a number of these sailcloth mats are decorated in oil-base paints, using the same folk motifs as on other hand-work. One such mat has a Germanic central star and whirling swastikas. Occasionally, the ends were left unpainted, and the warp threads on at least one example were drawn and knotted. Sailcloth mats with distinct Germanic overtones are rare, but several examples have been found in Lunenburg County.

Some very fine hooked rugs from this region employ the heart motif, in a slightly elongated form when compared with the wider heart generally found in Pennsylvania-German folk art. One example is embellished with six-point compass stars, a motif which has been given particular emphasis in Nova Scotia's Germanic regions.

Although South Shore quilts do not generally express a peculiarly Germanic sense, some from Lunenburg County employ the traditional motifs, especially tulips.

## Decorated Utilitarian Objects and Games

The artistic impulse of amateur and professional alike was often expressed in the simplest of objects, whether used for fishing, hunting or recreation.

A particularly interesting practice among Maritimers was that of making small "gum boxes." Usually made of spruce wood, they were used to carry balls of resin which were rolled into shape for chewing. In most cases, these small boxes were fashioned in the shape of books, with sliding lids on the top. In the Germanic settlements, such gum boxes were frequently decorated with distinctive motifs: hearts, trees, compass stars and diamonds. The techniques of decoration vary from chip-carving and relief-carving to painting.

Butter prints, found in every pioneer household, were often carved to impart a decorative pattern. From the Lunenburg area have come some of the most spectacular butter prints found in Nova Scotia. One of these has a central six-point compass star and geometric elements, surrounded by a circle of six deeply carved hearts. Such designs were also carved into cake or cookie boards, known as "*Springerle* boards."

Other decorated artifacts include the handles of knives used in the Maritimes for making basket splints and other utilitarian objects. These utensils, familiarly called "crooked knives," sometimes feature hearts, diamonds and other Germanic motifs carved in relief.

Wood was not the only material decorated in this manner; stone, bone and shell also received the imprint of the knife of the imaginative carver. Germanic motifs were incised into such varied objects as the slate panel of a sundial, a seashell, or powderhorns (see Plates 20, 24, 25).

The love of strong colour is evident in the ornamentation of many small utilitarian objects and games. Trinket and document boxes, for example, display vivid colouration and intensification of incised motifs. One of the distinguishing marks of the spinning wheels made by the Jung family of Lunenburg County is ring turnings with red and dark blue paint.

Among the most flamboyantly decorated articles in Lunenburg County are several decorated gamesboards, usually of the "Parcheesi" variety. Richly painted in many colours, these boards frequently have faceted stars and six-point compass stars, as in the examples shown in Plates 27-28. The large, square corners of these boards provided an excellent opportunity for the local artist, and the results are probably the most spectacular of Lunenburg County Germanic folk-art expressions.

## Gravemarkers

The German "foreign Protestants" were assimilated very quickly into the English culture, and they did not retain their native language very long. Nevertheless, some language idiosyncrasies remained:

> In the surrounding countryside, you still hear people — especially members of the older generation — speaking with a distinctive 'Dutch' accent, which has a lilt as cheerful as a hooked rug. The wonder is that any trace of it is left. They came from Germany, these pioneers, at a time when George II ruled Britain and Hanover. They settled the rocky shore with little more to furnish a house than a family Bible . . . . But nobody can read it because it's in German.[15]

Even as we interviewed people along the South Shore, we quickly became aware of a kind of accent or inflection foreign to our ears but scarcely identifiable as German as we know it.

Despite all this, South Shore cemeteries contain a substantial number of gravemarkers which are clearly products of the Germanic folk-art tradition. Early markers are located in burial grounds at Lunenburg and Mahone Bay, while others of a somewhat later date are to be seen at the village of First South and elsewhere along the coast. It is almost as if the deaths of relatives caused the surviving settlers to express themselves as they would have in their former homeland.

Some of the most Germanic gravestones still stand in the picturesque cemetery at Lunenburg, which is situated high atop a hill in the shadow of a most Teutonic-looking structure, the Lunenburg Academy. These early nineteenth-century stones are of a common shape — a rounded top with a bracket — and many are made of slate. They are quite tall, especially when compared to the later stones made in Ontario. Many were home-made by amateurs, some of whom were almost illiterate or quite naïve, while others were cut by professionals. In general, German markers are modestly decorated, with chaste design and primitive calligraphy, in dramatic contrast to the memorials of the English majority found here and throughout the Atlantic Provinces. English stones frequently employed established conventions popular in New England, such as death's heads and winged cherubs.

It is not difficult to recognize similarities of decoration between these stones and those found in Pennsylvania, Virginia and other regions where Germanic decorative arts flourished to a significant degree.[16] Among well-executed Nova Scotia headstones, for example, is the slate marker erected for J. George Iung (Jung) shown in Plate 38. The inscription is surmounted by a beautifully carved heart which is surrounded by entwined long-stemmed flowers. The decoration is firmly in the German folk-art tradition and would be equally at home in a similar cemetery in eastern Pennsylvania.

It is not surprising that Jung's stone has an English text, because he was a member of a famous wheelwright and spinning wheel manufacturing family, and commercial enterprises would have intensified contact with the surrounding English culture.

There are many other, less lavishly decorated stones whose austerity seems to echo the isolation and rigour of the lives of early South Shore settlers. The epitaphs might consist of little more than basic identification, and elaborate ornamentation might have been thought unnecessary or inappropriate. Even though the decorations on home-made markers were often crude, they were successful in imparting a degree of ornament which lifts them beyond the category of statistical records. One stone has both a heart and a tree, motifs much favoured in the Germanic decoration of textiles and furniture. The marker for Reb. [Rebecca?] Eliz. Meissner combines both the English and German traditions. At its top is a winged angel, common on English stones. Under the cherub are the large initials "M.S." The bottom features a full, wide heart which encloses the date of cutting the epitaph, seven months after the death. The text is in English, with the customary information of birth and death dates, but the spelling of the name Meissner is in the German form, using the double "s".

A skilful expression of local craftsmanship is the 1805 slate marker for Johan George Eisenhauer; it is the work of a sensitive designer and competent calligrapher. The focal point is a boldly carved tulip with a vigorous "S-curved" stem, resting on a curved horizontal flourish. The trefoil heart-shaped leaves are arranged asymmetrically, producing a lyrical effect. The earlier record of his name shows how non-Germans improvised a phonetic spelling for a Germanic name given verbally. According to the 1751 passenger list for the ship, *Pearl*, a George "Ysenda" from Wellemsfeld was among the company. Studying this name closely, one would rather quickly conclude that it does not fit well into any familiar ethnic name patterns. Sounding it aloud, however, gives an approximation for a recognizable variant. It was not uncommon for the "Y" to be used to indicate the "ei" sound in German. The relationship between "Ysenda" and "Eisenhaur" is not distant when sounded. This marker indicates that Eisenhaur came from "Wilhelmsfeld," giving further credence to the notion that they are one and the same name.

One of the latest German stones is a primitively carved slate marker in the cemetery at First South, Lunenburg County. Dated 1848, it is a naïve attempt to produce something more pleasing than a record. Its dominant feature is a heart with diagonal cross-hatching from which short rays emanate. The top is enclosed by a single line following the roughly semi-circular curve of the top of the stone. The bottom half of the circle is scalloped. The slate also reveals light incised lines, used as guidelines for the unevenly shaped and spaced letters. The cutter, possibly semi-literate, gave a strange spelling of a name, "Phillop

Cook" or "Cookmen," referring possibly to Koch or Corkum.

At an early date there was a tendency to Anglicize certain German names, sometimes producing unintended ironies of meaning. As early as 1770, names were being transformed into more comfortable English versions: Müller became Miller; Iung became Young; Koch became Cook. A more complex name, common along the South Shore, is Weihnacht, which in several instances became modified to Whynot. A rather strange epitaph on a twentieth-century granite marker is humorously ironic. Its first line reads "Whynot," while the second line follows with the inscription, "Love One Another."

Iron was used only occasionally and secondarily in the construction of Germanic gravemarkers along the South Shore. In the Bayview Cemetery at Mahone Bay, there are several cast-iron enclosures, like short fences, used to demarcate family or group plots. One such enclosure is a continuous sequence of joined hearts and crosses. Wrought-iron gravemarkers, like those in Ontario-German cemeteries, are virtually unknown in Nova Scotia, although a few commercially made, cast-iron markers are to be found in the Lunenburg area.

Nova Scotia's pervasive English culture quickly overwhelmed the much smaller pockets of Germanic heritage. However, the evidence provided by gravestones, functional objects, textiles, furniture and architecture shows that it did not completely negate traditional Germanic design impulses. These artifacts illustrate that things remembered are as strong as contemporary influences. For a stronger and more various panorama of these arts it is necessary to move further west into Ontario and yet closer to our own time.

1

1 *Romkey House, Lunenburg, Nova Scotia.*
Generally considered to be the oldest house
in Lunenburg, this home is built of log and
covered with clapboard. The dormer is a
nineteenth-century modification, cut into
what was originally a thatched roof.
Circa 1760.

2 *Interior Doorway, Zwicker House,*
*Lunenburg.*
These panelled doors in the central hallway
of the Zwicker house feature the applied
mouldings and corner blocks seen in several
fine homes in Lunenburg County. The
archway is particularly refined with chevron
reeding and outstanding marbleized painted
decoration. Late eighteenth century.

2

25

3

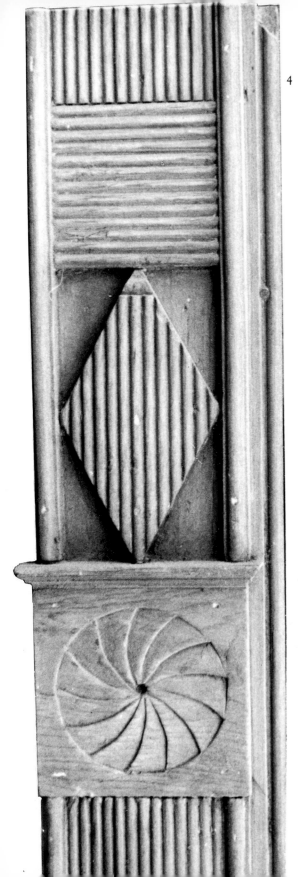

4

5

3 *Mantel, Hamm House, Hamm's Hill, Nova Scotia.*
The mantel of the Hamm House is distinguished by reeded details and lozenges. Visible on the removable fireboard are applied mouldings and corner blocks similar to those on the doors in Plate 2. Late eighteenth century.

4 *Architectural Detail, Lunenburg County.*
A section of reeded door trim incorporates the lozenges and whorls recalled from the Germanic design background of Lunenburg settlers. Late eighteenth century.

5 *Corner Cupboard (detail), Lunenburg County.*
The cornice of this pine open corner cupboard has a simple keystone into which has been carved the elongated heart often found on Germanic artifacts from the Lunenburg area. 1792.

6

6 *Open Dish Dresser, Lunenburg or Queens County.*
Many homes along Nova Scotia's South Shore once had pine dish dressers similar to those found in eighteenth-century New England houses. Some in the Lunenburg County area were given distinctive treatment, as in this example, with its chip-carved details, hearts and forty-three whorls. Late eighteenth or early nineteenth century.

7 *Table, Lunenburg County.*
Perhaps the most lavishly decorated pieces of furniture from Lunenburg Conty are various tables, such as this Sheraton example with turned legs and black decorative brushwork applied freely over a red background. Second quarter nineteenth century.

7

8

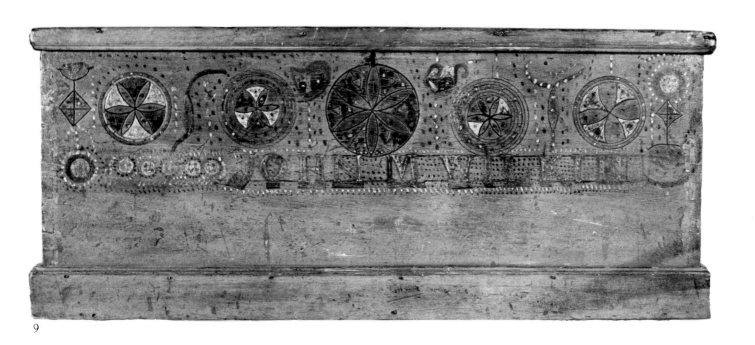

9

8  *Table, Lunenburg County.*
Made by a craftsman fond of the lathe, this table is a blending of traditional Germanic motifs (painted compass star, chip-carved fans) and personal eccentricity (lavish turnings, colour scheme). Second quarter nineteenth century.

9  *Storage Chest, Lunenburg County.*
Details on this pine storage chest found at Rhodes corners, Lunenburg County, reflect the eclectic nature of many decorated objects found in the region. Above the name "John M. Wilkin" are five incised variations of the compass-star motif. Nineteenth century.

*10 Desk, Lunenburg County.*
The free-spirited intermingling of traditional Germanic eleements with fanciful designs is seen in pieces such as this desk from St. Margaret's Bay. Painted reddish-pink and green, it features an applied heart and scrolls. Nineteenth century.

*11 Storage Chest, Lunenburg County.*
A painted counterpart to the applied decoration on the desk in the preceding illustration can be seen in the heart and scrolls on this simple pine storage box. Both pieces are highly colourful, using both green and a distinctive reddish-pink. Nineteenth century.

*12 Footstool, Lunenburg County.*
This small footstool has been transformed into an aesthetically pleasing object by its chip-carved rosettes, compass stars and other geometric designs. Nineteenth century.

*13 Footstool, New Brunswick.*
Reputedly found in the Saint John River Valley, this carved and painted footstool is evidence of the decorative energies of the scattered, small Germanic settlements of that province. Its dominant folk-art elements are hearts, six-point compass stars and a whirling swastika. Nineteenth century.

14 *Spinning Wheel, Lunenburg County.*
From the workshop of Frederick and John
Young (Jung) came many chairs and spinning
wheels found in Lunenburg area homes.
These spinning wheels are recognizable by
their fine turnings, accentuated by red and
black banding. Second quarter nineteenth
century.

15 *Reel, Lunenburg County.*
A fanciful treatment of an essential part of
the spinner's apparatus. With its scalloped
edges and punched and painted decoration,
this reel might almost be a caricature of a rural
housewife much shaped by the virtues of her
own cooking. Nineteenth century.

16

16 *Billethead, Lunenburg County.*
As figureheads gradually went out of vogue as
ornamentation on ships' prows, they were
frequently replaced by carved billetheads.
This polychromed example in blue, white
and red is carved in the form of a volute scroll
with egg-and-dart and acanthus leaf details.
Nineteenth century.

17 *Cutlery Tray, Queens County.*
Found at Liverpool, this birch cutlery tray is
joined by means of tiny wooden pegs. Its
features include a heart cut-out, as well as
incised concentric hearts and geometric
designs. Early nineteenth century.

18 *Trinket Box, Lunenburg County.*
Germanic in both colour and design, this
small pine box is boldly painted with double
compass stars in red, yellow and black set off
against a dark red background. Inside the lid
is the pencil inscription, "Abraham Hirtle,
First South, Lunenburg, N.S." Nineteenth
century.

19 *Trinket Box, Lunenburg County.*
Many small decorated objects testify to the
late perpetuation of folk-art expression in
Lunenburg County. This trinket box found at
Garden Lots has red and black stars, dia-
monds and hearts on a yellow background.
Early twentieth century.

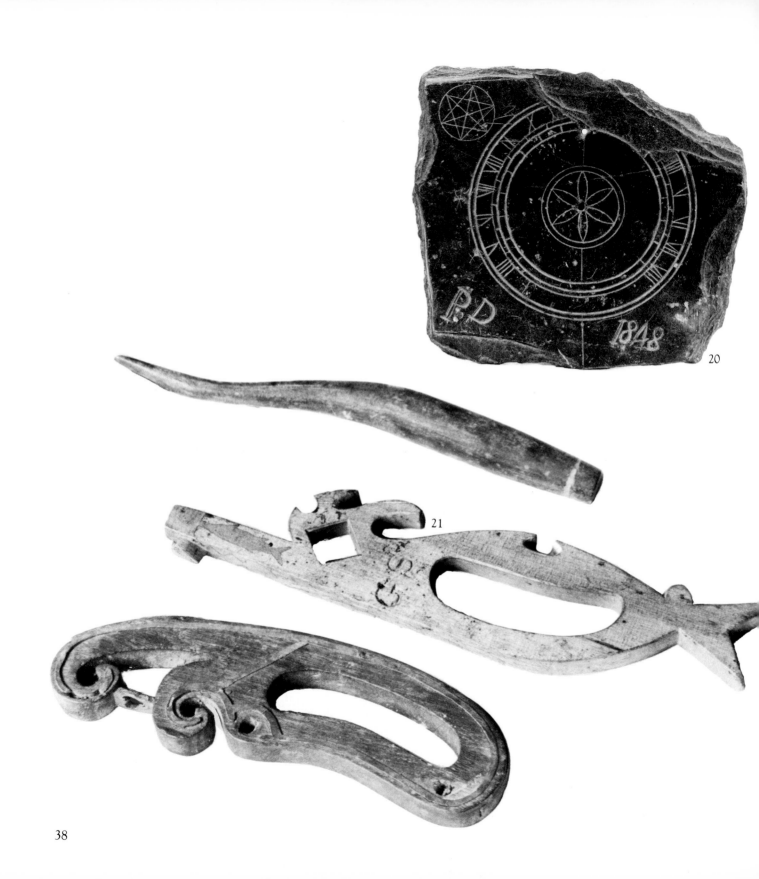

20

21

20 *Sundial, Lunenburg County.*
Perhaps no better indication of the idea that
art is timeless could be suggested than in the
embellishment of a sundial. Carved into this
slate panel are a circle of numerals, six-
pointed compass stars, other geometric designs, the initials "PD" and the date 1848.

21 *Mackerel Ploughs, Lunenburg County.*
The fusion of folk art and technology is
expressed in tools and utensils of the trades,
including the fishing industry along the
South Shore. These mackerel ploughs, used
to remove the marrow from the backbone of a
fish, employ, among other designs, a carved
heart, incised initials, inlaid lead bands and a
fish motif. Nineteenth century.

22 *Crooked Knife and Fish String Winder.*
These utilitarian articles were decorated
using different techniques. The crooked knife
has six hearts carved in relief on its handle,
while the fish string winder features chip-
carved hearts and floral elements. Late
nineteenth century.

23 *Busk, Lunenburg County.*
Similar to others found along the South
Shore, this birch corset-stay has a chip-
carved heart, whirling swastika and stylized
trees. Nineteenth century.

23

22

24

25

24 *Powder Horn, Lunenburg County.*
One of the finest powderhorns from
Lunenburg is this eighteenth-century example. It is engraved with a heraldic lion,
heart, tulip, the name Frasse Weber and the
date 1791.

25 *Shell, Lunenburg County.*
Four-point compass stars and bands of
overlapping half-circles are crafted on the
underside of this seashell from a home in
Lunenburg County. Nineteenth century.

26 *Gum Boxes, Lunenburg County.*
Spruce gum boxes, hollowed from a solid
piece of wood and fitted with a sliding lid,
were often given decorative treatment, as in
these boxes with carved hearts and stylized
trees. Late nineteenth or early twentieth
century.

26

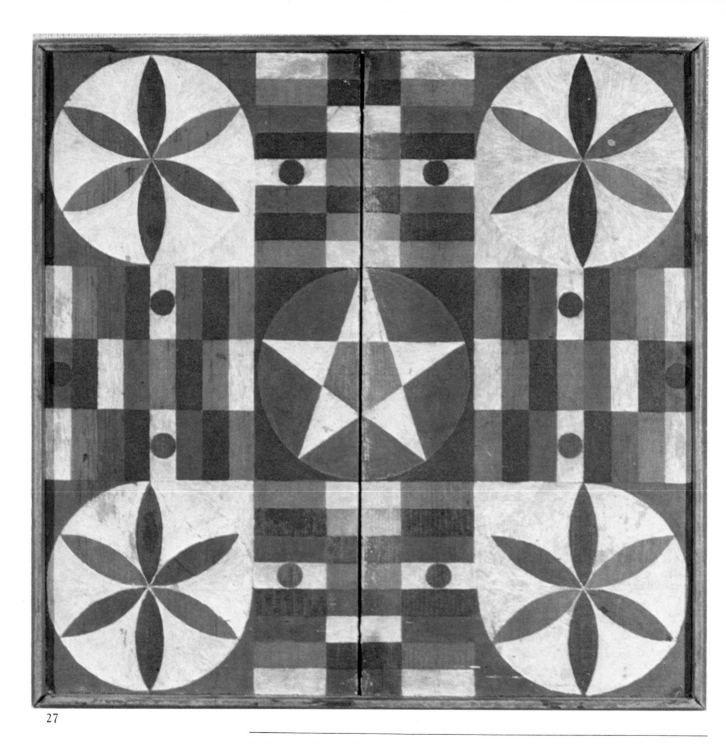

27

27 *Gamesboard, Lunenburg County.*
Made of pine, this gamesboard combines two dominant Lunenburg County decorative motifs, the central and six-pointed compass star. The compass stars and the rectangular blocks are painted in four colours: dark red, green, ochre and ivory. Nineteenth century.

28

28 *Gamesboard, Lunenburg County.*
Found at Lunenburg, this gamesboard
features the faceted red and yellow stars found
elsewhere (see Plates 27, 32) enclosed in
double circles on a green background. A
charming innovation is a house which has
been painted in the "home" section of the
board. Early twentieth century.

29 *Butter Print, Lunenburg County.*
This carved butter print is an outstanding
folk-art statement. Its central design com-
prises a six-point compass star, hexagon,
geometric extensions and arcs, surrounded by
six deeply cut hearts. Nineteenth century.

30 *Micmac Splint Box, Lunenburg County.*
Some decorated Micmac objects suggest an
intermingling of indigenous motifs with the
folk-art themes of Lunenburg's Germanic
settlers. This chip-carved box features compass stars and other geometric designs.
Nineteenth century.

30

31

31 *Hooked Rug, Lunenburg County.*
A favourite Lunenburg motif — the six-point
compass star — has been worked in this
hooked rug. Its strong colour scheme uses
burgundy red, yellow, beige and black. Late
nineteenth or early twentieth century.

32 *Painted Sailcloth, Lunenburg County.*
This painted sailcloth has a brightly painted
central faceted star, surrounded by four whirling swastikas and a border of intersecting half
circles. Further embellishment is achieved by
elaborate drawn-work at each end of the mat,
stained with red madder. Early twentieth
century.

33 *Birth-and-Baptismal Record, Lunenburg
County.*
This beautifully lettered and decorated
document is similar to examples found in
New England and may be the work of an
itinerant artist. It records the birth and baptism of Frederick Corkum, descendant of the
Corckum or Gorckum settlers who migrated
to Nova Scotia in 1752. After 1826. [Cour-
tesy Nova Scotia Museum, Halifax]

33

34 *Micmac Boxes, Lunenburg County.*
These quillwork boxes, all found in
Lunenburg County, have designs that include
hearts and whirling swastikas. Nineteenth
century.

35 *Micmac Cradle, South Shore, Nova Scotia.*
Reputedly made by a Micmac woman,
Christina Morris, this cradle is the most pro-
fusely decorated example of Micmac
quillwork known. Circa 1841. [Courtesy
Desbrisay Museum, Bridgewater, Nova
Scotia. Photograph courtesy Nova Scotia
Museum, Halifax]

34

35

36 *Cookmen Marker, Lunenburg County.*
A comparatively late example, this stone marker stands in the cemetery at First South, a small village just below the town of Lunenburg. Dedicated to an infant child of "Phillop Cookmen" (possibly Koch or Corkum), its particular charm arises from its heart motif with cross-hatched decoration and the primitively carved border. 1848.

37 *Johan Eisenhauer Marker, Lunenburg County.*
The tulip, a popular motif in the decorative arts of the Pennsylvania-Germans, is virtually unknown in Lunenburg Germanic folk art. This rare exception, a handsomely lettered stone in the Bayview Cemetery at Mahone Bay, commemorates Johan George Eisenhauer (1733-1805). 1805.

38 *George Jung Marker, Lunenburg County.*
One of the most graceful stones in the Lunenburg Cemetery is the marker for George Jung (1770-179?). An English text with bold Roman lettering is crowned with an exquisite motif of flowers intertwined around a Germanic heart. 1793 or 1794.

39 *Eliz. Meissner Marker, Lunenburg County.*
This tall slate marker in the Lunenburg Cemetery for Reb. Eliz. Meissner (1783-1802) was completed seven months after her death. It combines English influences (angel, English text, Roman lettering) with a Germanic incised heart motif. 1803.

**40** *Iron Plot Enclosure, Lunenburg County.*
This cast iron fence, designed to enclose a
family plot in the Bayview Cemetery at
Mahone Bay, is fashioned in the Germanic
design idiom with its joined heart and cross
motifs. Nineteenth century.

# 3 Ontario

Any consideration of the large influx of Pennsylvania-German settlers into southern Ontario (then called Upper Canada) during the late eighteenth and early nineteenth centuries must take into account both economic and religious phenomena. To understand why the Pennsylvania Germans moved westward and northward out of the Commonwealth of Pennsylvania, it is necessary to appreciate the continuity and the discontinuity of this group's outlook, or *Weltanschauung*, with that of the American ethos in general. Consistent with the American frontier spirit was the determination of the Pennsylvania Germans to transform a wilderness into a productive land where agricultural industry and spiritual labour could flourish. Inconsistent with the American mainstream, however, was a strong ethnocentric drive, intensified by religion, culture and language.

American history is marked by legendary heroes who prided themselves upon their solitary adventurism; one thinks of Daniel Boone in this regard. How different is the pattern of the Pennsylvania Germans, whose westward and northward movement had more the quality of a mass migration (if not a Biblical exodus). The varied accounts given by Arthur D. Graeff, G. Elmore Reaman, Lewis J. Burkholder and other authors reveal a pattern of initial scouting expeditions followed by the arrival of large groups with familial, religious and regional ties. The centrality of religious life, institutionalized in the Mennonite tradition in the meeting house, or *Versammlungshaus*, is to be seen in the early settlement of Waterloo County by significant numbers of Mennonites from Earl Township and the Weaverland Church area of Lancaster County, Pennsylvania. Similar patterns are discernible in the settling of large numbers of Dunkers (also known as Dunkards or Tunkards) along the north shore of Lake Erie, or of Bucks County Mennonites in Ontario's Lincoln County, along the south shore of Lake Ontario.

By and large, the Pennsylvania Germans resisted cultural absorption into the English-American cultural mainstream. This inner cohesion sustained them in Canada as well, most visibly in the religious life, dress, language and customs of the Old Order Mennonite community of northern Waterloo County.

While economic conditions were a continual rationale for leaving home and seeking out new lands beyond the Susquehanna River and Allegheny Mountains of Pennsylvania, financial considerations alone are not a sufficient explanation for the movement to Canada. On purely economic grounds, these industrious pioneers could have as easily gone to Ohio and the newly opened Middle West, as in fact others did. The decision to cross the Niagara River into the northern wilderness of Ontario was also, or perhaps principally, based upon a religious consideration — the ethical issue of pacifism. Evidence of actual persecution of Pennsylvania pacifists is lacking, but criticism by patriots of groups not supporting the American War of Independence would surely have been a source of continual annoyance and concern to Amish, Mennonites, Dunkers and Quakers. It is noteworthy that of all the Pennsylvania Germans who departed for a new life in Canada, pacifist groups were in the majority.

The immigration of Pennsylvania Germans into southern Ontario occurred over a period of approximately forty to fifty years, beginning in the mid-1780s, swelling at the turn of the century and diminishing to a trickle by the

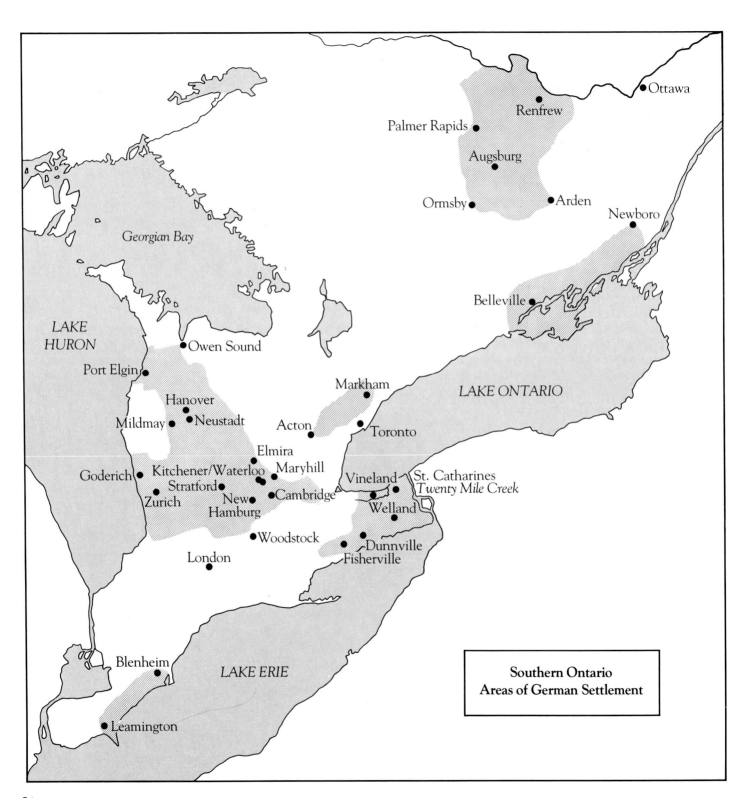

Southern Ontario
Areas of German Settlement

early 1830s. The earliest arrivals settled in the Niagara Peninsula, just across the Niagara River. They fanned out along the shorelines of lakes Ontario and Erie, settling in the present-day counties of Lincoln, Welland, Haldimand and Norfolk. Smaller numbers continued west along Lake Erie to a point just south of Windsor and Detroit. Although those Pennsylvanians who took the more southerly route along Lake Erie were largely from Lancaster and nearby counties, the pioneers at "The Twenty" — Twenty Mile Creek near its entry into Lake Ontario — were primarily from Bucks County.

A second area of settlement reached only a decade later was upper York County, north of present-day Toronto. Following the arrival of Lutherans and others, large numbers of Mennonites from Lancaster and adjacent counties migrated to Markham Township, while Dunkers from southeastern Pennsylvania settled in Vaughan Township, immediately to the west.

The third and largest area of Pennsylvania-German settlement, established initially in 1800, was Waterloo County, the "inland wilderness" along the upper Grand River, sixty miles west of Toronto and seventy miles northwest of the settlement at The Twenty in Lincoln County. After an exploratory visit in 1800 by the two pioneers, Samuel Betzner (born 1770) and Joseph Schoerg (born 1769), large numbers of settlers began to arrive in Waterloo County (then Waterloo Township). The majority of the Pennsylvania Germans to take up residence there between 1800 and 1830 came from Lancaster County, Pennsylvania, but a small yet significant number also migrated from Montgomery County, with sprinklings of families from Berks and other American counties.

Although the influx had nearly exhausted itself by 1830, throughout the remainder of the century there was a continual movement of families, relatives or friends from Pennsylvania to Ontario, particularly from Lancaster to Waterloo County. There was also a reverse motion back to Pennsylvania, testifying to an ongoing kinship of family, religion and culture on both sides of the Niagara River. This movement continues even today.

Among German settlers who found their way to Upper Canada in the 1780s, the earliest may well have been discharged veterans of Butler's Rangers, several of whom were European Palatines.[1] A significant number of these people established themselves in Stormont and Dundas counties in eastern Ontario, but their ranks also included such prominent figures in the early settlement of the western counties as Jakob Bahl. Bahl was a captain in Butler's Rangers (he eventually Anglicized his name to Jacob Ball), who settled at The Twenty in Lincoln County where he built a large mill that became the early basis of settlement in the area.

A larger Continental-German influx occurred in 1794 when William von Moll Berczy (1744-1813) led a group of 186 persons to upper York County. Unsuccessful in his original attempt to bring the group from Hamburg to the Genesee Valley in New York State, Berczy arranged for these families to settle at German Mills, a little to the west of present-day Markham.[2] This group of pioneers undertook the arduous task of connecting Markham to the Lake Ontario waterfront by building the early road eventually to be known as Yonge Street.[3] The impact of the Berczy settlers was a strong one in this sparsely populated land, in part because they arrived as a group. Despite the fact that Berczy experienced financial difficulties and eventually moved to Montreal where he died in 1813, the settlers who arrived under his leadership did establish the first inland settlement in upper York County.

An even larger immigration of Continental-German or Alsatian settlers took place in the 1820s. Many Lutherans settled just north of the Lake Erie shoreline in Welland and Haldimand counties, particularly near the later villages of Port Colborne, Stevensville and Fisherville;[4] other groups from southern Germany and Alsace went to Waterloo County. Although earlier arrivals had occurred by way of the United States (though briefly in the case of the Berczy group), the settlers arriving in the 1820s came directly from the Continent. After initial arrangements were made by Christian Nafziger to assure land grants in Canada, a group of Amish Mennonites left southern Germany in 1824. They took up a new life in Wilmot Township, just to the west of lands already settled by Pennsylvania-German Mennonites along the Grand River in Waterloo and Woolwich townships.

During this same period, a second group comprising Roman Catholics and some Lutherans departed from the German states in search of new opportunities in Canada. Catholic families from the same general region of southern Germany made the passage to North America and settled on land immediately adjacent to Amish and Mennonites in Waterloo County. One group of Catholic pioneers established themselves in eastern Waterloo County, around the present-day village of Maryhill (originally named Rotenburg and later called New Germany until 1941). Arriving in 1826, the first families in the area were the Fehrenbachs and the Scharbachs, who had come from Germany's Black Forest.[5] Other early pioneers included Gottlieb Brohman, Joseph Lauber, A. Weiler, his three brothers and Joseph Wendling.[6]

Still other Catholic-German immigrants founded the villages of St. Clements and St. Agatha in the western part of Waterloo County. Many older residents around St. Agatha still recall countless stories indicative of the side-by-side life and cooperative spirit of Amish and Catholic settlers in the region. One of the most illuminating of these stories of good will and spiritual kindredness is that of the close friendship of the Amish spiritual leader Peter Littwiller and the Roman Catholic priest Father Eugen Funcken. The "Amish bishop and the Catholic priest" held each other in such high esteem that on the day of Peter Littwiller's funeral in 1878, Father Funcken tolled the bells for his Amish friend as the procession passed in front of the open doors of the Catholic church in St. Agatha.[7] Local newspapers also printed Father Funcken's eulogy for his friend.

Through the 1830s, many Roman Catholic and Lutheran Germans continued to arrive in Waterloo County from the Continent. In the late 1840s and '50s, there was yet another influx of immigrants. Some settled in Waterloo County; others stopped briefly before moving on to newly opening lands to the north and west, in Huron, Bruce and Grey counties.

The chronological period of these extensive migrations coincides closely with the enactment of certain government policies in several German regions, particularly in the southwest German states of Württemberg, Baden and Hesse. In a detailed analysis of the problem of deepening poverty in the nineteenth-century German states, historian Gerhard Bassler has argued that several governments were eventually driven to the conclusion that funds normally required for the maintenance of welfare, police services and the administration of criminal justice in economically depressed cities could be better used to promote the emigration of the poor to North America. The distressing problem of severe destitution becomes evident in his observation that between 1824 and 1854 there was a two-fold increase of "totally impoverished communities" in Württemberg from 24 to 46.[8] In an 1847 response to the crippling economic situation, the governments of Württemberg and Baden, as well as those of

other German states, introduced intensive programmes of publicly assisted emigration. The practice was continued into the 1860s, finally provoking the predictable complaint from a Quebec immigration official that the failure of Canada to challenge this policy amounted to "a tacit admission of right to inundate it with the refuse of foreign pauperism."[9] Changes in German policy after 1855 reduced the flow of emigrants, and by the late 1850s the settlement of German settlers in Ontario (then called Canada West) was virtually terminated.

Among the victims of the economic decline in Europe came many of the weavers, cabinetmakers, potters, blacksmiths and other skilled workers who, in scattered settlements of both eastern and western Ontario, were to make a significant contribution to the Ontario-German craft tradition of the mid- and late-nineteenth century. From the ranks of "foreign pauperism" has come much of the very richness of Ontario's Germanic cultural heritage.

## Articles Brought Along

The stylistic similarities of architecture, furniture, folk and decorative arts in the Pennsylvania-German regions of southern Ontario and their counterparts in Pennsylvania make it apparent that these earliest settlers brought with them the techniques and trades of their forebears. To be certain, among them were many craftsmen who continued to practise skills which they had previously exercised in their Pennsylvania homeland.

Until recent research unearthed enough examples for comparative study, the relative number of Pennsylvania-made artifacts actually brought from the United States to Upper Canada by these pioneer settlers had not been clear. With the gradually growing pictorial documentation of artifacts found in the households of the Niagara Peninsula, York and Waterloo counties, several conclusions can now be drawn concerning "articles brought along."

The number of things actually made in Pennsylvania and carried as settlers' effects is smaller than has frequently been maintained. Most "brought-along" artifacts are of eighteenth-century manufacture. Apart from a few notable exceptions, large pieces of furniture, such as cupboards, tables, and wardrobes, were rarely imported into the remote settlements of Upper Canada. Among those articles actually carried to Canada from Pennsylvania, the principal items were: family Bibles and religious books of various kinds; some specimens of *Fraktur,* such as bookplates, birth records and small drawings (frequently stored in the pages of books); a few highly esteemed pieces of furniture; non-decorated textiles; and miscellaneous small articles and utensils.

The most common object brought along by Pennsylvania-German pioneers was the family Bible, sometimes augmented by the *Martyrs' Mirror,* songbooks, or other books of religious significance. Less common in number but closely associated with books were pieces of *Fraktur.* Interestingly enough, the largest numbers of *Fraktur* made in Pennsylvania have been found in Lincoln County, possibly indicative of the particular geographic origins of settlers there. Most had come from Bucks County where prodigious quantities of *Fraktur* had been produced in the schools once attended by these pioneers or their children.

There was at one time an unspoken tendency to assume that furniture found in southwestern Ontario was brought from Pennsylvania, particularly pieces of exceptional quality or whose stylistic features made them appear to be of early construction. Eventually, the comparative examination of inter-related pieces found in Ontario, as well as the growing recognition of the inhibiting factor of relative isolation upon stylistic change, has made it increasingly evident that most of this furniture is indeed of Canadian manufacture. Interesting examples are the stretcher-base walnut tables found in the Niagara Peninsula, at one time presumed to have been made in Pennsylvania. This view was gradually qualified in time as several similar tables came to light, including the dramatic discovery of a table in 1979 whose top was stamped on the underside, "J.H. Housser, Mak. C.W." From the "C.W." (Canada West) inscription, the date of the table can be bracketed between 1841 and 1867, indicating that even if made in the earliest possible year, its construction was much later than its style would suggest to the casual observer.

There are, of course, some exceptions to the rule that large pieces of furniture were not brought to Ontario in quantity by pioneer settlers. The tall-case clock is one such example; it was long regarded as one of the most valuable pieces of domestic furniture, and in some instances it was considered a family heirloom to be handed down from one generation to another. Large case-pieces (cupboards, wardrobes) or tables that can be definitely attributed to Pennsylvania origins have only rarely been found in Ontario households, and the few exceptions have been found along the shorelines of lakes Ontario and Erie, just across the Niagara River. Even less likely, then, is the idea that Germanic pioneers, trekking by horse-drawn wagons, crossing mountains and the ever treacherous Niagara River, should have attempted to carry cupboards or other furniture even further to the inland wilderness of Waterloo County. The trip entailed, among other challenges, the perils of the notorious Beverley Swamp between Dundas and the Grand River. It seems even more remarkable that so few Pennsylvania examples of the basic storage chest, or *Kiste,* have been found in Ontario. Given the usefulness of the chest during transport and for domestic storage, one might have expected large numbers to have survived early migrations. In view of the paucity of examples known, how much less probable is the transport of more cumbersome and less practical or essential furniture.

Among smaller objects which would have accompanied the first immigrants to Ontario, numerous functional textiles should be mentioned. To be sure, families carried such necessary items as blankets, table-cloths, towelling and clothing. Rare indeed are Pennsylvania-made decorated textiles, such as samplers or show towels, which were brought to Canada. The few known survivals include: a 1799 show towel from Lancaster County now at Doon Pioneer Village, a 1797 Risser sampler, as well as an 1804 Lehman show towel brought by a Pennsylvania family migrating to Markham Township in York County.

Other artifacts of Pennsylvania origin fall generally into the category of utensils and miscellaneous small items: tools, kitchen articles, decorated toleware, heckles, and (in rare cases) some pottery and even Stiegel-type glass, most dating from before the end of the eighteenth century. Some of these Pennsylvania artifacts no doubt served to influence styles and decorative techniques in the later production of domestic articles in Upper Canada, but by the time of the second generation of settlement, these articles would have been a decreasingly significant proportion of the household inventory. They were soon replaced by products made by craftsmen transposed to a new setting in the gradually retreating Canadian wilderness.

Given the greater distance travelled by Continental-German immigrants, it is not surprising that they imported even fewer large pieces than the Pennsylvania

Germans. If available space on a horse-drawn wagon was small, that allowed for each passenger on a trans-Atlantic voyage was still more confined. While a few pieces of large case-furniture are known to have been carried north along the Susquehanna, the prospect of cumbersome articles being brought across the Atlantic is more remote. Even the cabinetmaker, John Gemeinhardt (1826-1912), appears not to have imported any of the furniture he had made during his apprenticeship in Germany, apart from a hand-made box and the usual shipping or "immigrant's" chest which was used to carry effects.

Items clearly of Continental-German origin, which have been handed down through families of immigrants include: family Bibles, religious and other books; a few examples of *Fraktur,* such as bookplates, religious mottoes and drawings; miscellaneous small items, such as chip boxes or bride's boxes, family heirlooms or special presentation-pieces; and decorated storage chests.

Among books surviving from the time of initial settlement are various Roman Catholic and Lutheran religious works, mostly in German but also including some Latin texts. Amish settlers coming directly from the European mainland, or by way of brief excursions through the United States, likewise brought many religious books, including several "Froschauer" Bibles and other works from the early Reformation period.

A few examples of European *Fraktur* have been discovered in the Continental-German settlements of Ontario, usually recognizable by their style, subject matter, paper or vocabulary. Words such as *Kirche,* or church, would be used rather than the term *Gemeinde,* or congregation, preferred in Pennsylvania-German inscriptions done in Ontario. One of the more distinctive forms which has occasionally been found in Roman Catholic areas is the Mass Book; its German text is accompanied by elaborate decoration. These Mass Books, similar to those known in Austria and south Germany, are distinguished by colourful Roman Catholic Eucharistic imagery with lilies, crosses, chalices and other traditional liturgical motifs. Other books of European provenance sometimes have designs incised or sculpted from the ends or sides of the pages.

Among miscellaneous heirlooms, special presentation-pieces and other small decorated articles are small oval splint containers, sometimes called "brides' boxes," often lavishly painted on the tops and sides. One example, descended through generations of a family that had emi-grated from Alsace to Wilmot Township in Waterloo County, is exceptional, with painted tulips on the side and a girl standing among flowers and geometric designs on the lid.

Unlike the Pennsylvania-German artifacts, the most frequently found decorated object imported by Continental settlers is the immigrant's chest. There are perhaps as many as a dozen of these decorated chests still in the possession of families descended from European-German pioneers. The principal form is a heavy-lidded chest with three sunken panels on the front, normally painted with stylized flowers, sometimes accompanying a semi-religious or secular text. One immigrant chest passed down in a Waterloo County family reminds the viewer that failure to kiss a pretty girl whom one has just met is like stopping at a cool spring and not drinking thereof.

Additional miscellaneous effects, including clothing and various textiles, were doubtless among items brought from the Continent in these chests. It is likely that most eventually deteriorated and were replaced by locally made items.

## Architecture

The structures of Ontario-German settlements reflect both the Pennsylvania and Continental backgrounds of these pioneers and their descendants. The Pennsylvania Germans brought with them their taste for houses in the Georgian style. The earlier German house with steeply pitched roof and traditional three-room arrangement survived less frequently in Ontario, although a few examples remain today in the Niagara Peninsula and in York and Waterloo counties. Perhaps most distinctive of Pennsylvania-German structures is the bank-barn, built into the side of the hill to permit ground-level access to both upper and lower levels. Based on barns built by ancestors against the hillside of south Germany and Switzerland, this form was rarely utilized in Ontario by groups other than Germans. A tiny number of these barns also feature extended ("overshot") upper sections supported cantilever-style by extended beams over the lower level.

The Continental Germans, particularly in Waterloo, Huron, Bruce and Grey counties, adopted the Georgian-style houses and bank-barns of their Pennsylvania-German neighbours. The house-barn combination was built only rarely in Germanic areas of Ontario, appearing more frequently in the Mennonite villages of Manitoba and Saskatchewan. There are reports suggesting that a handful of such buildings may have once existed in Waterloo County, and the best example now known was located just north of the village of St. Clements. Unfortunately, it was recently severely altered, when its barn was replaced by a steel structure. Another modest structure still stands in the Neustadt-Ayton area of Bruce County. The roof line is continuous; the attached barn is the same height and width as the house.

With the arrival of the first pioneers from Pennsylvania, modest log houses were erected in the Upper Canadian wilderness. A few such houses survive today, but many have modern siding, and they are not always easily distinguishable from small houses of more recent construction. Many others have been altered or destroyed. Among the more substantial early log structures is the two-storey home built by Jacob Fry near Vineland in 1815. Recently, it has been moved to the grounds of the Jordan Museum of the Twenty. Known locally as the birthplace of Samuel Fry (1812-1881), an outstanding Lincoln County Pennsylvania-German weaver, it features clapboard sheathing and a centre-wall fireplace.

The earliest extant dwelling in upper York County is the log house of Philip Eckhardt, surveyor and millwright, built shortly after his arrival west of Markham in 1794. When first erected it was two-storeys high with a steeply pitched roof and deep overhang supported by floor beams extending beyond the walls. The structure has since been drastically modified by the elimination of one floor and the addition of dormers and modern siding.

One of the most imposing log buildings was the Christian Schneider homestead, reportedly built at Doon in 1807 after the arrival of this pioneer, his wife and eight children from Franklin County Pennsylvania. Now demolished, this large house had a two-storey verandah and steeply pitched roof. Perhaps its most important architectural detail was the "pent roof," or protective overhang along the tops of one end of both floors. This was relatively commonplace on early houses in eastern Pennsylvania, but unique in Ontario.

Perhaps the best representations of Pennsylvania-German architecture surviving in upper York County are several massive barns dating from the early nineteenth century. Three prominent examples are those built by the Baker, Stong and Schmidt pioneers of Vaughan Township. The largest is the Schmidt-Dalziel barn, built by Johannes Schmidt in 1809. John Dalziel later purchased it

in 1828 and it was used as a stock barn for over one hundred years. This immense structure, now part of Black Creek Pioneer Village, is made with heavy logs and employs the overhanging forebay seen on Swiss and southern German prototypes.

One of the finest examples that has survived in Vaughan Township of a Pennsylvania-German farmhouse is the "second house" of Daniel Stong. Built in 1832, it exhibits careful craftsmanship with its multi-panelled interior doors, beaded panelling, refined moulding and trim. It is more closely related than most Ontario examples to early Germanic houses in Pennsylvania, retaining the central chimney, interior-wall hearth, built-in bake oven and three-room floor plan (kitchen, parlour, master bedroom) on the first level. The house is constructed of massive hewn timbers covered with clapboard siding.

Several interesting frame dwellings were also built in Upper Canada. One was built in 1820 by Joseph Schneider close to what is presently downtown Kitchener. It is said that most of the materials used in the construction of this large home were hand-crafted. Remodelled at mid-century, it is now a historic site, honouring the founder of Kitchener, and is being restored. In upper York County is a smaller home, the one-and-a-half storey frame dwelling built near Markham in 1825 by the elder Christian Hoover (1798-1885); it has since been moved to the grounds of the Markham District Historical Museum.

The Pennsylvania-German homes of a later period testify to the improved fortunes and relative affluence of a prospering agricultural community. The transition from survival to comparative comfort appears to have taken place by the 1830s or 1840s. Several brick farmhouses in the Vineland-Jordan area, built between the approximate dates of 1837 and 1845, are of large proportions and exhibit refinements not possible a half-century earlier. An outstanding example from this later period is the Jacob High house, which was built along the road rising sharply out of Vineland at its southern outskirts. Dating from 1837,[10] it is one of the earliest brick houses in Lincoln County, and it retains features from yet earlier Pennsylvania-German Georgian-style houses. Attached to this and other homes in the area is a characteristic *Doddy* or *Grossdoddy* house, traditionally used to accommodate elderly family members when they retired and transferred farm responsibilities to a son and family.

Slowly but surely, aesthetic considerations in houses built by second and third generation Germanic settlers became more evident. Not only was attention increasingly given to details in both exterior and interior, but also choice of location became an important factor. Built in 1844, the David Fretz House is picturesquely situated adjacent to the harbour where Twenty Mile Creek joins Lake Ontario. Nearby stands a rare Ontario example of an independent brick bake oven with overhanging roof (Plate 42). Such structures have long attracted the attention of students of vernacular architecture in Pennsylvania. This particular oven is the only Ontario-German specimen presently known to us.

The Samuel Moyer home (Plate 41), built near Campden around 1840 to 1845, shares many features with the High and Fretz houses, including arched windows at each end, returned eaves and fine details. A notable variation in this brick building is the placement of two doors at the front, recalling similar Pennsylvania examples. The usual symmetry of the Georgian house is extended here in the arrangement of windows and doors. Although the reasons frequently given for the purpose of the two-entrance house in Pennsylvania are varied, a Moyer descendant recalls that the original owner used one side for religious meetings. This anecdote may give greater insight into temporary use than initial purpose. In any event, the two-door house is a rare occurrence in the Niagara Peninsula.

These and several additional brick homes in the region have much in common, and at least two of them (Fretz and High) are believed to have been constructed by a builder named Culp.[11] Common to these houses are arched windows, similarity of umbrages (recessed, sheltered spaces), plaster ceilings on porches, wainscotting on back porches, raised brick basement entrances, twelve-over-eight window sashes whose panes measure nine by seven inches and other details of moulding and interior trimwork. Each house also has a false chimney at one end of the roof to create symmetry. Several have cooking fireplaces in addition to other heating fireplaces. The Moyer house has the unusual feature of a corner fireplace, set at a forty-five degree angle to the walls on either side.

Waterloo County was settled by both Pennsylvania and Continental Germans. This mixture resulted in architecture representative of their differing traditions, but more often in detail rather than overall conception. Brick was certainly in use here by the 1840s, but this was also a period of ambitious stonemasonry, and stone houses and public buildings became more common.

Several brick homes were conceived and executed along rather grand lines. The tanner John Wissler (1810-1870) and the miller Jacob S. Shoemaker (1798-1875) built imposing homes in 1842 and 1840, respectively. Shoemaker, originally from Montgomery County, Pennsylvania, came to Canada as an assistant to Abraham Erb, founder of Waterloo, before establishing himself as a miller and imaginative entrepreneur in the village of Glasgow, later amalgamated into the town of Bridgeport. In 1840, he built what is one of the most ambitious Pennsylvania-German Georgian brick houses in Waterloo County. Both structures have stucco facing which was carefully lined to emphasize the Flemish-bond brick beneath it. They share other meticulous refinements such as well-crafted mouldings, shutters, umbrages and interior details, the most notable of which are fine plaster ceiling medallions.

The Shoemaker house, the larger of the two, has a central hall which runs the entire length of the structure. It also has fluted doorways, sidelights and overhead fantransoms. An extraordinary feature is the attic floor, which is made of brick laid over a beam-and-plank subfloor.

Alongside these fine brick homes are many Pennsylvania-German stone houses built in increasing numbers toward the middle of the nineteenth century. Many feature five bays, walls of variegated fieldstone, deep-set windows and doors and the twelve-over-eight window panes characteristic of early houses in the region. Some have the date of completion incised into a millstone or other stone set into the side wall under the gable.

One outstanding stone farmhouse is that of John Brubacher, built in 1850 just northwest of the village of Waterloo. Constructed of variegated fieldstone, it is finished with large corner quoins. Like many stone houses in the region, the front wall enclosed by the first-floor verandah is faced with plaster. With its symmetrical fenestration and sound proportions, it is one of the more successful architectural statements in the Pennsylvania-German countryside of western Ontario. Its beauty is augmented by its scenic hilltop location overlooking the Laurel Creek watershed.

Among public buildings erected by the Pennsylvania Germans in western Ontario, one of the most imposing is the Fryfogel Inn built by Sebastian Fryfogel (1791-1873), the first settler of Perth County. Located along the well-travelled Huron Road, just west of the border with Waterloo County, this 1844 building is an exceptionally fine expression of the Georgian style retained to such a late date by the Pennsylvania Germans of Ontario. A somewhat larger inn, which has been in continuous use since it was built in the early 1850s, is the Blue Moon Hotel in Petersburg. Like the Fryfogel Inn, the Blue Moon is of simplified Georgian proportions, but it also retains some of the Neoclassical elements of the earlier Georgian style. These features are evident in the more pronounced return of the roof eaves and in the simple columns and pediments flanking the four doorways on the north facade of the building.

Perhaps more significantly than other buildings, it is the religious architecture of the Pennsylvania Germans in Ontario that reveals the degree to which this migration was made up of Mennonites and, in smaller numbers, Dunkers. For them the dominant religious structure is not the church, but the meeting house or *Versammlungshaus*. The Conestogo Meeting House, a simple structure with white horizontal siding, located a few miles west of the village of St. Jacobs, is a typical example.

The buildings of the Continental Germans in Waterloo County are concentrated primarily in Lutheran, Roman Catholic and, to a lesser extent, Amish areas. It is true that the Continental settlers tended to construct domestic and public buildings in a manner and style similar to that of the Pennsylvania Germans, but some departure is frequently evident. As in the case of the Pennsylvania settlers, the Continental immigrants maintained a conservative architectural tradition. Like other pioneers, they quickly replaced original log structures with more substantial houses of frame, brick or stone. The Georgian style with its simple lines and architectural symmetry, much favoured by the Pennsylvania Germans, was perpetuated to a still later date (into the 1880s) by Continental Germans in the regions to the north and west of Waterloo County. The houses built by German settlers, in contrast to those of their Scottish and English neighbours, continued to be constructed of variegated fieldstone, sometimes modified by ashlar masonry.

Although the houses erected for or by Continental-German settlers resembled those of their Pennsylvania-German neighbours, a few details occasionally suggest regional differences of origin. A notable example is the

appearance of the diamond or lozenge panel on doors (or on furniture). The authors have encountered this form of panelling on rare occasions in areas settled by Amish immigrants of Swiss or Alsatian ancestry, particularly in the Wellesley area of Waterloo County and more frequently in homes of Catholic-German families near Maryhill (see Plate 52). This kind of enhancement is visible on the Perth County log home erected in 1862 by George Fischer. Its doorway is of particular interest, framed by flat pilasters with applied lozenge motifs and featuring a lintel with dentil moulding. The keystone and the caps above the pilasters have carved six-point compass stars.

A number of stone farmhouses around the village of St. Agatha in Waterloo County are essentially one-and-a-half storey buildings with a characteristic row of large cut stones arranged formally between the top of the front verandah and the lower edge of the roof. It is interesting that this feature appears in homesteads of both Amish and Roman Catholics, groups which originated from virtually the same region of southern Germany. Another distinctive detail of several stone houses in this region is the use of double (side-by-side) windows at front and sides.

A good example of Alsatian or Swiss-inspired architecture in Waterloo County is the former Embassy Hotel in St. Agatha, now a restaurant. It has been recently modified, but remains distinguished by a dramatically extended roof supported at the front by angled posts buttressing the roof edge and the wall. The door is flanked by sidelights and a tripartite arch.

Among religious buildings built by Continental Germans in this region, a group of three churches could be the work of a single individual or team of builders. Located within approximately fifteen miles of each other in western Waterloo and eastern Perth counties, these are St. Agatha Zion Lutheran Church (1863), St. John's Evangelical Lutheran Church (1872) near Bamberg, and St. Anthony's Roman Catholic Church (1863) between Shakespeare and Tavistock. These churches are based upon a refined Georgian prototype, but they have been given a quaint provincial interpretation. Each church has most of its early furniture, and the interior of St. Anthony's is virtually unaltered, retaining its original pews, altar, sanctuary furniture, movable confessional screen and accessories. This beautiful little country church, but for the shortening of its spire,[12] is one of those rarely fulfilled dreams in which an early architectural jewel has escaped natural calamities and the spectre of modernization.

Somewhat smaller but no less aesthetically appealing than this trio of churches is the nearby Shrine of the Sorrowful Mother in St. Agatha, situated adjacent to the cemetery of St. Agatha Roman Catholic Church. Erected ca. 1858-60, this attractive neo-gothic chapel is rarely used but nevertheless well maintained to the present day. Among its fine features are windows with gothic tracery and spire with a scrolled wrought-iron cross similar to gravemarkers in the cemetery. The religious prints mounted along the length of the ceiling are a poor-man's counterpart to the lavishly painted ceilings of European churches. A talented woodcarver fashioned several reliquaries and the altar itself.

Some of the most effective stone structures made by the Continental Germans are found in Bruce and Grey counties. When areas of Carrick Township (Bruce County), Normanby Township (Grey County) and the surrounding country were opened to settlers during the 1850s, great numbers of German Lutherans and Catholics, as well as some Amish and Mennonites from Waterloo County, purchased land. The first houses in the 1850s and 1860s were log or frame. But by the late 1860s and 1870s there appeared a surprising number of fine stone houses in the countryside and in the villages of Ayton, Neustadt, Hanover, Formosa, Carlsruhe and Mildmay. Most have date stones located just beneath the peak of the roof.

Among notable examples here are the Friedrich Ploethner house built in 1868 and the George Schenk house of 1871 (Plate 58). In the case of Ploethner and Schenk, both Continental-German immigrants, part of the family took up permanent residence in Waterloo County, while other members continued on to the Neustadt-Ayton area. These and other houses in the area have a high degree of refinement not commonly found in Waterloo County stone houses, particularly the finely glazed sidelights and transoms enclosing front doorways. A glazing arrangement consisting of two rows of facing arcs is found on numerous houses here, as well as on the entrances of hotels in Neustadt and Mildmay. A few stone houses in both Bruce and Grey counties reveal the influence of Ontario's gothic revival in the form of centre gables, yet many remain reasonably true to the simple lines and symmetry of Georgian homes built a half-century earlier.

Within the sphere of public architecture serving the religious needs of Continental-German communities in Ontario, several churches are especially noteworthy. In the town of Formosa, Bruce County, the Immaculate Conception Roman Catholic Church was originally a simple log structure built in 1857. Nearly two decades later, a recognized architect, Joseph Connolly, an immigrant from Ireland, was hired to design a more magnificent edifice. Connolly had already achieved distinction with his design for the Church of Our Lady of the Immaculate Conception in Guelph, modelled after Cologne Cathedral, and from 1870 to 1890 he provided plans for several churches and cathedrals in Toronto, London and Kingston. The Formosa church was constructed over a decade, with the outer shell done in 1880 and completion by 1883. The exterior is rather simple, with a somewhat austere square tower. The interior commands considerable interest. Its gothic altars were carved by Nicholas Dürrer (1834-1908), a farmer and cabinetmaker residing just north of the village. It is reputed that many children witnessed Dürrer carving this altar, as well as the communion rail and other carvings in his home. Dürrer is also known for his carved altars in Roman Catholic churches in Mildmay and in St. Mary's Church in Kitchener. In 1904, the interior of Immaculate Conception Church was decorated by M.E. Von Mach Company of Detroit at a cost of $4,500. The oil paintings were done by Joseph Barth,[13] who studied art in Munich.

For the most part, the strongly Germanic accentuations of architectural styles and building techniques visible in eighteenth-century Pennsylvania structures had been largely dissipated by the time southwestern Ontario was settled. A rather muted expression of Germanic background is faintly evident in the occasional bank-barn with overhanging forebay; in the three-room first floor arrangement of some farm homes; in the rather late perpetuation of an English-Georgian architectural style favoured by the Germans of Pennsylvania; in a predilection for stone houses with walls of variegated fieldstone; in the utilization of bold interior colour (blue, dark red, green and ochre) of which distressingly few examples remain; and in the infrequent retention of distinctive details of moulding, panelling and carving on doors or interior woodwork. From the earliest log houses, such as that of Philip Eckhardt erected in upper York County during the 1790s, to the stone houses built by the Continental Germans in Bruce and Grey counties into the 1880s, we have been left a diversified architectural record of southern Ontario's German pioneers and their descendants.

## Furniture

Of all the artifacts left to us, Ontario furniture exhibits the greatest intermingling of Continental- and Pennsylvania-German craftsmanship. In several geographic regions these groups worked alongside each other, or even within overlapping communities. In other areas, they were more isolated.

The Pennsylvania Germans formed strong cultural, religious and craft traditions in the three principal areas of the Niagara Peninsula, upper York County (Markham and Vaughan townships) and Waterloo County. The Continental Germans dispersed themselves more widely over the province, producing recognizable bodies of furniture in several centres. These regions form a geographical band just north of Lake Erie in the Niagara Peninsula, near the communities of Stevensville, Port Colborne, Dunnville and Fisherville; in Waterloo County, including adjoining townships in Oxford and Perth counties; in the "Huron area" (Huron, Bruce and Grey counties); and also in eastern Ontario, particularly in lower Renfrew and upper Lennox and Addington counties.

Turning attention first to the Pennsylvania Germans, it can reasonably be said that furniture made and used by them consisted in large part of English forms with Germanic interpretation. In this respect, the furniture parallels the architecture of their settlements.

To be certain, some pieces of Pennsylvania-German furniture are traceable directly to German prototypes, as in the massive clothes cupboard, or *Kleiderschrank*. This almost standard component of the Waterloo County farm home is much more Germanic than the English-inspired linen press favoured in the Pennsylvania-German households of Lincoln County. But the form has been so simplified that it is only a distant echo of the prototype.

The Pennsylvania-German furniture of Ontario, surviving examples of which are almost exclusively of nineteenth-century manufacture, tends to be governed stylistically more by Hepplewhite, Sheraton, American Empire and even early Victorian influences than by the strong Germanic baroque style which had still manifested itself in some eighteenth-century Pennsylvania furniture. The "Germanization" of these English forms is more pro-nounced in Waterloo County or Markham Township than in the Niagara Peninsula, and is achieved by details of colour, decorative painting, ebonizing and distribution of mass and elements of composition.

Of the three areas of Pennsylvania-German settlement, furniture made in the Niagara Peninsula attained the greatest degree of refinement and sophistication. The comparatively formal quality of this country furniture derives in part from a mixture of superb craftsmanship, severe design and the extensive use of black walnut as primary wood used for exterior show.

It is probable that the earliest professionally made Niagara Peninsula furniture dates from not much earlier than 1820, or from the second generation of settlement in what thirty years earlier had been wilderness. Among the earliest pieces made in Lincoln County are chests of drawers attributed to the cabinetmaker David Simmerman, who is reputed to have made a tall walnut chest signed "MM" for the bride of Samuel T. Moyer in 1821,[14] and another for Mary Bricker on the occasion of her 1826 marriage to Abram Tohman in Waterloo Township.

Also active at or very shortly after this time was the Mennonite craftsman John Grobb (1800-1885) of Louth Township. Several signed examples provide material evidence for the attribution of many pieces to him. Other identified cabinetmakers of the region include Albert Lane, Jacob Fry, Jacob Houser and J.H. Housser. Another craftsman who reportedly specialized in both house and furniture painting was Israel Moyer.

A distinctive Niagara Peninsula furniture form is the linen press, made in two sections. In nearly every known instance, these pieces have three drawers in the bottom section and two doors above. All have well-developed cornices, mouldings, quarter-columns (usually reeded) and either plain or ogee bracket feet. Neither the Pennsylvania-German settlements of Waterloo nor of York County produced anything comparable to these Lincoln County linen presses.

Wall cupboards in the Niagara Peninsula were made from both pine and walnut. Most of these do not have the characteristic "pie shelf," or arched work area separating top and bottom sections, found commonly in similar cupboards from York and Waterloo counties. Many Niagara examples have drawers in the top section, or in both sections, while in Waterloo and York counties, drawers occur only in the base. Several of these cupboards are of exceptionally fine proportion and workmanship, frequently mounted on well-articulated ogee bracket feet.

A form rarely encountered in the Niagara Peninsula is the corner cupboard.[15] Its scarcity is somewhat surprising because it is often found in other Pennsylvania-German areas of Ontario, particularly Waterloo County.

Among other refined pieces from the Niagara Peninsula are blanket chests, chests of drawers and desks. Blanket chests share many similarities of design and construction with those made in Bucks and other counties of Pennsylvania from which settlers of this area had emigrated at the end of the eighteenth century. But the tradition of painted decoration, widespread in Pennsylvania, seems not to have been imported; few folk-painted chests of Niagara provenance are presently known. Instead, the aesthetic appeal of Lincoln County blanket chests is concentrated in their clean form and black walnut construction. Many have pronounced Chippendale design features, notably well-developed bracket feet, reeded mouldings and quarter columns. Many have two or three drawers, while a few are made without drawers at all, yet they retain the quiet refinement of the more elaborate examples.

Quite a few walnut chests of drawers from the Niagara Peninsula retain the Chippendale design elements of reeded friezes, quarter columns, lapped drawers and fine details. Most have flat Chippendale bracket feet, although a few comparatively sophisticated examples have sturdy ogee bracket feet. These chests of drawers, as well as a smaller number of desks of related design, are among the finest pieces of Pennsylvania-German furniture made in Upper Canada.

Another strong Pennsylvania-German form that continued to be made and used in the Niagara Peninsula was the heavy kitchen table with drawers and removable top (a practical feature which allowed for easy cleaning). While such tables were made in all Pennsylvania-German areas of Ontario, it is only in the Niagara Peninsula that examples are known with "box" or "H" stretchers. Generally made of walnut, these tables have turned legs, lapped drawers, cleated tops and resemble counterparts in Pennsylvania. One stretcher-base table is stamped "J.H. Housser Mak C. W." indicating that it was made at some time during the surprisingly late period from 1841 to 1867.

Furniture made by or for Continental Germans in Ontario is frequently so similar to that of the Pennsylvania Germans that it differs from the latter only in detail.

Often, Continental-German furniture is recognizable by its greater departure from the rectilinear in favour of the curvilinear, in "baroque" elements such as elaborate scrollwork, carved pediments, cabriole legs and variations and inversions of curved lines. Further refinements might take the form of lozenge or diamond types of panelling, diamond-shaped pulls, carved motifs, elaborate inlay, applied flat columns and other Classical Revival or Biedermeier elements.

Although the Niagara Peninsula furniture tradition was dominated by the work of Pennsylvania craftsmen, there is also a distinctive body of Continental-German furniture, particularly in Welland and Haldimand counties and including some pieces made somewhat later in Lincoln County itself. It is from areas around Stevensville, Port Colborne and Fisherville that some distinctively Continental furniture has come to light, but in considerably smaller numbers than Pennsylvania-German examples.

Perhaps the most conspicuous expression of Alsatian or south German influence is to be seen in the numerous clothes cupboards or *Kleiderschränke* found in the region. It has already been noted that few of these are known within the Pennsylvania-German communities of the Niagara Peninsula. They preferred the linen press for this function. It is rather in the Continental-German areas of the Peninsula that the *Schrank* appears to have been used for clothes storage. Several pieces from lower Welland and Haldimand counties have been found which exhibit distinctive Continental design features such as scrolled, flared or unusually shaped feet or applied lozenges and geometric elements characteristic of German Neoclassical prototypes. A Lincoln County example, reputedly the work of G. Bender,[16] reflects strong Continental influences in its architectural elements (triangular pediment, massive feet) and its rounded case and cornice.

Although Niagara Peninsula wall cupboards normally fall within the Pennsylvania-German design idiom, a notable deviation features large lozenge panels on its doors, revealing Continental influences (Plate 63).

The Ontario-German furniture tradition of upper York County is almost exclusively dominated by Pennsylvania-German craftsmen who entered Vaughan and Markham townships at the beginning of the nineteenth century. Furniture from this area reveals a diverse range of skill and refinement, from the striking sophistication of the figured maple desks and chests of John or Ebenezer Doan from the Sharon area[17] to the naïve charm of the fancifully painted cupboards and chests by John Barkey who worked in the Mennonite community near Markham. The few known Doan pieces are refined expressions of the cabinetmaker's art with powerfully shaped ogee bracket feet, lapped drawers, quarter columns and cases lavishly fashioned of bird's-eye maple.

Numerous pieces of furniture made by individuals for home use have been recorded in upper York County. Notable in this category are several tables, cupboards and other pieces attributed to the Vaughan Township settlers Henry Snider (1807-1876) and his sons Jacob and Henry, as well as the Bakers and Cobers.[18]

The Markham area produced an "earlier" and a "later" body of furniture, the former of heavier and more decidedly Pennsylvania-German styling, the latter a diluted mixture of Pennsylvania-German form and contemporary tastes.[19] In the former group are several corner and wall cupboards with massive cornices, lapped doors and drawers, deep fielded panels, inset end panels (on the wall cupboards), deeply overhanging countertops on base sections and heavy bracket feet. The "later" Markham area wall cupboards, particularly those by John Barkey, are of much lighter construction, with simplified cornices, narrower proportions and almost delicate feet shaped from the stiles rather than an outside bracket base. In these later examples, the protruding counter-top of the earlier cupboards, built up with complex mouldings, has been almost totally eliminated. A similar diminution can be seen in two groups of Markham chests of drawers. Several earlier examples feature graduated rows of lapped drawers with the upper two rows consisting of five smaller drawers. These large case-pieces are mounted on bracket bases or heavily turned feet (already a surrender to American Empire influences). The later chests of drawers, several attributed to the Barkey cabinetmakers, are of generally lighter proportion, shortened from five to four rows of drawers. The five-drawer arrangement in the upper rows has given way to a simple splitting of the top row into drawers. The most conspicuous evidence of American Empire influence in these later pieces is the appearance of backboards, rounded stiles and turned feet. These chests are prevented from falling wholly into the category of "Empire" furniture by the whimsical carving and imaginative feather-grain painting of cases and drawer-fronts.

There are several pieces from this area which become a genre of their own by virtue of having been decorated in the manner of traditional Pennsylvania-German folk art. One important example is a wall cupboard from nearby Goodwood, in Ontario County, with strong Neoclassical features and six-pointed stars cut into its upper stiles. (See Pain, Plate 1002). Another is a superbly decorated desk from Markham or Vaughan townships, with compass stars, geometric designs and wood-grain patterning painted on its sloped front and sides (Plate 64).

In Waterloo County, a furniture-making tradition developed which enlisted the creative energies of both Continental and Pennsylvania craftsmen. While it is true for the most part that these two groups were more or less geographically distinct and tended to produce "for their own," in at least a few instances there was a pattern of crossing-over. An interesting case is the Swiss-born chairmaker Jacob Hailer (1804-1882), whose well-known slat-back chairs have not only been found in Continental- and Pennsylvania-German households, but also in English homes in Waterloo County.

One of the earliest Waterloo Pennsylvania-German craftsmen was the carpenter and builder Samuel Bowers (died 1855). He operated a cabinetmaking firm in Berlin (Kitchener) at a very early date. Perhaps the earliest and longest lasting enterprise had its beginnings in the 1830s when two brothers, John Hoffman (1808-1878) and Jacob Hoffman (1809-1864), opened a cabinetmaking business on land given to them by Bishop Benjamin Eby. These businesses, in addition to Jacob Hailer's chairmaking shop, placed furniture-making at the centre of Berlin's early commercial history. Judging by the extensive advertising done over the following decades by the Hoffman firm (engaged in various partnerships) and eventually continued by Jacob's son, Isaac Hoffman (1835-1898), the firm sought to produce a wide variety of furniture in the newest and most fashionable styles. In 1845, another local craftsman, Georg Jantz, advertised a mixed offering of traditional furniture, including *Schränke*, and more stylish pieces, such as *Fränzosische Stühle* ("French chairs," otherwise known as sabre-leg or *klismos* chairs) of Neoclassical design.[20]

An important Pennsylvania-German furniture-maker operating in Waterloo County, outside the village of Berlin proper, was Abraham Latschaw (1799-1870), who worked at Mannheim and New Hamburg.[21] In 1854, Latschaw undertook the ambitious task of building for the then high price of $68 a large inlaid corner cupboard for Jacob Bricker (1818-1909). Its form is a highly eclectic fusion of Chippendale and American Empire elements, but its inlaid stars and tulips are from the Pennsylvania-German design tradition.

Cupboard types found in Waterloo County include wall cupboards, corner cupboards, and — less commonly — hanging cupboards. Wall cupboards, unlike their Lincoln County counterparts, normally have a pie-shelf area between upper and lower sections. They are often of excellent proportion and design, made of both hardwood (cherry) and painted pine. The usual form has two or three drawers in the base, although a few rare examples are known with seven drawers in an arrangement of three across and four down the centre between the doors. Top sections have either solid ("blind") or glazed doors. Most have simple feet carved either from the stiles or from an applied outside bracket base. Only two are currently known with ogee bracket feet, and these are much simpler in design than those found on Niagara Peninsula cupboards.

Corner cupboards are found only rarely in Lincoln and upper York counties, but they appear to have formed an essential part of the household inventory in Waterloo County. A few with solid doors are known, but most have glazed doors above and drawers and solid doors below. Like the wall cupboards, they are usually made in two sections. Early pieces tend to be distinguished by stepped-down window mullions, heavy cornices, applied mouldings, outside bracket feet and fielded panels. Later versions often have flat mullions, simple cove-cornices, little or no applied moulding, feet cut from stiles and flat panels. Though a few hardwood pieces have been found, most corner cupboards are made of pine, usually with a simple red stain or paint, but on rare occasions with multi-coloured finish (Plate 67). Later examples, like wall cupboards, were generally given a mustard-and-ochre grained finish.

The *Kleiderschrank*, or clothes cupboard, is one of the most recognizable "Waterloo" furniture forms. The large surface area of such pieces lends itself to the creative use of geometry, as witnessed in the extensive panelling of doors, stiles and ends of several larger examples. A number of well-designed *Schränke*, possibly from the workshop of Abraham Latschaw, feature ogee bracket feet (identical to those on the two wall cupboards discussed above), extensive panelling, elaborate cornices above friezes decorated by inlay, or painted, applied mouldings and other refinements. Several pieces are constructed of

carefully selected figured cherry or of pine with skilfully painted feather-decoration. Later examples tend to be of lighter construction and proportion, with flat panels and feet shaped from end stiles. Some of these simpler pieces are distinguished by their well-executed painted decoration.

Tables found in Waterloo County's Pennsylvania-German households resemble those of the Niagara Peninsula with removable cleated tops over a base with two or three drawers. Hardwood examples in Waterloo County are made of cherry rather than walnut, although pine was more commonly used than hardwood. Stretcher bases, seen occasionally on Niagara Peninsula tables, are not generally found on kitchen tables made in Waterloo County.

Several Waterloo chests of drawers and desks demonstrate competent craftsmanship. Important early examples include an 1817 cherry slant-front desk inlaid with the name of its maker or owner (Moses Eby) and a beautifully shaped heart motif in the Pennsylvania-German design tradition. Other desks and chests of drawers testify to a vigorous cabinetmaking industry prior to mid-century. Related in detail to these pieces are blanket chests with lift tops and (optionally) drawers at the base. In time, the early Waterloo County chests, with their sturdy bracket feet, applied mouldings and lapped drawers, gave way to pieces with flush drawers, simple mouldings and factory-painted finishes, a change that also occurred in the Markham area.

Traditional furniture taste was perpetuated in Waterloo County longer than in the other Pennsylvania-German regions of Ontario. Factory-made cupboards and blanket chests were produced into the early twentieth century by such firms as the Waterloo partnership of Isaac Hoffman, Adam Klippert and Martin Wegenast; the preference for traditional furniture has really never died in Waterloo County. Even today there are local craftsmen, like Sidney Fry of Conestogo, who continue to make for Old Order Mennonite neighbours and friends, chests of drawers, blanket chests and special pieces of traditional furniture modelled closely upon pieces used by previous generations.

In the Catholic-German areas, there developed a tradition of furniture-making which resembled that of the Pennsylvania Germans in general impression, but differed in detail. Numerous pieces of case-furniture found around Maryhill have raised lozenge or diamond-shaped panels; still more distinctive are several wardrobes whose elaborately shaped panels resemble the panelling of the front door of the Goetz House in Maryhill (Plate 86). Other pieces from Catholic-German settlements are distinguished by cabriole or flared legs, while a remarkable table from the village of St. Clements features a sliding tambour door modelled after a Louis XVI *poudreuse*. [22]

The furnishings made in Amish regions of Waterloo County, particularly in the Petersburg-Baden area of Wilmot Township, also reflect south-German or Alsatian design influences. A local cabinetmaker produced a number of pieces upon which are stencilled dates, places and names. Similar pieces with stencilled names and dates have also been found in the Catholic-German area around Maryhill. Among identified examples are many panelled wardrobes, such as that made in 1852 for Elizabeth Litwiller, daughter of Bishop Peter Litwiller of Petersburg. [23] We have also seen cupboards from this area which are stencilled in a similar manner as well as smaller objects including mirror or picture frames. It may well be that these objects, especially those bearing feminine names, were intended as marriage presentation-pieces, but firm evidence for such an assumption is lacking.

From the vicinity of Wellesley, a few miles to the north of Petersburg and Baden, there comes another group of related Continental-German furniture. These pieces have also been found in the Amish settlements of adjoining Perth County. Deserving particular attention are the large panelled wardrobes with rounded corners and inset flat panels on the doors and sides. In some cases the upper door stiles are restrained, shaped in a modified Louis XV manner. A few resemble furniture made in French Canada and probably are of direct Alsatian influence.

A most notable example of furniture decorated in the south German or Swiss style is a panelled wardrobe found near Baden. It came down through Amish settlers. Of local design and construction, it is boldly painted with baskets of flowers on each panel and floral designs on the stiles and cross members (Plate 84). Sadly, this wardrobe was cut in half about thirty years ago. The remaining portion provides evidence of the perpetuation of Continental decorative conventions in the New World.

Some Continental-German furniture makes use of elaborate inlay, as in the case of two well-known tables found near the village of Erbsville (Plate 85). Several pieces from adjoining Perth County, including a cherry

wall cupboard signed "John Schweitzer, North Easthope Township," indicate a relatively widespread practice of decorating furniture with inlaid motifs.

Two late cabinetmakers of Continental-German background are Christian Gerber (1845-1928) from the Amish area near Wellesley and John K. Lemp (1860-1938) of Tavistock, Oxford County. Christian Gerber learned cabinetmaking from his father John (1809-1889). Copying a desk made by the elder craftsman in the 1860s, Christian set out to make five desks and three chests of drawers for his five sons and three daughters respectively. These were made at a late date (one piece is dated 1900), but are virtually identical to the American Empire styles adopted and modified by his father thirty years earlier. The name of a son is lettered on the lid of each desk, along with the date of its making, and each one is stencilled, ebonized and flamboyantly painted, sometimes in imitation of figured maple and other hardwoods, or simply in an abstract manner (Plates 82, 83). John Lemp, on the other hand, made several eight-foot high clocks which are an eclectic blend of baroque carving, German clockmaking and Victorian washstand design (Plate 91). Working in the 1920s, he retained some of the traditional wood-carving skills which characterized the work of German craftsmen-carvers employed in the numerous furniture factories of Berlin (Kitchener).

Further to the north and west, furniture of strong Continental-German design was made from the middle to the end of the nineteenth century in Huron, Bruce and Grey counties. Bruce County, especially around Mildmay and Formosa, has been the source of many pieces with elaborate scrollwork and baroque features. Furniture from this area utilizes the cabriole leg, a form generally unknown in Pennsylvania-German examples.

John Gemeinhardt (1826-1912) was an inventive craftsman from Huron County. He emigrated from Germany and settled at Bayfield along the eastern shore of Lake Huron in the 1850s. Listed originally as a carpenter, by the 1880s he had established a cabinetmaking business. There he produced a modest body of furniture for the local market, generally of Germanic construction and style. In addition, he made a number of specialty pieces, including bedroom suites, parlour tables and chairs for each of his four daughters when they married. It is these specialty pieces which reveal his conservative approach to style and use of the carving, ebonizing and techniques associated with traditional Germanic craftsmanship. Although the bedroom suites were made more or less in the manner of Eastlake and other factory furniture of the late nineteenth century, he introduced refinements of shaping and carving undoubtedly learned during his apprenticeship forty years earlier in Germany. Especially representative of Biedermeier design are his four superb chairs with sabre or *klismos* legs and lyre motifs (Plate 94). Another excellent example of Neoclassical workmanship which had been in vogue in Germany during his apprenticeship is a watch-holder (Plate 95) consisting of an arched pediment supported on four turned columns. Gemeinhardt's work is a dramatic instance of the *retardataire* phenomenon by which traditional techniques, modes and designs were retained by an immigrant cabinetmaker nearly three-quarters of a century after they had ceased to be stylish in urban centres.

In Bruce County, many examples of elaborately inlaid furniture suggest the work of several craftsmen, among them Nicholas Dürrer (1834-1908), the altar-carver from Formosa, and John P. Klempp (1857-1914), who emigrated from Germany by way of Waterloo County to the village of Neustadt in the 1870s. Engaged both as a hotel proprietor and cabinetmaker, Klempp produced a surprising number of meticulously inlaid wardrobes, cupboards, desks, chests of drawers and smaller pieces during the late 1870s and through the 1880s. Many of them feature heavily scrolled aprons and intricate inlay patterns using traditional Germanic motifs. In addition to these inlaid pieces, usually butternut or cherry with maple inlay, Klempp also produced some painted furniture, such as a wardrobe made for his own use. This piece combines traditional Continental-German baroque styling with elements of American Empire, perhaps even Victorian design and strong innovations of his own conception. The result is a rather loose amalgam of traditional, contemporary and idiosyncratic elements. In their eclecticism, several of his creations attain a novel folk-art quality, in the eccentric notion of the phrase, while others are markedly ethnic and traditional.

The cabinetmaker Friedrich K. Ploethner (1826-1883) was also engaged in business as a weaver and farmer. Like others in the Bruce-Grey County area, he had passed through Waterloo County en route from Germany in the 1850s. Born at the village of Neustadt, near the Czecho-slovakian border in eastern Germany, Friedrich and his brother August emigrated to Preston, Waterloo County, in 1854. While August remained behind in Preston, tak-

ing up weaving there, Friedrich journeyed north in 1856 or 1857, settling almost midway between the villages of Neustadt and Ayton, in Normanby Township, Grey County. During the 1870s, he produced a significant group of well-crafted pieces of furniture. A number of items possibly made by Adam Pletsch, Friedrich Ploethner, or both in collaboration, reflect a strong Germanic design vocabulary. These and other smaller pieces suggest the persistence of traditional techniques in the remote Germanic settlements of Canada which were to be dissipated only at the beginning of the twentieth century.

A few Continental Germans also established themselves in eastern Ontario, inhabiting several small villages in Renfrew, Lennox, Addington, and Frontenac counties. In the hamlets of Palmer Rapids, Augsburg, Rankin and Germanicus in Renfrew County, German craftsmen produced distinctive furniture forms and styles. Food lockers, cupboards, wardrobes, cradles, benches, chairs, couches, dough boxes and other small furnishings were all among their products. The most traditional of these are food lockers with wooden grills and baroque pediments. One of these is virtually covered with sponge-painted decoration and stylized trees on the pediment (Plate 101). Frequently, it is hand-made primitive furniture which retains the most pronounced traditional design or construction elements, as in several couches from Renfrew and Frontenac counties, or a plank chair attributed to August Boehme of Palmer Rapids. Perhaps one of the most appealing examples of Continental-German furniture from eastern Ontario is a primitive wall cupboard, also attributed to August Boehme, with its carved rosettes, hearts and baroque pediment (Plate 102).

These examples indicate that traditional designs and forms seem to have survived so long as one or two craftsmen still worked from memories of earlier pieces, and so long as the village market was able to remain relatively immune from mass manufacturing and cosmopolitan tastes emanating from the growing urban centres.

## Fraktur and Drawings

One of the most distinctive and recognizable types of Pennsylvania-German folk art is manuscript illumination, known more familiarly as *Fraktur*. Developing from an earlier period in Medieval Europe when the flowing Carolingian cursive script was replaced by a more ornamental lettering (called loosely, "gothic," "black-letter" or *Fraktur*), this decorative printing flourished in Germany, Switzerland and, later, Pennsylvania. In addition to hand-lettered texts, there appeared many hand-drawn decorations: hearts, stars, tulips, birds and other elements. Appearing originally as book margin decoration, these motifs eventually became as prominent as the text itself and in many cases overpowered or even replaced it altogether.

This *Fraktur* tradition was continued in the various documents found in the religious and domestic settings of Anabaptist regions. Typical decorated forms were the birth record (*Geburtschein*), the combined birth-and-baptismal record (*Tauf-und-Geburtschein*), the family register (*Familien-Register*), the marriage certificate (*Heiratschein*) and the bookplate (*Bucherzeichen*). An additional form, associated with the school, was the writing-specimen (*Vorschrift*), lettered and decorated by the schoolmaster, to be copied by his pupils. Because they are the work of professionals, these *Vorschriften* are among the finest examples of *Fraktur*. Typically they employ alphabets, numerals or a passage from the Scriptures and accompanying decorative motifs.

While *Fraktur* has its origins in the folk-art traditions of Switzerland and southern Germany, it flowered in Pennsylvania in the eighteenth and nineteenth centuries. From there, it was carried to Maryland, Virginia, the Carolinas, Ohio and Ontario, when these areas were settled in the late eighteenth and early nineteenth centuries.

The earliest known indigenous Ontario *Fraktur* specimens have been found in the Niagara Peninsula, principally in Lincoln County and to a lesser extent in Welland, Haldimand and Norfolk counties along the Lake Erie shoreline. Early schoolteachers, such as Samuel Moyer (1767-1844), his cousin, Jacob Moyer and Abraham Meyer were most likely the artists who produced many of the drawings and illuminated songbooks from the Vineland-Jordon area of Lincoln County. It is from this region that the few rare Ontario *Vorschriften* originated, reflecting the work of both teachers and pupils. The most prominent type of *Fraktur* associated with Lincoln County is the decorated songbook; numerous superb pieces were done by teachers in the Mennonite Singing School at Vineland (called the Clinton School). These songbooks closely resemble earlier examples brought along from Bucks County, Pennsylvania.

It is possible that they were made by schoolteachers who had previously taught or been pupils in Pennsylvania parochial schools under such famous teachers as Johann Adam Eyer. [24]

An itinerant *Fraktur* practitioner, known as the "Ehre Vater Artist," apparently travelled far and wide, living in Pennsylvania, but making trips through Maryland, the Carolinas and Ontario. On a brief journey in the early nineteenth century along the Lake Erie shoreline, he did numerous birth records for pioneer families in the area. Other miscellaneous specimens found in Welland County indicate a modest activity there, practised in both Pennsylvania and Continental-German settlements.

A second region in which the art of *Fraktur* was developed to a significant degree is upper York County. Examples are known there among the Mennonites of Markham Township and also among the Dunkers of Vaughan Township, just to the west. The dominant type of *Fraktur* associated with the area is the birth-and-baptismal certificate. The earliest group of such pieces, produced between the known dates of 1807 and 1812, were hand-lettered and decorated for early families who had migrated to York County from Pennsylvania. There is also a number of small drawings by the same hand bearing the names of pupils to whom they may have been given as awards. These early certificates and drawings are the most refined *Fraktur* specimens from this county; they are clearly the work of a professional scrivener who was probably following the long-accepted practice of rendering a service for a small fee to augment his modest teacher's salary.

Another Markham Township artist, also likely a school teacher, was Joseph Lochbaum,[25] who was active in Pennsylvania and possibly in Ontario. Sometimes dubbed "The Nine Hearts Artist" or "The Cumberland Valley Artist," he appears to have travelled to Upper Canada in the 1820s or '30s stopping briefly in Markham before moving on again. Some dozen examples of his work are presently known. Like his forerunner, he produced hand-drawn birth-and-baptismal certificates for several families in the Markham-Stouffville area. These certificates are uniquely designed. Each features an arrangement of nine hearts enclosing a religious text and pertinent biographical information. His work was later copied by at least two other artists active in the 1840s or 1850s.

The certificates produced in the 1820s or '30s by these two earliest York County artists are the result of a frequently repeated situation in which a non-Mennonite schoolteacher or professional scrivener practised *Fraktur* for Mennonites. This is illustrated by the fact that these artists employed forms normally intended for baptisms in Lutheran and Reformed Churches. Mennonites do not practise infant baptism. Hence, the use of a certificate which records both birth and baptism (the latter information is generally missing from these examples) suggests the adaptation of a form from one religious group for use in another.

The last in a trio of Markham Township *Fraktur* artists was Christian L. Hoover (1835-1918), an individual who seems to have taken up the art almost against his own wishes. In 1854 when he was nineteen, Hoover fell seriously ill and was confined to bed in order to recover from a form of intermittent fever.[26] Unable to engage in farm work, he occupied his time during a lengthy period of convalescence by lettering and drawing birth records for his brothers, sisters, relatives and friends. He produced at least one marriage certificate, for his oldest brother, Abraham (married to Veronica Groff in 1851), as well as some drawings and a school copybook whose pages he filled with *Fraktur* motifs. The copybook drawings were done during the period from 1852 to 1854, while the large certificates are dated 1854 (the sole exception is a birth record for Elisabeth Bercki dated 1854). Christian Hoover's *Fraktur* career was truly brief; it appears to have been terminated immediately upon his recovery in 1855. It was in fact the end of a creative era. Except for a few birth and marriage certificates made by Christian's younger brother, Samuel Hoover (1838-1915), which were closely copied a few years later from the 1854 works, little *Fraktur* was produced in Markham after 1860.

The third principal region of *Fraktur* activity in Ontario's Pennsylvania-German communities was Waterloo County. The majority of examples found there can be attributed to a quartet of artists: Abraham Latschaw (1799-1870), Isaac Z. Hunsicker (1803-1870), Anna Weber (1814-1888) and Joseph D. Bauman (1815-1899). Latschaw and Hunsicker could be considered "professionals," while Anna Weber and Joseph Bauman were "amateurs," producing drawings and decorated texts primarily for family, friends or visitors.

*Fraktur* in Waterloo County flourished from 1820 to 1890. A Montgomery County, Pennsylvania, schoolmaster named Jacob Schumacher had executed family records for several Waterloo County pioneer families, but the earliest indigenous *Fraktur* in this region is the 1823 work of Abraham Latschaw, a Berks County scrivener and cabinetmaker who settled at Mannheim in Wilmot Township. His bookplate/family genealogy, for the Bible of Bishop Benjamin Eby, is undoubtedly the masterpiece of Waterloo County *Fraktur* illumination. After the one-year period during which he produced few but outstanding pieces of *Fraktur*, Latschaw apparently abandoned this pursuit in favour of his cabinetmaking business, which he continued over the next thirty years.

Possibly the most prolific Waterloo County artist was Isaac Z. Hunsicker, active from the 1830s to almost 1870, the year of his death. He arrived sometime between 1832 and 1835 from Montgomery County, Pennsylvania, where he had earlier produced *Fraktur* in the Skippack area. Hunsicker was a schoolteacher in Berlin, where he executed various small drawings as awards for his pupils. He also produced several fine bookplates, birth certificates and marriage records. His most extensive work, however, was in the lettering of family registers, frequently done on the blank pages reserved for this purpose between the Old and New Testaments of family Bibles. Nearly every major family name in Waterloo County is represented by a Bible lettered by Isaac Hunsicker. Because of these family registers, Hunsicker produced more known specimens of *Fraktur* than any other scrivener in southwestern Ontario. One exception might be Wilhelm Gerhard (1864-1913); he inscribed family registers on large sheets for persons in virtually every Germanic community west of Toronto.

An unusual artist was Anna Weber, who began work late in her life. She had been stricken with a chronic illness, and loneliness may have motivated an interest in producing simple drawings as gifts for hosts, friends and children. Others were sometimes sold to visitors for a modest fee. Most of her work is somewhat coarse, and her palette is generally limited to four colours (characteristically, violet, yellow, blue and green, with occasional variations). The earliest signed and dated work is her own songbook, decorated in 1866. Her pictures appear to have been produced in nearly every year from 1870 until her death in 1888. Many possess a special charm, combining flowers and animals from everyday observation within Pennsylvania-German conventions.

An interesting contemporary of Anna Weber was Joseph D. Bauman (1815-1899), who according to family recollection produced drawings and decorated texts for his grandchildren and friends, and illuminated family Bibles.

Many of his drawings are literal copies of printed forms, while others appear to have been influenced by the earlier work of Hunsicker, whose work Bauman probably saw in the family Bibles of neighbours and relatives. Among common subjects done in *Fraktur* by Bauman are printed texts with hand-drawn pictures of Adam and Eve, as well as birds and other motifs which he borrowed from mass-produced birth certificates. In contrast to the rather muted colours used by Anna Weber, Joseph Bauman's drawings were normally executed in brilliant reds and yellows.

By the time Bauman died in 1899, the Pennsylvania-German *Fraktur* tradition had, for all practical purposes, come to a close in Ontario. A few isolated individuals, however, continued to produced occasional pieces of expert calligraphy well into the twentieth century. In recent years, the art has been reintroduced in some rural schools of the Old Order Mennonite community in Waterloo County.

It is of interest to note the extreme variations in the careers enjoyed by Ontario *Fraktur* artists. In contrast to the sustained activity of Isaac Hunsicker (some forty years) or Anna Weber (twenty-two years) are the tantalizingly brief flourishings of Christian L. Hoover or Abraham Latschaw. One cannot help but wonder how much richer the Ontario *Fraktur* tradition might have been if an artist of Latschaw's stature had devoted a full life to calligraphy and drawing for the surrounding community.

In addition to *Fraktur*, other forms of graphic art have been found in Ontario-German communities, though such examples are rare in contrast to non-German areas, or in comparison with settlements in Pennsylvania. The domestic or farmyard naïveté of the Grandma Moses type is generally not found in western Ontario, but a few amateur landscapes of considerable primitive charm are known, including the example done by Orvie Shantz of Lexington in Waterloo County (Plate 129).

Interesting drawings have survived occasionally in children's school books or "scribblers." Among amateur artists of unusual talent are the young Benneval G. Martin (1876-1935) and his son, Absalom Martin (1902-1977). Three books done by the elder Martin when he was a pupil at Three Bridges School west of St. Jacobs in the 1890s indicate his artistic interest in natural subjects that would be familiar to a farm boy in Waterloo County. These include several renditions of roosters and horses, often accompanied by lettering in the *Fraktur* style. Like other schoolboys of his time, Benneval appears to have been infatuated with the coming of the Grand Trunk Railway. His books contain several charming portrayals of railway cars. One pencil drawing done in 1890 shows the first passenger train to run between Berlin (Kitchener) and Elmira. Absalom shared his father's interest, and around 1915 he produced a delightful drawing of a rooster, similar to those later fashioned in wood by the St. Jacobs woodcarver, David B. Horst.

Strenuous farm work, severe climate and religious self-effacement might seem to some observers to be antithetical to the expression of artistic energies. Yet the high value placed on family history, the expressions of kindness and appreciation among relatives and friends and the love of both the beauty and the goodness of nature, all favoured the artistic impulse. In addition, the general belief in doing all things well has long provided a climate for the flowering of folk art through the realization of the human instinct to embellish nature.

## Textiles

Ontario-German textiles may be divided into several categories. From a functional point of view they can be classified according to whether they were made by professionals or amateurs. More formally they might be divided along the lines of type, technique and materials. From an aesthetic perspective they could be sorted out by design and decorative vocabulary.

Among the principal decorated textiles made and used in Germanic areas are weaving (coverlets, blankets, tablecloths), needlework (samplers and embroidered towels), pieced and appliquéd work (quilts, chair cushions) and hook work (rugs, mats). The large woven pieces were made by professionals for a local market. Other forms were generally done by amateurs, working at home. Samplers and embroidered towels were normally worked by young girls, while quilts and hooked rugs were created by women of all ages.

Weaving was practised mainly by men who filled custom requests during the winter months when the demands of farming were comparatively light. Most Ontario-German weavers were trained on the Continent and were primarily Lutheran, or less frequently, Roman Catholic. The number of Mennonite or Pennsylvania-German weavers in Ontario was small, but there were several capable craftsmen.

On the basis of designs, it is often difficult to isolate Pennsylvania-German from Continental-German weaving in Canada. Mechanical devices have no ethnic boundaries. The weavers of Upper Canada, whether in the Niagara Peninsula, Waterloo County or the Huron area, copied and used pattern drafts from cards easily obtainable from Pennsylvania. It is not unheard of, for example, to find an Ontario coverlet with an American eagle perched atop a stars-and-stripes shield. Production for the local market frequently utilized whatever was popularly available, making precise identification of weaver or area difficult.

The two basic fibres necessary for day-to-day living in pioneer communities were wool and linen. As soon as sheep could be raised on the farm, wool was sheared, cleaned and treated for spinning by the girls in the home. Fulling, a process of compacting wool fibres, was not done in the home but at a fulling mill. Linen, on the other hand, was the result of a painstaking, lengthy process.[27] Nine months were required for flax to go from seed to fibre, and then the strands had to be broken from the stem and combed. The short (tow) and long (linen) threads had to be separated and stored until spinning time in winter. Linen was used to make cloth, but it was an important yarn for coverlets, too, as it was used as the lengthwise threads, the warp. Although some coverlets were made with both wool warps and wefts, this was the exception rather than the rule. At this time cotton was scarce, but after the invention of the cotton gin supply increased enormously and cotton replaced linen as warp material.

The harsh winters of Ontario ensured a market for woven wool blankets, but the early plain or tabby weave blankets of utilitarian character were not particularly attractive. Weaving of this type probably dates back to the early nineteenth century in the Niagara Peninsula; many horse blankets were also produced. But because the bed was a prominent feature in the log cabin, it soon acquired more decorative covering. Some of the finest nineteenth-century coverlets were made by Germanic weavers in the popular indigo blue and white colours.

The first Jacquard loom was introduced into Canada in 1834 by the German-trained Wilhelm Armbrust, who advertised his "new and fancy loom" in a St. Catharines newspaper.[28] He produced many fine coverlets, often recognizable by a "Four Roses" motif, as well as stars, hearts, carnations and flowering trees. A particularly distinctive mark on his coverlets is a cartouche containing two hearts suspended between two pillars.[29] Shortly after his marriage around 1848, it seems that he stopped weaving.

Another important weaver in the Niagara Peninsula was Edward Graf (1826-1904), who bought Armbrust's equipment and patterns. His son, Albert, assisted him in the business at Gasline, Humberstone Township, Welland County, east of the town of Port Colborne.[30] Dated Graf coverlets are known from the period 1853 to 1870 and can be identified by the appearance of the pattern name in a corner, including the "Double Rose," "Bird's Nest" and "Birds of Paradise."

One weaver active around Welland during the first half of the nineteenth century has yet to be named. Numerous similar coverlets by his hand have been found in this region, dating from the 1830s and 1840s. They are identified by the device of a heart lying sideways in the corner.[31]

Other weavers of Continental-German background in the Niagara Peninsula were Hans Peter and a female practitioner, Mrs. Jacob Benner. Examples of their work may be found today in the textile collection of the Royal Ontario Museum.[32]

The most fully documented weaver in Canada is Samuel Fry (1812-1881), a Mennonite from Bucks County, Pennsylvania. Account books, patterns and examples of his work are preserved in the Jordan Museum of the Twenty and also in the Royal Ontario Museum. Fry travelled to Bucks County to learn the trade and commenced business when he returned to Lincoln County in 1836. One known example of his weaving is his own woollen blanket, marked "S F" and done in lozenge twill. Several pieces of clothing made from cloth woven by Fry are preserved in public collections, including his wedding suit, made of all-black wool. Part of another marriage outfit, a pair of trousers made for David Housser, was reputedly woven by Fry around 1843.[33] In contrast to his own sombre, conservative suit, it was made of white cotton with red and blue stripes. Other handwoven articles surviving from the Vineland-Jordan area are a cotton dickey made for John Rittenhouse when he married Elizabeth Funk in 1826. This and other pieces are still in the hands of descendants in the Markham area.

Yet another Mennonite from Pennsylvania, Moses Grobb (1806-1877), worked around Vineland during the approximate period of 1853 to 1872.[34] According to

Ontario Census listings he was both a weaver and fruit merchant. Most of his Jacquard-woven coverlets are dated and of fine workmanship and design. Further inland, many weavers of distinction were actively fashioning blankets and other woven goods in the Waterloo County area. Among Continental-German immigrants was August Ploethner who worked in the town of Preston (Cambridge). He is well known for his wide Jacquard coverlets in monochrome, often a bright red. Toward the end of the nineteenth century, he worked in more brilliant if not garish colours. A brother, Friedrich, may have worked with him briefly before moving further north and west to set up a business of his own in Grey County.

Daniel Knechtel was a fully trained professional weaver who emigrated from Pennsylvania during the American Civil War and settled at Roseville in Waterloo County. His coverlets frequently employ the "Wild Turkey" pattern, popular also in Pennsylvania. His use of a motif found earlier in Pennsylvania supports the notion that Jacquard coverlet patterns were in fact imported from the United States.

Wilhelm Magnus Werlich, from Wildenspring in Germany's Thuringia, arrived in 1850, bringing pattern books with him from the Continent, which he used for weaving coverlets in Preston, Waterloo County.[35] He continued working from his log cabin weaving shop until 1912.

Among Waterloo County's best known craftsmen are William and John Noll of Petersburg, the first Roman Catholic weavers in the county. In 1848 they were both listed in the Census under this trade, and many outstanding examples can be attributed to them. Frequently, the name of the maker is woven into one or two corners, while the recipient's name also appears in the cartouche. One of the earliest dated Noll Jacquards is dated 1868; one year later one of Waterloo County's distinctive historical artifacts was produced — the coverlet for Father Eugen Funcken, spiritual pioneer of the Roman Catholic settlement at nearby St. Agatha and founder of both St. Jerome's Academy and the St. Agatha orphanage. This fine coverlet was woven when John Noll was eighteen and his brother William twenty. The "Four Roses" motif on many of the Noll coverlets suggests that they may have been made as part of a wedding trousseau. It is possible that some of their border designs came from contemporary china patterns. William also made horse blankets, while both weavers produced clothing materials, sheets and

carpeting well into the twentieth century.

Not far from the Nolls in Petersburg was the weaving establishment of Johan Lippert and his son, Henry, who continued the business well into the twentieth century. The "Church" pattern is a motif associated with their work.

Beyond Waterloo County, Germanic settlements were gradually established in the Huron area, which included the counties of Huron, Bruce and Grey. Like other regions of Ontario, the professional weavers active in these counties are often difficult to identify. In Keep Me Warm One Night, for instance, Harold and Dorothy Burnham refer to an unknown weaver of blue and white Jacquard coverlets active near Neustadt-Hanover.[36] Recent research indicates that this weaver may in fact have been Friedrich K. Ploethner (1826-1883), brother of August Ploethner of Preston. The family of Friedrich Ploethner moved, about 1856 or 1857, from Preston to Lot 6, Normanby Township in Grey County.[37] Surviving examples of his work include several Jacquard coverlets and tablecloths. Preserved by descendants is an account book with entries of Weber-Arbeit (weaving work) from the years 1868 to 1883. Like his brother, he produced handwoven goods for the local market. Sadly, his loom was chopped up for firewood (a not uncommon fate) in the 1920s.

The Ontario-German handweaving tradition prospered in three principal areas — the Niagara Peninsula (primarily Lincoln and Welland counties), the Waterloo County region, and the Huron area — for approximately the century bridged by the dates 1825 and 1925. Surviving evidence is restricted almost to the woven artifacts themselves, with only a few looms and related utensils preserved in museums.

The outstanding form of Pennsylvania-German needlework in Ontario is unquestionably the decorated hand towel, familiarly called a "show towel." This art form is primarily a Mennonite tradition, found only rarely outside areas of Canada settled by persons from this religious background. It is not found in regions of Lutheran or Roman Catholic settlement in Ontario, nor is it evident in the German communities of the Maritimes or the Prairie Provinces, although a version of it is known in Hutterite colonies. Even within Ontario's Pennsylvania-German regions, it flourished only in Waterloo County and around Markham. Its practise in Lincoln County seems to have been infrequent, during a brief period of time. From the observation of known Pennsylvania examples, it appears that the custom was well developed among Mennonites from Lancaster County, who settled in Waterloo and York counties, but it was less common among those from Bucks County who settled Lincoln. It is found occasionally also in the Amish-Mennonite settlements of Waterloo, Oxford and Perth counties, probably influenced by or derived from the Swiss-German Mennonite settlement of the area.

The show towel is essentially a long piece of linen upon which traditional decorative folk-art motifs have been embroidered, usually in a cross stitch. Some consist of separate sections which have been added, given a fringe and faggoted. Earlier towels normally have designs worked in two colours, red and blue; the use of three or more colours was a later development. Dyed cotton thread was used on earlier towels rather than silk or wool which became popular after the middle of the nineteenth century. Decorative motifs were most likely copied from earlier prototypes. The bottom edge was sometimes drawn and then worked into a kind of needle lace. One example has the bottom threads pulled and worked in macramé groups.

In most cases, the name of the maker and the date appear across the top panel. Frequently, one section of a towel features an arrangement in which a central motif is flanked horizontally by identical designs. Dominant motifs are eight-pointed stars, trees, flowers, plants emerging from pots or urns, tulips, birds and hearts. One charming departure from convention shows a cat with its tail tightly curved around it. A distinctive focal point seen on many towels in Pennsylvania and Ontario is a pattern comprising the letters OEHBDDE (or a close variant) encircling or emanating from a heart; it almost resembles a "spider." The letters form an acronym for the religious aphorism *O Edel Herz Bedenk Dein End* (O Noble Heart, Consider Thy End). Although this "code" is found commonly on show towels, only on one rare known example do the actual words themselves appear.

From surviving towels, it is evident that they were made by women of all ages, but the art was normally practised by girls in their teenage years. The youngest maker known to us is Anna Burkhardt (1816-1833), who at the age of nine worked a show towel dated 1825 near the village of Waterloo.[38] A survey of extant show towels indicates that the prime flowering of the art occurred during approximately the half century from 1825 to 1875. Outside this range of dates, individual pieces have been

documented from as early as 1820 in Markham Township, while the latest known date is on a 1906 towel from Waterloo County. A few earlier examples of known Pennsylvania provenance have been found, including one dated 1799 in the collection of Doon Pioneer Village.

There are conflicting opinions concerning the use and placement of show towels. One popular theory holds that it was hung on a roller in the guest bedroom for "show" only. Beneath this fancy towel was an ordinary one for daily use. Another view claims that they were hung on the door of the parlour or master bedroom. Interviews with descendants indicate a popular preference for the first usage. However, more direct evidence or first-hand recollection is missing. In support of the second theory, the authors have found two households with parlour doors retaining original wooden or brass pegs once used for this purpose (see Plate 137).

Although there must at one time have been many decorated towels in Ontario, no more than two hundred are presently in public or private collections. Unlike *Fraktur*, which often remained intact because it was stored between the leaves of books, show towels were vulnerable to the deterioration caused by exposure to light, dirt and repeated washings. Many surviving towels are so faded that one can scarcely decipher the faint patterns of light blue, brown (once dark blue) and pink (originally red). In a few contemporary cases, owners have been sadly forced to consign the faded remains to the dustrag collection.

Closely related to show towels but having more direct counterparts in English and Scottish decorative arts are embroidered samplers which displayed the young girl's skill with the needle. Although Germanic and English samplers are often similar in design, the former are sometimes recognizable by small variations. Occasionally the letter "J" is absent; there is a tendency toward a more limited vocabulary of folk-art motifs similar to that used also on show towels and in *Fraktur*, frequently in a symmetrical arrangement.

The number of Ontario-German samplers is rather small. Among important examples is an 1827 piece by Susanna Byer (Plate 140) and a small, vertical, undated sampler by Anna Beam of Lincoln County. One of the most important Waterloo County examples was made and dated 1827 by Fanny Bricker, daughter of Old Sam Bricker whose legend has been brought to life in Mabel Dunham's *The Trail of the Conestoga*. All of these seem to have been influenced by English prototypes, and they employ alphabets, numerals and a verse. Early pieces used cotton thread, but later examples were often done with wool on a punched-paper backing. This was the same base used for the popular Victorian needle-craft, Berlin-work, which was originally done on open-weave canvas. That the creative skills of young girls in Germanic settlements of Ontario were enlisted in the making of some fine textile work can readily be seen from the comparatively few surviving examples.

By the late nineteenth century women in virtually all North American communities engaged in quilt-making, and one cannot easily speak of it as a unique cultural occupation. The wide diffusion of patterns made it almost impossible to maintain a strong ethnic design tradition. Often, only nuances will differentiate the work of cultural or religious groups. Such nuances may include colour predilections, certain occasions or motivations and in some cases, choices of motifs or subjects. For example, in Pennsylvania, "Amish" quilts are clearly distinctive. The designs suggest Joseph Albers' paintings, using bold colours arranged in concentric squares against which extremely fine quilting is done in feather or other patterns. In Canada, there has never developed a specifically Amish quilt tradition. Indeed, the work of Old Order Amish quilters in Perth County is scarcely distinguishable from that of their Mennonite neighbours in adjoining Waterloo County.

Both pieced (patchwork) and appliquéd quilts answered the requirements of thrift, although the latter type was generally reserved for more special occasions. Scraps of new material saved from the making of clothing were preferred because they would wear longer. The common idea that Mennonite quilts must necessarily be predominantly black and drab is unfounded. (Very young Mennonite children often sport vivid print dresses, aprons and hats.) Some "Star" quilts found in the Germanic communities of Ontario and those with geometric designs are extremely colourful. The brilliant reds and yellows literally tease the eyes, a phenomenon also embraced by the modern "Op Art" movement. There is yet another example from Zurich in Huron County where a noble attempt has been made to create a completely original design. The maker cut out 108 hearts from solid red, blue and gold cotton and appliquéd them randomly in neat rows against a white background. The effect is spectacular if a bit disconcerting.

The quilting tradition is still alive and well in Waterloo County. We have been shown the "hope chests" of several young Mennonite girls where some magnificent quilts lie awaiting a new home. Many quilts of traditional patterns in new and synthetic cottons filled with polyester batting are being made daily, mostly by Mennonite ladies, although it is interesting to note that there is at least one exception that we know of to this division of labour according to sex. One older Mennonite couple north of Waterloo maintains a small cooperative business to supplement their income. The husband traces and cuts out all the individual pieces, while the wife stitches the blocks together on the sewing machine. They then send the completed quilt top "out" to be quilted by another party.

Recently Nancy-Lou Patterson was commissioned to design a very large banner for St. Peter's Lutheran Church in Kitchener. The actual stitching and quilting was done by a group of Mennonite ladies from the St. Jacobs area. Hanging in the sanctuary above the altar is a fine tribute not only to the designer, but also to the many hands that assisted in its making.

One of the largest auctions of the summer is the Mennonite Relief Sale held annually since 1967 in New Hamburg, not far from Kitchener. Proceeds from this sale assist the Mennonite Central Committee work. Probably only second in popularity to the mountains of cheese, sausages, fritters, shoo fly pies — all those foods that "really schmeck" — are the magnificent quilts made specially for this sale. People come from all over Ontario, if only as spectators, to watch them being auctioned. These quilts often command handsome prices.

Quilting may continue to survive for many years in the Germanic communities of Ontario. Quilting bees provide a unique social occasion for the ladies to get together and engage in good conversation. There is a sense of fellowship and sharing which those of us who have never plied a thimble and needle can envy; above all, it must be soul-satisfying to work together to produce a practical and aesthetically pleasing object.

Newer materials have always been preferred for quilts; used garments, on the other hand, were recycled in hooked rugs. Hooked rugs of every conceivable design were turned out across the width and breadth of North America in the late nineteenth century. Many were made according to commercial patterns, but because the design could be worked rather freely upon a burlap backing, these rugs allowed more diversity of both individual and cultural expression than quilts. Several examples pictured here bear strong resemblance to other folk-art forms, or incorporate motifs of long-standing acceptance in the Germanic decorative tradition: paired birds, eight-pointed stars, pinwheels and geometric designs.

One exceptional rug-maker was Maria Beck Warning (1832-1918) of Brunner, Ontario. Large birds, ducks, roosters or other animals occupy the centre around which is a border often formed by diagonal striping. Most of her rugs are dated and are among the finest examples of the skill as practised in Ontario.

It is worthwhile to mention one interview with a Mennonite lady now in her nineties. She has been hooking rugs, similar to the commercial variety, for years. Her eyesight is failing; yet she is persistent and continues to hook. However, there has been a dramatic change of subject. She admits that she cannot discern specific areas, even of colour; today, with gay abandon, she proclaims with a chuckle that she has "gone abstract." As a result her latest rugs resemble non-objective paintings. No doubt she is unaware that she is currently working in a Riopelle or Pollock style!

## Pottery

Pottery occupies an interesting position in the Ontario-German decorative tradition. Certain objects, notably samplers and show towels, were created primarily for aesthetic reasons, while others, such as quilts and *Fraktur*, occupied a middle ground between art and functionality. A third category contains such things as iron and pottery which were made for primarily utilitarian purposes but which occasionally had some degree of ornamentation. Pottery was first and foremost a craft born out of necessity.

Like their non-German counterparts, many potters of Lincoln, York, Waterloo and Huron area counties produced clay containers for the practical purposes of food storage. Although a few German names are associated with Ontario stoneware potteries, the majority made earthenware. While many commonplace articles — storage jars, jugs, flowerpots, plates, bowls and the like — were given only a simple glaze with little concern for decorative effect, a substantial body of Ontario-German earthenware is recognizable by its mottled, speckled or specially drawn decoration, sometimes in two or more colours. In other cases, aesthetic appeal is achieved less by glazing than by form. Although there were small Germanic settlements in eastern Ontario, it is only in the

southwestern part of the province that there developed a distinctive Ontario-German pottery craft.

The Niagara Peninsula was an easily accessible region for American immigrants, including several potters. There were, of course, non-German potters working in this area, such as John Martindale and the craftsmen who operated the Thorold Pottery. The few Pennsylvania-German potters had relatively successful businesses, but, unlike their more isolated counterparts in Waterloo County, they were generally forced out of business at an early date due to improved methods of food storage and the changing public taste in favour of mass-produced china.

John Kulp (1799-1874), a Pennsylvania German, established a pottery at Grimsby in Lincoln County in 1829.[39] In 1868 he moved with his son to Elgin County where he continued to farm and to make pottery, returning to the Niagara Peninsula in 1870. The only clearly documented piece of Kulp pottery presently known is an earthenware storage jar with a clear lead glaze which has been signed on the bottom.[40]

Daniel Orth (1817-1902) was one of the major potters of Lincoln County, taking up the trade before 1851 near Campden in Clinton Township. Although he has been frequently called a Pennsylvania German, it rather appears that he was a Continental craftsman who came to the Niagara Peninsula by way of New York State.[41] Like many other craftsmen, he farmed most of the year, and during the winter months he produced several varied types of pottery, ranging from utilitarian crocks to specialty items. A number of earthenware spaniel dogs have been found, some examples of which are signed and dated. Orth may have been one of the last remaining German potters of the Niagara Peninsula; he continued to work until his death in 1902.

Benjamin Lent (born 1802), active in New York State and New Jersey prior to coming to Lincoln County, operated a pottery in Louth Township during the late 1830s and early 1840s.[42] The surviving earthenware produced at the Lent works include several pieces with incised or stamped decorative motifs, such as the unusual feature of painted accents to simulate sgraffito decoration. These pieces are among the most interesting examples of Ontario redware in the Pennsylvania-German folk-art tradition.

An important early potter working in the Pennsylvania-German region of Markham Township in York

County was Cyrus Eby (1844-1906), son of "Potter Sam" Eby (1805-1847) of Waterloo County. Cyrus was recorded, after 1862, as producing wares in Markham, where he rented facilities for two years.[43] Of the pieces made in Markham by either Cyrus Eby or his predecessor, Philip Ensminger, is a decorated storage jar with the inscription "Markham Pottery 1862." This rare piece is decorated much in the manner of *Fraktur* or needlework, with such Pennsylvania-German motifs as an eight-pointed star, paired birds and stylized trees. In 1867, Cyrus went to Conestogo, assisting his brother, William, before eventually moving further north to take up potting at Chippawa Hill in Bruce County. Joseph Wideman was another Markham potter of Pennsylvania-German background. He maintained a pottery in conjunction with farming just to the west of the village.[44]

Waterloo County was the centre of a strong pottery-making enterprise which enlisted the skills of more than a dozen men of both Pennsylvania and Continental-German origin. The overwhelming majority were Continental craftsmen, although it appears that Pennsylvania-German potters may have had both the first and the last word, chronologically speaking.

On the basis of material evidence, the earliest potter in Waterloo County was working in the 1820s. An earthenware tobacco jar found in recent years has inscribed on its base "Waterloo September 17, 1825 Upper Canada Jacob Bock." Bock (1798-1867), a Mennonite who migrated from Lancaster County, Pennsylvania, in the early 1800s settled initially at the Christian Reichert homestead near Freeport and eventually moved to New Dundee where he served as deacon of the Blenheim Mennonite Church from 1841 until his death.[45] Characteristic of these straight-sided earthenware jars is the application of press-moulded figures of St. Ambrosius in low relief.

An additional pre-1830 specimen of well-designated provenance is a redware barrel with the inscription "Waterloo 1827." It is tempting to assign this piece also to Bock's hand. The handwriting on this barrel, however, differs somewhat from the inscriptions on the Bock jars, making such an attribution uncertain. At the same time, it is an intriguing thought that two potters may have been active at such an early date in Waterloo County.

Among Pennsylvania-German potters working to a late date in the same region, the best known is William K. Eby (1831-1905) of Conestogo. He and his younger brother Cyrus had most likely learned the craft from their father

while growing up in the village of New Hamburg. In 1855, William opened a pottery in Markham. He sold it two years later to John Byer and purchased land from Burton Curtis at Conestogo in 1857.[46] Even at the most active period of his career, William was at most a part-time potter, carrying on the business during the winter months, alternating with farming in the spring, summer and fall. For several years prior to building a house, the family lived in cramped but warm quarters on the second floor of the pottery.

It is evident from anecdotes told by descendants that the Eby pottery served not only as a place of business but as somewhat of a social centre as well. Simeon Martin (born 1892), grandson of William Eby, remembers many lively stories concerning day-to-day life at the Conestogo pottery. Rural Waterloo County was a favourite stopping-place for the scores of transients making their way across Ontario during the late nineteenth and early twentieth centuries. Many were offered the exceptional hospitality of Mennonite households. Simeon Martin can recall hearing his grandfather tell of more than one such transient who would come to the pottery during the winter months, knowing that a warm night's sleep could be had near the kiln which was continuously fired, day and night.[47]

Like most village potters, William Eby produced a general line of utilitarian earthenware, among which were drain tiles, storage crocks, plates,[48] pitchers, bowls, flower pots and other common things for daily use. In addition to this functional pottery, he made a smaller number of specialty pieces primarily for his immediate family, friends, children and grandchildren. Among these are his finest and most colourful works. For grandchildren he made miniatures: pitchers, spittoons, bowls and other pieces. Many of the articles made for the family were finished in a distinctive dark green glaze, like a small and unusual "harvest ring" (*Ringkrug*). This earthenware "canteen" resembles a large lifesaver, hollow, with an opening stopped by a cork. It could be carried on an arm or tied to a belt while a person was away from the house for a while. Presumably it was filled with water. In addition, he made a small number of pieces for the table of his own family and relatives, such as covered sugar bowls, spoon holders, cups without handles, saucers, and even candle holders. Upon the bowl of one spoon holder is the word "Spoon holder" in a green glaze, but to the uninitiated it appears more like a large eggcup. These are all treated with a clear glaze revealing a pinkish clay body with blue and green decorative marks. These are among the rarest and most appealing of known examples of Eby redware. Experiencing a general decline in commercial production toward the end of the nineteenth century, the business eventually closed in 1905 upon William Eby's death. This was the last Pennsylvania-German pottery in Ontario.

The Continental-German tradition in Waterloo County was represented by a considerable number of potters working in the towns of Berlin (Kitchener), Waterloo and in the surrounding hamlets of the region. Possibly the most imaginatively decorated pottery made in this country came from the workshop of Adam Biernstihl (1825-1899), an Alsatian immigrant who was active in both Lexington and Bridgeport. His products are generally distinguished by boldly drawn glazing, often in the form of blue and green daubing against a clear buff base, which itself is frequently spattered with brown slip. This potter was comparatively innovative, using a butter print to impress designs upon a flower pot. One of the most spectacular Biernstihl pieces is a very large bowl made for a daughter; on the base are two chickens primitively drawn in green and the names "Emilie Biernstihl Bridgeport." This decorated redware bowl is one of the most charming pieces of Ontario-German folk pottery.

Yet another exceptional instance of decorative work is an earthenware bank, possibly made by Adam's son, Henry Biernstihl. It is made in the form of a tree with perched birds, similar to examples found in Germany and Pennsylvania. The glaze is marbleized and has the initials "H B." It is dated 1876, the year in which Henry set up business as a potter in the village of Milverton in Perth County.[49]

Another Continental-German potter who made limited use of blue and green colour against a light background was Joseph Wagner, who along with his father, Anselm, maintained a workshop in downtown Berlin (Kitchener). A small number of signed works is known, including a large spatter-decorated milk pitcher stamped "Joseph Wagner, Maker Berlin, Ont." Also of unusual decorative interest is a storage jar identical in form, colour and glaze to another signed Wagner example. Lacking any colour variations, its focal point is an applied heart.

The Wagner father-son partnership was the dominant Berlin pottery operation during the second half of the nineteenth century. Nearby Waterloo had a counterpart

in the joint business of John Jacobi (1816-1869) and his son, Daniel (1850-1905). The Jacobis made an extensive line of flowerpots, crocks and the usual utilitarian jars, but they also produced distinctive pieces, many of which have been preserved by descendants. These include numerous miniatures, milk pitchers, umbrella stands and several objects with applied sponged marks. Many are decorated with dark brown spotting against a clear glaze revealing the pinkish clay body. Others, such as plant stands, incorporate brown and green spatterings on a buff base.

Other potters of Continental-German extraction were John Groh of Kossuth, Michael and Henry Steumpfle of Preston (Cambridge), Joseph Adam and son Joseph Jr. of Hawkesville and St. Clements, and Xavier Boehler and sons Joseph and Henry, in New Hamburg.[50] The importance of the Boehler pottery in providing the early work experience for various potters who later took up the craft in other communities has been pointed out by David Newlands:

> In 1860 Ignatz Bitschy worked at the New Hamburg pottery; he later established his own business in Mildmay, Bruce County. In 1862 Abraham Martall worked with Boehler; he later owned a pottery in the village of Colborne, Norfolk County. Henry Schuler, who later took over the John M. Marlatt pottery in Paris, Ontario, learned the pottery business under Xavier Boehler's watchful eyes.[51]

It seems a fitting conclusion to the story of pottery-making in Waterloo County that circumstances required the collaboration of a Continental- and a Pennsylvania-German potter early in the twentieth century. According to a story told by Simeon Martin of St. Jacobs,[52] in 1902 his grandfather, William Eby, was called to assist Daniel Jacobi in meeting a large order of small earthenware barrels to be sold as specialty items at the Berlin Sugarfest that year. The results were marked "Berlin Sugarfest 1902" and were among the last products of the Jacobi pottery. This collaboration in the waning years of Ontario earthenware potteries is a rare instance of a close relationship in otherwise distinct traditions.

The preponderance of Continental-German potters was even heavier to the north and west of Waterloo County, notably in the counties of Perth, Huron, Bruce and Grey. Although potters of European or Pennsylvania-German lineage also worked in areas south of Waterloo County,[53] these craftsmen were active in essentially non-German settlements. Potters in the Huron area, on the other hand, were busy meeting the requirements of large numbers of German immigrants arriving there in the decades after 1850.

The most important establishment in Huron County was the Huron Pottery at Egmondville, founded in 1852 by the Alsatian immigrant, Valentine Boehler, brother of Xavier Boehler of New Hamburg.[54] While most of the earthenware produced by Valentine and his successors was for the local market, some of his wares were sent as far afield as Manitoba.[55] The most distinctive features of Huron Pottery earthenware are the applied floral motifs that appear on many large flower pots. Cast from sprig moulds, these details give some of the pieces a quality vaguely similar to the "art pottery" which came into vogue at the end of the century.

To the north, potters of Germanic origin, such as John Kuehner, worked in Grey and Bruce counties. He had moved from Waterloo County to Hanover.[56] Various examples of pottery have been found in the vicinity of Mildmay and Formosa, a Catholic-German area of Bruce County, which are possibly the work of the Boehler-trained potter Ignatz Bitschy, who was active at Mildmay from 1886 to 1903.[57]

From the early nineteenth to the early twentieth century, an impressive domestic pottery tradition flourished in Ontario. Of the earthenware made during this period, it is the work of Ontario-German craftsmen, both from Pennsylvania and the Continent, which attained the greatest diversity and boldness of design and colour. This decorative enhancement is consistent with the artistic enrichment of other utilitarian objects created in these communities.

## Decorated Utensils and Accessories

The greatest decorative impulse is sometimes reserved for the smallest objects, perhaps because carving or painting is more easily accomplished on smaller areas. Then too, there may be fewer inhibitions about decorating objects for personal use. Aesthetic judgments need not be a factor in the ornamentation of purely utilitarian objects. Even where religious convictions might invoke a hesitant attitude toward flamboyant decoration, the vanity involved in painting a tulip on a heckle might be less evident than that implied in painting the same motif on the larger expanse of a wardrobe or cupboard door.

No simple distinction can be made between Pennsylvania- and Continental-German decorations on domestic utensils and accessories. Extant examples are ordinarily the work of amateurs who surely would not have suspected that their handiwork would in a later time come to be highly prized by historians and collectors.

Some of the simplest articles that received decorative treatment were connected with special festive events. An example is the decorated cookie or *Springerle* boards from several Lutheran settlements near the Lake Erie shoreline. Mrs. Viola Waddel recalls the annual Christmas parties in the two Lutheran churches at Fisherville, Haldimand County, which were the occasions for making the numerous *Springerle* boards still found in homes in that area. "Every year there was a party at the Lutheran churches for children of the congregation. Each little boy or girl was given a bag containing a popcorn ball, an apple and several *Springerle* cookies pressed from fancy boards."[58] Some of these boards are the work of known makers in the Fisherville-Rainham Centre area, one being William Nagel (1871-1938), the father of Viola Waddel. Mrs. Waddel kindly provided us with the following recipe for *Springerle* cookies.

*Springerle Cookies*
  8 eggs
  4 cups granulated sugar
  2 heaping tsp baking soda
  ½ cup cream
  1 tbsp melted butter
    pinch of salt
Beat one hour. Add enough flour to make a stiff dough. Add salt. Roll out dough. Press down onto board. Let stand overnight. In morning add 1-2 tbsp anise seed before baking. Bake until brown at 300° F.

According to her, these cookies were and still are made using many eggs, lots of sugar and heavy cream. (Doubtless this would have provided enough cookies to satisfy even the most voracious appetite.) A few *Springerle* boards have been found elsewhere in Ontario, but almost exclusively in areas of Lutheran settlement.

One folk-art expression nearly extinct today is the weathervane. Older persons remember that back in the 1920s, weathervanes, in the form of nearly every kind of farm animal, could still be seen on barns and small buildings. Harsh weather, vandalism and the salvos of hunters stumbling across easy targets have all but annihilated this art form. Happily, an exceptional weathervane in the shape of an animated horse, mounted on the barn behind the Honsberry house in the village of Jordan Station in Lincoln County has remained to the present day, as has an identical example just down the street. Most wooden weathervanes have long since disappeared, although an unusual trumpeting Gabriel from the Neustadt area has managed to survive. From this same area have come several finely carved whirligigs and a combination whirligig-weathervane (Plate 180) made by Justus Dierlamm. A superb Ontario whirligig (Plate 179) from the Fisherville area in the Niagara Peninsula was made near the turn of the century by William Hartwick (Hartwig), a cabinetmaker with a creative flair.

An apple peeler from Markham counters the notion that such an object would not lend itself well to the decorative impulse. The large wooden base is dramatically embellished with tulips growing upward out of hearts, an eagle, confrontal birds and the name and date "David Byer, 1843." This utensil is one of the most singular examples of Pennsylvania-German folk art in Ontario.

Waterloo County is particularly well blessed with a broad cross-section of small decorated utensils and accessories. A significant number of iron hinges and cooking utensils display interesting variations in both form and applied decoration. Locksmiths, like Andrew Wolf of Berlin and John Peter Wilker (1809-1889) of Petersburg (named after Wilker), made attractive functional locks of the Rohrer type, many with fine scrolled handles and ornamental work. Latches, forks, spatulas and other household utensils also received decorative treatment.

Stencil-painting, a nineteenth-century form of decoration, was popularly applied not only to the walls of houses, but also to farm wagons and children's sleighs. A rare example of wall stencilling in Waterloo County survives in the parlour of the David Eby house constructed about 1834 just west of Waterloo. At a later date, Emmanuel Soehner (born 1898), a local craftsman, decorated the interiors of several Lutheran churches and houses between 1915 and 1918 using his own hand-made stencils. He operated an automobile repair garage in Floradale from 1924 to 1949, where his grandfather, Henry, and his father, Philip, had had a wagon-making shop. After his retirement in Elmira, Emmanuel took up the hobby of making children's sleighs which he decorated with striping and floral designs. He continued this kind of work until past the middle of the twentieth century, a remarkable extension of a traditional art form.

Yet another known stencil artist was Eckhardt Wettlaufer (1845-1919), a wagonmaker by trade in Sebastopol, South Easthope, Perth County. He ran a shop combined with a cider mill and made stencilled wagons and sleighs. A descendant recalls that in the 1890s he decorated children's wagons, including five special wagons for his grandchildren. Perhaps his pièce de résistance was a beautifully painted crokinole board made about 1875 for his son, Adam (born 1871). Adam was only a child, and the family remembered that it hung on a bedroom wall, rarely used.

## Woodcarving

Few examples of handicraft have provided a greater measure of pride and enjoyment than woodworking or whittling. Unlike *Fraktur*, pottery-making or iron work, almost everyone tried it. A few became accomplished, however, and they were known, admired and remembered by many of the "older" generation.

Woodcarving was surely the most "natural" of arts amenable to the creative instincts of a young boy on an Ontario farm. And yet the finest work was produced frequently by men in their sixties and older. Like a young boy, the older man on a farm had leisure time; past were the years of paternal duty and responsibility for domicile, farm and family. Unlike the young boy, an older man may possess a refinement of sensitivity in many areas of art and knowledge which gives to his work a special expressiveness and beauty. The older man has, finally, the particular advantage of a newborn liveliness in his work deriving from his new position as teacher as well as learner.

Woodcarving is by no means an art form unique to Ontario-German communities. Indeed, in the Canadian context it is more likely to call to mind the great religious works produced by generations of French-Catholic craftsmen in Quebec. The work of Ontario's carvers, particularly of Mennonites from Waterloo County, is distinguished by their choice of subject, application of colour and use of selected motifs from the Pennsylvania-German design tradition. A further distinction, invisible in character, resides in a certain set of motivations related to Old Order Mennonite and Amish understandings of hospitality, kindness and a caring attitude toward strangers and sufferers. Just as many of Anna Weber's drawings were done for the children of those who provided for her, so too the works of at least two woodcarvers were an expression of appreciation to those families who opened their hearts and homes to them.

The principal types of carving done in the Mennonite communities were small farm animals, wooden chains, copies of items commonly found in magazines and instructional manuals, a variety of boxes, shelves and utensils. Easily carved basswood was most popular, with the instrument being a well-sharpened penknife. Sometimes the basic shapes were cut out with a coping saw.

One challenge animating whittlers was the ball-in-cage made by carving out a block of wood so that a movable ball was encased within a "cage" formed by the remainder of the block. A skilled carver might repeat this operation several times along the length of a board, producing a number of ball-in-cage sections in succession. One St. Jacobs carver showed the writers a block containing seven such segments that he had whittled.

A popular yet difficult subject was the wooden chain whose links were fashioned from a single long piece of wood. By carving consecutive links in a "closed" position, the finished chain could be drawn out so as to significantly exceed the length of the board from which it was cut. Frequently, these chains were decorated in some way, and they have been known to reach a length of more than eight feet.

The carving of decorative motifs into furniture was not common in Ontario's Mennonite communities. However, the heart cut-out appears on some smaller pieces, such as cutlery boxes or cabbage cutters. A number of cradles have been found in each of the areas of western Ontario Germanic settlement where one or both ends are decorated with these cut-outs. The motif is not without functional considerations, as it provided a handle as well. One such cradle from Waterloo County has the wonderfully wide or fat heart so often associated with Pennsylvania-German *Fraktur*. A late owner of this piece recalled her mother's interpretation of the design: "The heart is wide because it represents the idea that the love of a child makes for a full heart." While this is truly a beautiful thought, we should also remember that it was easy to describe two adjacent circles and then join the bottom to form the design.

Fretwork is found occasionally in Germanic areas; many examples are known from Waterloo and Oxford counties, particularly in the Tavistock vicinity. Employing a mechanical notching technique, a meticulous craftsman could cut out a number of designs in distinctive arrangements. One carver even produced fretwork verses, such as Biblical texts or the Lord's Prayer.

Every country kitchen in Waterloo County had some form of hanging wall box to hold papers, letters, combs, candles, matches, salt, spices or small articles in daily use. These boxes offered a man or boy an opportunity to show his decorative talents. Still, it is difficult to determine the beginnings of the custom of making decorative wall boxes in Ontario-German communities. Simple functional pieces of this type were made throughout the nineteenth century, but the application of decorative motifs appears to have developed not much before the beginning of the twentieth century. After this time the skill was taught as part of "Manual Training" for boys in school.

Of particular interest is an itinerant Ontario woodcarver who went by the name of Frederick G. Hoffman (1845-1926). His exact identity and background have never been established, but since many of his works were signed, "Philadelphia," we assume that was his previous residence. There is considerable speculation among those who remember him concerning why he chose to come to Waterloo County. One theory is that he escaped from a penitentiary, successfully eluded pursuing dogs, and finally arrived there. Whatever the story, "Fritz" as he was known in German, was an enigmatic figure — obviously an educated transient, but unlike most tramps he was fastidious and would never do any kind of work in the barn. He became well-trusted and was regarded as a member of the household by the Mennonite and Amish families with whom he stayed during the approximate period from 1895 to 1926. In return for room and board, he fished in the summers and "made wood" (chopped wood) in the winters during the early 1920s. He usually spent the winters in Amish homes near Punkeydoodles Corners, an area bounded by Waterloo, Perth and Oxford counties, and it was there that he appears to have done most of his woodcarving. He alternated his visits by travelling on foot to the Mennonite families in Woolwich Township, where during his final months he did some carving in the Menno Hoffman (born 1863) and Amos Martin households.[59]

Fred Hoffman carved chains, wooden pliars, baskets and wall ornaments. His characteristic subject was a hanging wall shelf, which owners generally call a "bracket" — a form popular around the turn of the century. Nearly all used horseshoe shapes, some in series, others carved or incised. Even small sewing or trinket boxes were decorated with a row of carved horseshoes, often carefully notched and painted. Most of his carvings are signed and dated in a florid script; some also record the names of recipients written in pencil.

When Fred Hoffman became critically ill, the unhappy decision had to be made to take him to the House of Refuge in Kitchener. Mrs. Ivan Cressman can still remember the day when in the company of her brother, Isaiah, her father, Amos Martin, and Menno Hoffman, Fred left their home for the last time. Two months later, on May 18, 1926, the news reached their door that he had died and that his body had been sent to the Toronto Medical College. With the passing of the man who had come to be much loved by Mennonite and Amish families at opposite ends of the county came a deep sense of regret.

The older generation, looking back on those days some fifty years ago, treasures the many fond memories of this fascinating guest, as well as the carved brackets that he left behind. Fred also made pencil drawings in children's school books; all of them appear to be copied from seed catalogues, magazines, and children's story books. It is possible that he drew them, and then the children coloured them. His life and work are in some respects reminiscent of Pennsylvania's colourful figure, Wilhelm Schimmel (1817?-1890), but fortunately Fred Hoffman was spared the degradation and despair that were Schimmel's lot.

A "school" of carvers in Waterloo County continued to produce wall brackets in the Hoffman manner. One family of four brothers (Levi, Irvin, Orvie and Elam Shantz), who were born and raised in the Wissler House at Lexington in the early 1900s, carved a number of these brackets and comb boxes between the 1920s and 1940s. At least one of these was copied from a 1921 shelf made by Christian Burkhardt, a neighbour and frequent visitor to the Menno Hoffman home where Fred Hoffman stayed. The Shantz brothers also made extensive use of notch-carving, horse-shoes and radiating-star motifs.

Another woodcarver who worked in this area of Waterloo County was a farmer and maker of farm gates, Daniel B. Hoffman (born 1877). A younger brother of Menno Hoffman, it was Daniel who found time to carve brackets for his children or friends upon request, when he retired. Despite some stylistic modifications and nuances, his indebtedness to the designs of Fred Hoffman is apparent in the continued pattern of chain motifs and horseshoes.

Possibly the most versatile of Mennonite woodcarvers in Waterloo County was David B. Horst (1873-1965) of St. Jacobs.[60] His ingenuity is displayed in the small carved animals he produced in the late 1930s and early 1940s. It is remarkable that these enchanting creatures were made after 1935, following a stroke that left him paralyzed on one side. He was, in fact, in his sixties when he began to carve seriously. Friends recall how he supported the piece with his lame hand while he carved or painted with the other. Many of his animals were made for small children, for friends and family, and for visitors who might ask to take one home as a memento. In the case of a visitor, a small remuneration was often given in return. As a rule, he used basswood, which was easy to carve. But on one occasion at least, he used a pine board salvaged from the demolition of his grandfather's house to carve a memento for his sister. These Horst pieces are skilfully carved and make subtle use of simple water-colours, sometimes stippled. The bases (made from scraps) are ornamented with spots of red and green. The faces of his chickens, horses, squirrels, cows and other animals are often wonderfully expressive. Because he was working within the confines of the Old Order Mennonite community, Horst's woodcarvings were recognized by a wider public only after his death. His art is a testimony to the spirit of an earlier folk tradition that was carried to the more northerly outposts of the Canadian countryside by generations of immigrants. It is difficult to make hard and fast aesthetic judgments, but it is probably accurate to say that Horst's work represents the highest level of Pennsylvania-German woodcarving found in Ontario.

Daniel Kuepfer, an Amish craftsman from near Millbank in Perth County, participated in the same tradition. He carved numerous small animals, and his tiny birds on heart-shaped bases are probably the most successful (Plate 188). John Hummel (1892-1970) also belongs in a discussion of important Ontario-German carvers. Hummel lived in Maryhill, and following a disabling accident, turned to woodcarving in the 1960s. He carved many small animals and birds, including several particularly appealing bird-trees (Plate 187).

Although many individuals must have fashioned pleasing pieces from wood during the entire history of Germanic settlement, the number of articles surviving from the early years is small. Fortunately for later generations, it has been possible to obtain relatively comprehensive information on the lives and works of several traditional carvers whose work is of exceptional beauty and refinement.

# Gravemarkers

The practice of commemorating the buried dead has a long history in the western world. Even under pioneer conditions this custom was not overlooked and was sometimes observed through the erection of markers of strong decorative interest. Out of necessity the first settlers of southern Ontario were forced to fashion markers from whatever material was practical and locally available, at first using rectangular wooden slabs or crudely hewn stones. White sandstone, relatively easy to carve and plentiful, quickly became popular for headstones throughout all of Ontario in the nineteenth century. Early Pennsylvania-German stones tend to be vertical slabs with architectural shapings at the top, or of the "tombstone panel" shape seen on many Germanic immigrant chests. The cruciform marker is conspicuously absent in Ontario's Pennsylvania-German cemeteries, most of which are Mennonite burial grounds, due to the general Anabaptist aversion to pictorial imagery.

The rigours of establishing first-generation farms and homes in Upper Canada left relatively little time or inclination for the decoration of objects, including gravemarkers. When conditions became easier, though, both professional and amateur artisans began to embellish their tombstones. Many markers in Waterloo County, in particular, employ simplified folk motifs often seen in Pennsylvania cemeteries. Among these are the six-pointed compass star, the quatrefoil or four-petalled flower seen frequently in *Fraktur*, the sun, the heart, trees and tulips. Unlike some of the more highly decorated stones in Berks County and elsewhere in Pennsylvania, there are no cherubs, death's heads or *memento mori* to be seen on Ontario-German markers. Modest adaptations of previously established conventions, such as the weeping willow tree, a very popular Neoclassical device, were used probably not so much as esoteric symbols as appealing, easily carved decorations. The *arbor vitae*, or real tree-of-life, with central trunk and drooping flowers or tulips is not seen on the first settlers' markers. Where a decorative motif is used, it is normally placed at the top, in rigid axial symmetry, a practice consistent throughout the Germanic decorative tradition.

The characteristic epitaph favoured by the Pennsylvania Germans in Ontario consisted of simple identification, often beginning with the words *Hier ruhet* (Here lies), with birth and death dates, and the age at death given in years, months and days. This format may still be seen today on markers inscribed in German for Old Order Mennonites in Waterloo County. In rare cases, some early stones were inscribed on both sides. The elegies and doggerel rhymes popular among the English were seldom used, though some are to be found in the Blair-Preston (Cambridge) area where the first Conestoga wagons arrived from Pennsylvania. One cemetery in this region contains an epitaph which is an unusual departure from the normal, simple descriptive format; it records that "His Death was caused by falling off a wagon." The casual observer today might dismiss it with even a degree of humour, but such accidents were not infrequent in pioneer times. Isaac R. Horst, in *Up the Conestogo*,[61] devotes a section to "Tragic and Violent Deaths," among which are many victims of wagon accidents.

Both the Roman and *Fraktur* alphabets were used for epitaphs on Ontario-German gravemarkers, and English and German were often employed on different markers for the same family. Some professional stonecutters were obviously capable of working in both languages and in a variety of lettering forms. One such person was the Berlin cabinetmaker and stonecutter, John Hoffman (1808-1878), who placed advertisements in early issues of the German language newspaper *Canada Museum* and its successor, *Der Deutsche Canadier*:

### JOHN HOFFMAN

hereby announces to the local public that he is now prepared to furnish gravestones of all popular sizes at a cheap price. He cuts desired letters in either German or English, likewise at a cheap price. He also continues to pursue the business, as before, of sign painting, and inscribes names — in both languages — on wood and in metal, and labels grain bags and barrels; and he seeks the friendly business of his local fellow-citizens. He will strive at all times, to all those who bring him work, to give as complete satisfaction as he can.

City of Berlin, the 23rd of February, 1839.

Some Pennsylvania-German gravestones are harsh reminders of tragedies that befell early communities. At the Blair Cemetery is a memorial erected to the memory of John Bricker (1796-1804), son of old Sam Bricker, both principal characters in Mabel Dunham's *The Trail of the Conestoga*.[62] A devastating diphtheria epidemic claimed this young boy and countless others shortly after the Pennsylvania Germans first arrived in the Waterloo County wilderness. Later, in 1834, the residents of this inland settlement in Upper Canada eagerly awaited the arrival of a travelling circus. "Every wagon carried its quota of children... their eager faces illumined with the light of childish delight."[63] The next morning it was discovered that one of the showmen had been critically stricken with cholera. This marked the beginning of a deadly plague that consumed hundreds of men, women and children. Many unmarked graves were dug and coffinmakers were reported to have been hammering for nights. In such times, it is possible that volunteers rather than trained artisans cut some of the tombstones, as that for Elizabeth Bricker, one of the victims.

Some of the earliest Pennsylvania-German grave-markers in Ontario are in the Mennonite Burial Ground at Vineland, Lincoln County; several date from the late eighteenth century. A number of early stones display crudely cut initials or the names of such families as Grobb, Fry (or Frey), Moyer and Kulp, who still inhabit the area. Two primitive markers have carved initials accompanied by semi-circles like a sun motif or perhaps a simplified version of the *Ur-bogen* found on Pennsylvania tombstones.

York County, too, has burial grounds associated with Dunker and Mennonite churches in Vaughan and Markham townships, respectively. The principal Pennsylvania-German cemetery in the county is that of the Wideman Church, just north of the town of Markham. There are comparatively few markers of Germanic character in this burial ground, but several do have inscriptions in German. A marker for Jacob Berky (Plate 207) features a sun motif which is almost identical to that found on the stone for Daniel Cressman located in the Wilmot Centre Cemetery, Waterloo County. The sun and its many ideograms have long been revered in Pennsylvania-German folk art. In a slightly more elaborate context, it appears on gravestones in Lancaster and Northampton counties.

The most highly decorated markers in the Pennsylvania-German tradition are found on some of the stones in the East End Cemetery which serves Kitchener's First Mennonite Church. Both English and German inscriptions are used on these stones, and they are graced by such motifs as a calligraphic tulip, trees of life, a wide heart and even an eye. We have found that almost all of these rather special stones were for young children. Motifs like these are not found in other Waterloo County cemeteries.

The variety of calligraphic styles that occur repeatedly on different stones, and in some cases in different

cemeteries, indicates that a number of stonecutters worked fairly widely in Waterloo County. A singular, primitive style appears in more than one cemetery; it uses a crude Roman alphabet frequently with confused upper and lower case letters and punctuated with wide Greek crosses. Others show a well-trained *Fraktur* hand (always in German), but with occasional problems such as alignment or spacing; in one case a misspelled name was corrected by inserting the letter above the error.

Among the more unusual markers are those with elements of Masonic imagery or mixed influences. Perhaps the most unique one is a marble stone, now eroding badly, in Wellesley Township, Waterloo County. The epitaph is carved in the form of a cryptic puzzle which works out to be a tribute to a doctor's two wives. Measuring fifteen letters across and fifteen letters down, the cryptogram commemorates Henrietta (1842-1865) and Susanna (1840-1867). "Two better wives a man never had. They were gifts from God and are now in Heaven. May God help me, S.B., to meet them there."[64]

By mid-century, Pennsylvania-German influences had been so diluted that gravemarkers in these communities were no longer easily distinguishable from the Victorian forms popular in urban and non-Germanic areas.

In contrast to the rather chaste quality of Pennsylvania-German gravemarkers are the iron crosses in the Roman Catholic cemeteries of western Ontario. The form is well represented in Waterloo, Huron and Bruce counties.[65] Copied from prototypes in an Alsatian homeland, these crosses are flamboyant in their elaborate scrollwork and applied decorative elements.

Wrought-iron crosses were made by several native village blacksmiths in such communities as New Germany (Maryhill), St. Agatha, St. Clements, Zurich, Formosa, Deemerton, Riversdale, Chepstow, Mildmay and Carlsruhe. They are generally constructed as a single frame, with double or triple bars articulating a Latin cross sometimes as high as two metres. Set firmly into the ground, sometimes in a cement base, they resemble iron "trees" against the cemetery landscape. Around the basic armature are placed decorative coils, open C-curves, orbs and spear- or lance-like shapes. Some markers also feature fleurs-de-lis and lozenge shapes, motifs found on Alsatian furniture and architectural decorations.

The most dramatic memorials in these Roman Catholic cemeteries are the paired-angel crosses found at both St. Boniface Cemetery, Maryhill, and at St. Clements.

They are identical, surrounded by large, flat stylized holly leaves. The confrontal angels were cast by a sensitive designer, because their faces are quite expressive and their postures are spirited. They are reminiscent of motifs employed in the coverlets made by Continental-German weavers and in Pennsylvania-German *Fraktur*, like the pieces done at the "Clinton School" in Lincoln County. This motif is also found in the marble markers at Formosa and other Roman Catholic settlements. The top of nearly every iron marker is a cross, sometimes arising from a heart created by arcs on either side. A white Corpus appears on some along with two other figures.

German epitaphs usually adorn these iron markers. They are extremely brief — merely identification and dates carved on a small marble slab or imprinted upon a metal plate which is mounted at the crossing. In the Carlsruhe cemetery, a deviation from this arrangement is seen in the form of a long, slender marble slab extended horizontally along the whole length of the transverse arms of the cross.

Iron crosses found in cemeteries north of Waterloo are of somewhat different design. Of later vintage, they tend to be more baroque, less restrained. Very tight coils are used, and even the frame is undulating. In the Zurich area, the entire shape of the cross is changed; the arms are very wide and resemble more a Greek cross.

The tradition of using wrought-iron crosses seems to have begun late and lasted for only a short time in Ontario. Most have death dates in the 1890s or early 1900s. Those that are continually repainted in some cemeteries have remained in excellent repair, while others have suffered from both exposure and neglect.

A few Germanic gravemarkers are to be found in other parts of Ontario but they are less decorative. At Petawawa, Golden Lake and Locksey, some stones with German inscriptions survive. By the early twentieth century, both the Pennsylvania-German and Continental-German decorative traditions had given way to mass-produced Victorian-style gravemarkers. Still, a visit to a cemetery in Germanic settlements in Ontario provides a stimulating encounter with a folk-art spirit which transcends even the reality of death.

As we approach the bicentennial of the arrival of the first Germans in Upper Canada, we cannot help but be a little amazed at the fact that a lively tradition of decorative and folk art has survived within this cultural strand of Ontario life for fully a century and a half or more. Even within the more restrictive range of artifacts actually illustrated here are textiles as early as the 1827 samplers by Susanna Byer and Fanny Bricker and as late as a 1936 sampler by Maria Schwartzentruber. *Fraktur* illustrations span a period from an 1804 Lincoln County songbook to a hand-lettered family-register done in Grey County around 1880. Furniture strongly grounded in the Ontario-German community craft tradition include an 1817 desk made by Moses Eby and another made by Christian Gerber in 1900. In these and other examples we have visible testimony to the vitality of a Germanic ethos shaping art and custom long after tastes had changed again and again in urban centres.

The survey of Ontario-German communities and regions includes two significant groups, the Pennsylvania Germans and the Continental Germans. Although much unites these groups in language, customs and culture, several differences are discernible in decorative and folk-art expressions. Possibly the most conspicuous distinction can be seen in furniture, where the heavy baroque forms frequently preferred by Continental craftsmen stand in marked contrast to the simpler and plainer outlines of Pennsylvania-German pieces. Gravemarkers provide an interesting parallel. Pennsylvania Germans tended to favour stones of rather simple shape with occasional inscribed flourishes, such as the heart, tree or tulip. Continental Germans, especially in Roman Catholic areas, commemorated the dead with wrought-iron markers of exuberant baroque form. In each category, it is almost as if Pennsylvania craftsmen chose to decorate the surface, Continental craftsmen the profile, of a chest or a monument.

Other distinctions have to do less with forms than with the very practise of certain craft traditions. Two cases in point are *Fraktur* and needlework. The art of *Fraktur* is confined almost exclusively to the Pennsylvania-German communities of Ontario, except for a few instances in Continental-German areas of the lower Niagara Peninsula, Waterloo County and the Huron area. In the textile arts, the decorated show towel was produced only in Pennsylvania-German regions of the province. A further qualification is that this folk art form flourished extensively in Waterloo County, but scarcely at all in Lincoln County, reflecting a similar disparity from an earlier period between Bucks and Lancaster counties in Pennsylvania.

Other distinctions within the broad Ontario-German culture are related to religious traditions. Sculptural and pictorial representations of religious subjects in Roman Catholic communities grew out of a tradition largely eschewed in Mennonite or Amish areas, where folk art expression was and is dominated by the substitution of stylized motifs and conventionalized design arrangements. Once again it is in gravemarkers where this distinction is most graphically exhibited, reflected on the one hand by three-dimensional representations of Christ, the Holy Family or various Biblical figures on Roman Catholic iron gravemarkers, or expressed on the other hand by simple floral or geometric symbolism on Mennonite headstones.

The persistence of Germanic customs and artistic expression in Ontario is attributable in part to factors of numerical strength and religious ethos. Unlike the comparatively small Germanic communities of Nova Scotia, some areas of Ontario not only received large numbers of German pioneers at an early date but also continued to be populated by a steady stream of additional German immigrants for a half century or more afterward. This is especially true of Waterloo County, where the combined immigration of Pennsylvania- and Continental-German settlers meant a continued swelling of the ranks, beginning in the early nineteenth century and persisting even into the twentieth century. The religious factor has served also to perpetuate the German language and traditional ways in rural areas of Waterloo and Perth counties, particularly as expressed in the conservative posture of Old Order Mennonites and Amish. While in nearly every small town and village of Waterloo County the Pennsylvania-German dialect is spoken commonly on the street, in the urban Kitchener-Waterloo community itself one is very likely to encounter not only this dialect but also High German, reflecting both the Pennsylvania- and Continental-German groups who transact their daily business there. It is not inconsistent with this late perpetuation of linguistic distinctiveness that vestiges of the Germanic decorative arts and folk traditions have survived until the present day in this culturally rich region of Ontario.

41 *Moyer House, Lincoln County.*
A rare example of the two-door house seen
also in eastern Pennsylvania is this one-
and-a-half storey brick home near Campden.
It boasts fine woodwork and ornamental
painted trim and doors reminiscent of the
work of the furniture painter Israel Moyer.
Circa 1840 to 1845.

42

**42** *Outdoor Bake Oven, Lincoln County.* Situated behind the brick house of David Fretz which overlooks Jordan Harbour, this structure is possibly the only surviving Ontario example of a Pennsylvania-German style outdoor bake oven with overhanging roof. Circa 1845.

**43** *Christian Hoover House, York County.* This frame house features an overhanging front roof extended to form an integral verandah. Built by the elder Christian Hoover (1798-1885), it is the birthplace of the Markham Township *Fraktur* artist Christian L. Hoover (1835-1918). Circa 1825.

**44** *Schmidt-Dalziel Barn, York County.* This immense bank-barn of heavy log construction with overhanging forebay is among the finest Swiss or south-German barns in North America. Along with the buildings of the adjoining Stong farm it forms the nucleus of Black Creek Pioneer Village in Vaughan Township, at the north edge of the city of Toronto. 1809.

43

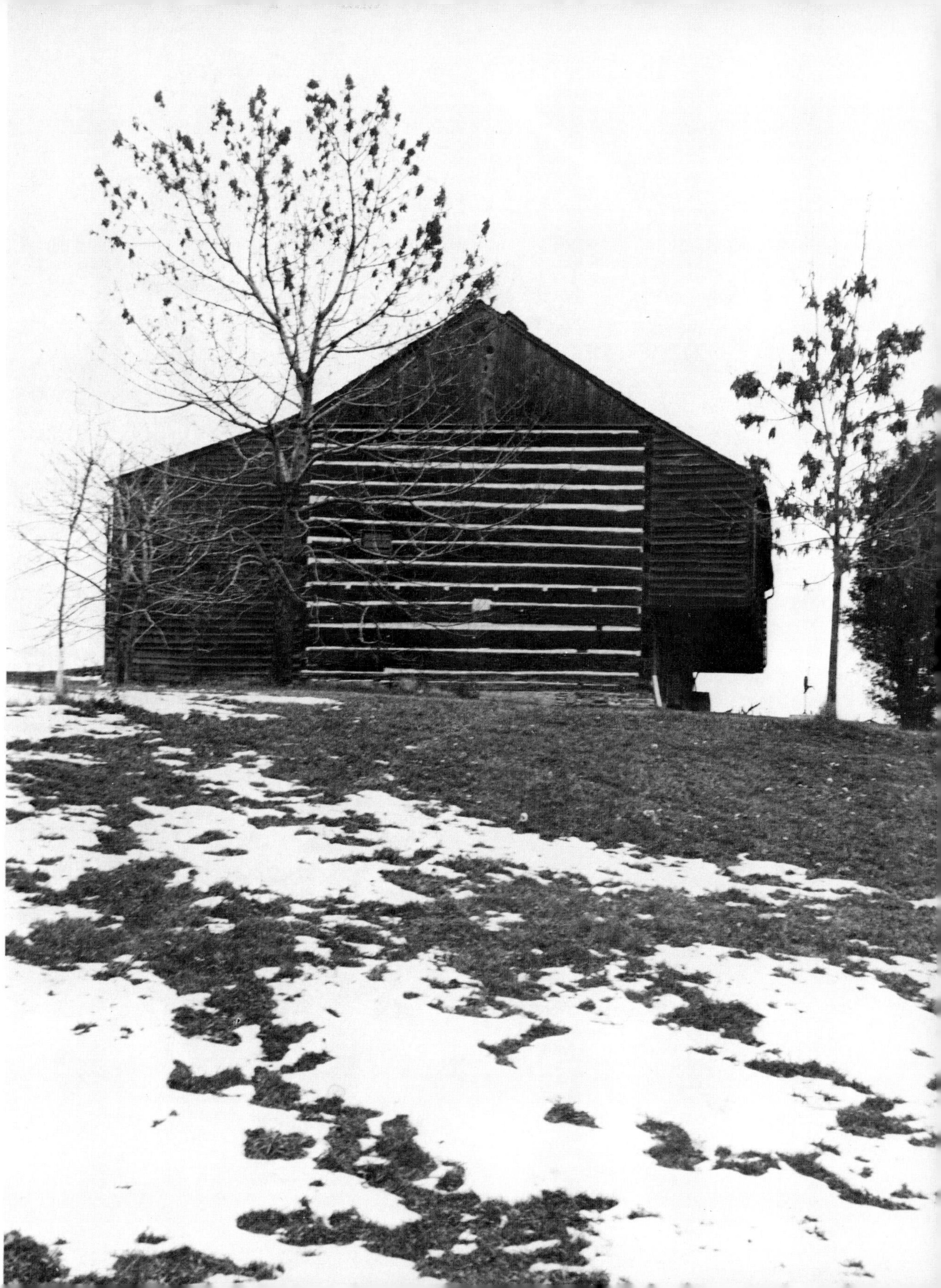

45

46

47

## 48

49

45 *Christian Schneider House, Waterloo County.*
Demolished in recent years, this two-storey house was built by one of the Schneider brothers who arrived in the Doon area of Waterloo County in 1806. Its modest pent roof extending along one end was a rarity in Ontario. 1807.

46 *Joseph Schneider House, Waterloo County.*
This large house was built as the second home of the founder of Berlin (Kitchener), Joseph Schneider (1772-1843), a brother of Christian Schneider (see Plate 45). The house was remodelled by the family in the mid 1850s. It is of frame and rough-cast construction, built in the Pennsylvania-Georgian style often seen in Ontario. Circa 1820 or earlier.

47 *Jacob Shoemaker House, Waterloo County.*
Possibly the finest brick house built by Pennsylvania Germans in Waterloo County is this imposing Georgian-style home erected by Jacob S. Shoemaker (1798-1875), founder of Bridgeport. This view of the east facade shows its detailed roof mouldings, returned eaves, symmetrical fenestration, multi-panelled doors, sidelights and fan transom.

48 *John E. Brubacher House, Waterloo County.*
One of the most pleasing fieldstone farm-houses in Waterloo County is this home built by John E. Brubacher (1822-1902), now part of the campus of the University of Waterloo. Like many stone houses of the period, the front wall beneath the verandah roof is faced with plaster and painted. 1850.

49 *Fryfogel Inn, Perth County.*
Several public buildings retain the simple Georgian proportions favoured by Pennsylvania Germans in Ontario to a late date. This brick inn was built by the Swiss immigrant Sebastian Fryfogel (1791-1873), who became the first settler of Perth County. 1844.

50

50 *Conestogo Meeting House, Waterloo County.*
One of the least changing structures in Ontario is the Old Order meeting house. The Conestogo Meeting House was erected near St. Jacobs in 1894. Its traditional style is virtually indistinguishable from those constructed as late as the middle of the twentieth century. 1894.

51 *House-Barn, Waterloo County.*
A rarity in Waterloo County is the house-barn combination found in central and eastern Europe. This rare example, known locally as the "Hinsperger House," was seriously altered in the 1970s. Mid-nineteenth century. [From a photograph taken about 1950]

52 *Doorway, Goetz House, Waterloo County.*
This front door on an inn built about 1830 in the Roman Catholic village of Rotenburg (now Maryhill) features lozenges, intricate panels, "endless-chain" carving and other elements of Continental-German design in Waterloo County. Circa 1830.

51

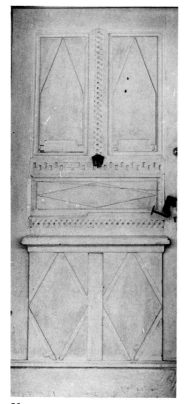
52

53

54

53 *Barn, Waterloo County.*
Even a strictly utilitarian structure received some form of ornamentation from time to time. Three heart cut-outs in the dormer window of this barn near Maryhill are reminders of the south-German folk-art background from which the settlers of this area had come. Mid-nineteenth century.

54 *Embassy Hotel, Waterloo County.*
This two-storey hotel was built by Anthony Kaiser in St. Agatha to replace an earlier structure destroyed by fire in 1854. It is strongly reminiscent of Alsatian or south-German prototypes, particularly in the dramatically overhanging roof. After 1854.

55

56

57

58

55 *St. John's Evangelical Lutheran Church, Waterloo County.*
Located near the village of Bamberg, this quaint church is undoubtedly the work of a builder or team of builders who also constructed two nearby churches. It is conceived in the Georgian style, with effective incorporation of round-headed windows, spire and fan-transom above its panelled door. 1872.

56 *St. Anthony's Roman Catholic Church, Perth County.*
North of Tavistock, near the junction of Waterloo, Oxford and Perth counties, is this truly delightful fieldstone Georgian church. It has finely constructed round-headed windows and naïve fanwork graces its front doorway. 1863.

57 *John Fisher House, Perth County (detail).*
This one-and-a-half storey log house near the village of Bornholm in Perth County contains numerous Germanic design details. The dated keystone with six-pointed compass star above the front door is especially interesting in this context. 1862.

58 *George Schenk House, Grey County.*
This large stone house was erected a decade and a half after its builder, George Schenk (1835-1914), reputedly walked from Mannheim in Waterloo County to take up life in the Neustadt-Ayton area of the comparative wilderness of Normanby Township. 1871.

59

**59** *Immaculate Conception Church, Bruce County.*
Catholic-German congregations in Mildmay, the Carlsruhe area and Formosa in Bruce County erected several large churches in the late nineteenth century. Immaculate Conception Church in Formosa has many refinements, such as paintings by the commercial church decorator Joseph Barth and a superb wooden altar carved by the local cabinet-maker Nicholas Dürrer (1834-1908). 1876 to 1883.

**60** *Linen Press, Lincoln County.*
An unusually refined walnut linen press, this impressive Lincoln County piece found its way into the American market and was recently returned to Canada after being sold at an auction in Ohio. On its base is the pencil inscription "Jacob G. Kulp." Early nineteenth century.

60

62

63

**61** *Wall Cupboard, York County.*
Evidence of the trend toward lighter proportions and simplification of Pennsylvania-German furniture of the Markham area can be seen by comparing this later cupboard with that in Plate 62. Probably made by John Barkey, this example has the excellent painted decoration characteristic of much of his work. Third quarter nineteenth century.

**62** *Wall Cupboard, York County.*
This cupboard of heavy Pennsylvania-German proportions, from Whitchurch Township in York County, features lapped drawers and doors. Its robust character is further emphasized by a strong scalloped bracket base, fielded panel doors, fluted stiles and well-developed cornice. Early nineteenth century.

**63** *Wall Cupboard, Lincoln County.*
Of pine construction, this wall cupboard is similar to other Lincoln County examples in overall conception. However, it differs markedly from them in the use of raised lozenge panels on upper and lower doors, a design element associated not with the Pennsylvania background but rather with that of Alsace and southern Germany. Early or mid-nineteenth century.

**64** *Slant Front Desk, York County.*
This pine slant front desk from Markham or Vaughan Township is an exceptional example of the Pennsylvania-German folk-art tradition. Signed "Samuel Snider 1839," it features bold abstract painting, geometric designs and brilliant use of colour. 1839.

**65** *Corner Cupboard, Waterloo County.*
Built into the Daniel H. Weber homestead (1837) south of the village of Conestogo, this architectural corner cupboard resembles earlier Pennsylvania examples with its fan doors, fluted columns and arch, and heavy built-up cornice. Second quarter nineteenth century.

65

66 *Corner Cupboard, Waterloo County.*
A fine expression of subtlety in design and
detail, this pine cupboard features an elaborate cornice, spool-turned decorative moulding, four square, raised panels on each door
and a brown-and-mustard paint scheme.
Second quarter nineteenth century.

67 *Corner Cupboard, Waterloo County.*
Bold Neoclassical characteristics define this
imposing Pennsylvania-German corner cupboard. The visual impact of this architectural
cupboard is intensified by a three-colour
scheme of red, blue and yellow, as well as
effective use of reeding, fluting and mouldings. Second quarter nineteenth century.

67

103

68 *Corner Cupboard, Waterloo County.*
This massive cherry corner cupboard reflects the transition from the Neoclassical period to the heavy American Empire styling. A handwritten note attached to an upper shelf reads: "This corner cupboard was made to order and all made by hand for Jacob Bricker — son — in the year 1854 by Abraham Latschaw. Total cost about $68." 1854.

69 *Desk, Waterloo County.*
Among the earliest documented furniture from Waterloo County is this cherrywood desk with maple inlay made by Moses Eby (1799-1854). Its outstanding features are its inlaid stars and diamonds, drawer banding and, in particular, its decorated front, with name and date enclosed in a large heart. 1817. [Courtesy Doon Pioneer Village]

70 *Chest of Drawers, Waterloo County.*
This tall chest of drawers is striking evidence of the refinement occasionally achieved by Pennsylvania-German cabinetmakers in Waterloo County. Its sound proportions are complemented by its ably executed details. Second quarter nineteenth century.

69

70

105

71

71 *Chest of Drawers, Waterloo County.*
This pine chest of drawers of simple Sheraton styling has willow trees painted inside hearts on the drawer fronts, stylized trees on the end panels and feather-grained decoration, all in a dramatic red-over-orange colour scheme. Second quarter nineteenth century.

72 *Storage Chest, Waterloo County.*
This pine storage chest, found in Waterloo County, exhibits construction methods, cut nails and other details which suggest a date considerably later than Pennsylvania proto-types. Its painted decoration employs geo-metric designs against an orange background. Second quarter nineteenth century.

*73 Table and Bench, Waterloo County.*
This pine Sheraton-type table and bench retain their original ochre colour. In the traditional Pennsylvania- or Continental-German kitchen, the bench is kept flush against the wall. Second quarter nineteenth century.

*74 Cradles, Waterloo County.*
These pine cradles are good examples of both the similarities and differences found in the Pennsylvania- and the Continental-German design traditions. The cradle on the left is from the St. Jacobs area and retains decorative elements of the Pennsylvania tradition. The cradle on the right comes from Maryhill and exhibits qualities of the more complex Continental-German baroque style. Second quarter nineteenth century.

*75 Footstool, Waterloo County.*
This painted and stencilled pine footstool falls within the category of "presentation-pieces," frequently made for members of a craftsman's family. It bears the name "Mary Schuh" and was most likely made for this small girl (born 1851) by her father Jacob Schuh (1831-1875), a cabinetmaker in Berlin (Kitchener). Circa 1855.

73

74

75

76 *Clothes Cupboard, Waterloo County.*
An outstanding statement of sophisticated
Pennsylvania-German craftsmanship in
Waterloo County is this large cherry clothes
cupboard, or *Kleiderschrank*, possibly by the
cabinetmaker Abraham Latschaw. Its arrangement of fielded panels reflects a
thorough mastery of proportion and decorative geometry. Second quarter nineteenth
century.

77 *Clothes Cupboard, Waterloo County.*
A simple type of *Kleiderschrank* is found
frequently throughout the Waterloo County
area. The example illustrated here is indicative of the gradual simplification of form
which occurred after mid-century. It is distinguished by its flamboyant feather-grained and
abstract painted decoration. Third quarter
nineteenth century.

78

**78** *Hanging Shelf, Waterloo County.*
Found near New Hamburg in Wilmot Township, this pine shelf with original blue-green paint exhibits strong Continental-German design characteristics in its shaped back and brackets, primitive Neoclassical cornice, incised floral motifs and six-pointed compass star. Mid-nineteenth century.

**79** *Pail Stand, Waterloo County.*
This pail stand with its original red paint has been given considerable style by virtue of its beaded edges, shaped ends and complex scrollwork along the front of the legs. Nineteenth century.

79

80

**80 Box-Bench, Waterloo County.**
A pine bench which functions also as a chest, this piece was made in the Amish-Mennonite area between Wellesley in Waterloo County and Millbank in Perth County, a region settled by Continental-German immigrants. Late nineteenth or early twentieth century.

**81 Decorated Chair, Waterloo County.**
This crisply decorated chair is closely related in stencilling to other half-windsor and arrowback examples from the same county. In addition, this chair features exceptional grain-painting and striping in red, black and green. Nineteenth century.

81

82 *Desk, Waterloo County.*
Made by the elder John Gerber (1809-1889),
who lived near Wellesley, this pine desk is
considerably more delicate in execution than
most American Empire pieces from which it
is derived. It is vigorously decorated with
painted abstract motifs, ebonizing and
simulated figured and birds-eye maple finish.
Circa 1865.

83 *Desk, Waterloo County.*
This desk by Christian O. Gerber (1845-
1928), who copied it from the work of his
father (see Plate 82), represents the late con-
tinuation of traditional styles. 1900.

82

84

84 *Clothes Cupboard, Waterloo County.*
Sadly, one of the most striking examples of painted furniture found in Waterloo County was sawed into two sections about 1950. Only one half survives today. The painted baskets of flowers and stylized floral motifs on the drawer and stiles are strongly reminiscent of Swiss or south-German prototypes. Second quarter nineteenth century.

85 *Table, Waterloo County.*
Found in the village of Erbsville in Waterloo County, this table is constructed of figured cherry and is given decorative appeal by inlaid maple diamonds, hearts and stars. Second quarter nineteenth century.

86 *Clothes Cupboard, Waterloo County.*
Originally among the furnishings of the Goetz house at Maryhill, this maple *Kleiderschrank* features elaborate panelling in the form of lozenges, pentagons and triangles. Nearly identical treatment can be seen in the design of the front door of the Goetz house (see Plate 52). Second quarter nineteenth century.

85

86

**87 *Open Corner Cupboard,***
***Wellington County.***
This small pine dish dresser from near Mount Forest, at the junction of Wellington and Grey counties, is reminiscent of German prototypes in its primitively scalloped sides. The outstanding feature is its folk-art bird and stylized tree enclosed within a primitive zig-zag border. Third quarter nineteenth century.

**88 *Dough Box, Grey County.***
From Eidt family settlers near Neustadt in Grey County, this pine dough box may have been made locally, or by ancestors in Waterloo County who moved to Normanby Township. Its lid, front and sides are painted with six-point compass stars. Second or third quarter nineteenth century.

**89 *Desk, Grey County.***
On the lid of a cherry lift-top desk, John P. Klempp has created a particularly pleasing arrangement of folk motifs. Within a border is a central tulip tree with confrontal birds flanked on each side by horses. Circa 1875 to 1885.

**90 *Clothes Cupboard, Grey County.***
Numerous inlaid case-pieces and accessories are likely the work of the Neustadt cabinetmaker and hotel proprietor John P. Klempp (1857-1914). The large *Kleiderschrank* pictured here has elaborate baroque shaping of the base and his characteristic elaborate embellishments. Circa 1875-1885.
[Courtesy National Museum of Man]

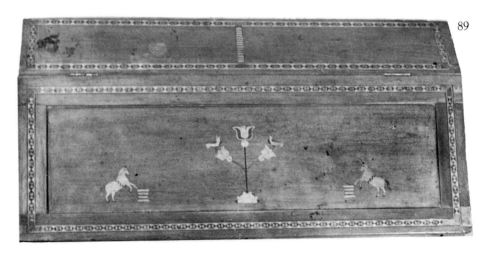

91

**91 Clock, Oxford County.**
During the early 1920s, John K. Lemp (1860-1938), a Lutheran-German carpenter living in Tavistock, made four clocks of monumental proportions for members of his immediate family. He is shown posing in the shadow of one of his creations in a photograph taken around 1928.

**92 Bed, Grey County.**
This pine bed from the Clifford-Ayton area of Normanby Township retains vestiges of Biedermeier design in its pediments. It has boldly fielded panels at each end, and is given strong impact by the original dark red painted finish. Third quarter nineteenth century.

**93 Table, Grey County.**
Found near the village of Ayton, this small two-drawer kitchen table with cleated top resembles those made in Pennsylvania-German areas of Lincoln, York and Waterloo counties. An unusual feature is the striking black and red painted finish. Third quarter nineteenth century.

92

93

94

95

96

**94** *Lyre-Back Chair and Footstool, Huron County.*
This and the following six illustrations record the ingenious workmanship of John Gemeinhardt (1826-1912), a German immigrant cabinetmaker in Bayfield, Huron County. Within a broader range of commercial products are several superb pieces he made for himself and his family. Among these are four lyre-back chairs fashioned for each of his four daughters in the 1880s and 1890s. This chair and the scalloped footstool with cabriole legs are remarkable instances of the *retardataire* phenomenon. Late nineteenth century.

**95** *Watch Holder, Huron County.*
One of the most unusual objects made by John Gemeinhardt is this wooden watch holder. It is a superb miniaturization of an architectural conception. The four turned columns and arched pediment are designed to mount and display a pocket watch. Late nineteenth century.

**96** *Tall Desk, Huron County.*
This "butler's" desk is among several pieces believed by Gemeinhardt's descendants to have been made for his personal use. Its interior reflects his architectural interests with its central arcade and a facade which is carved to resemble masonry blocks. Late nineteenth century.

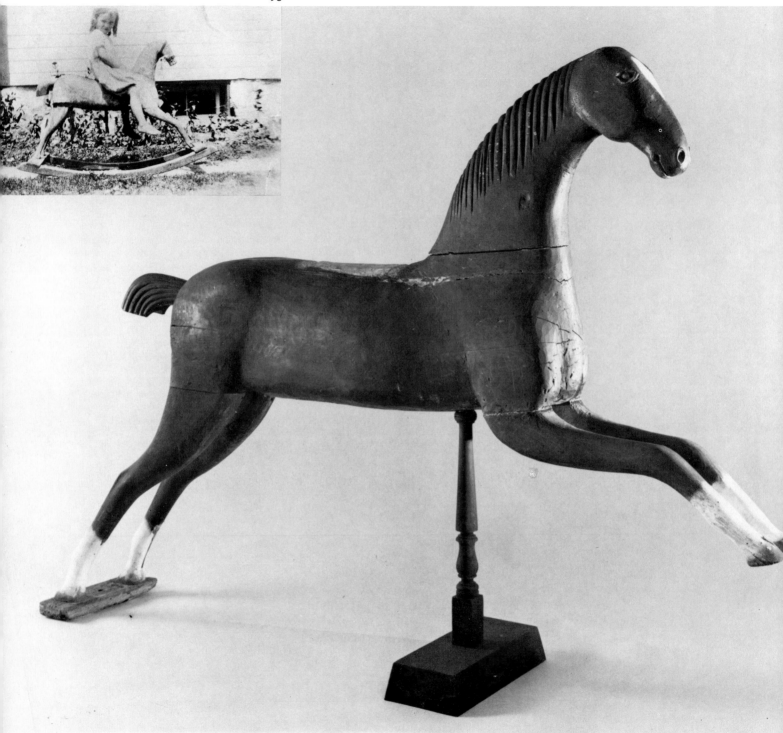

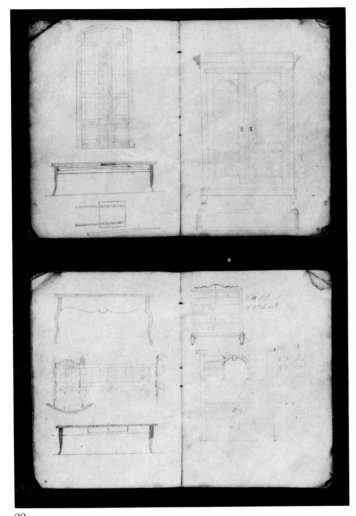

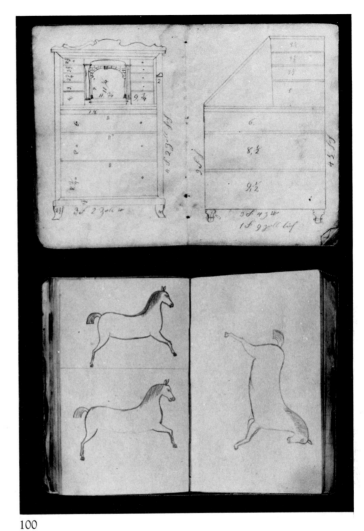

99

100

97 *Horse, Huron County.*
Perhaps the masterpiece of John Gemeinhardt's art as woodcarver is this large horse. It was intended as one of a set of six for a carousel made for a patron in nearby Grand Bend, but is believed to be the only surviving example. Late nineteenth century.

98 *Rider and Horse.*
This photograph shows Evelyn Gemeinhardt, a granddaughter of the cabinetmaker, seated on one of the carved horses originally planned for the carousel. This example was modified for family use by the addition of rockers. Circa 1925.

99 *Gemeinhardt Sketchbooks.*
Various pencil sketches in the drawing books of John Gemeinhardt reveal the diverse talents of this Bayfield cabinetmaker, including a doorway, a large Germanic wardrobe, a "draw" table, chests of drawers, a child's bed and a preliminary sketch for the footstool illustrated in Plate 94.

100 *Gemeinhardt Sketchbooks.*
A second cabinetmaker's sketchbook features preliminary drawings for numerous pieces of furniture preserved by Gemeinhardt's descendants. An important example is the sketch of the tall desk in Plate 96, shown here in exact detail. At the bottom are three pencil sketches of the carousel horse in Plate 97. Late nineteenth century.

101

101 *Food Locker, Renfrew County.*
Found near Augsburg in Renfrew County, this food locker is a striking eastern-Ontario example of Germanic furniture. Its sponge-decorated finish is remarkably similar in appearance to Ontario-German decorated earthenware pottery. Late nineteenth century.

102 *Wall Cupboard, Renfrew County.*
Reputedly the work of August Boehme of the Palmer Rapids area of Renfrew County, this pine cupboard is of primitive yet charming workmanship. Its pediment, base and sides are scrolled, and its facade is embellished with rosettes and cut-out hearts. Second half nineteenth century.

103 *Plank Chair, Renfrew County.*
From the Boehme family of Palmer Rapids, this plank chair with tapered and chamfered legs has an elaborately shaped back and cut-out heart similar to Germanic styles of a much earlier date. Second half nineteenth century.

104 *The Boehme Family.*
This remarkable photograph shows members of the Boehme family posing in front of their log house at Palmer Rapids. The real point of interest is, however, a background detail: visible on the porch is the plank chair shown in Plate 103. Circa 1900.

104

103

105 *Illuminated Songbook, Lincoln County.*
The earliest known dated and place-marked
example of Ontario *Fraktur* is this songbook
from the "Clinton School." It is possible that
some of these early *Fraktur* specimens were
drawn by the schoolteacher-scrivener Samuel
Moyer (1767-1844). 1804. [Courtesy Jordan
Museum of The Twenty]

**106** *Drawing, Lincoln County.*
The appearance of human figures in Mennonite *Fraktur* is a rare occurrence. This example, made for Magdalena Meyer, is especially appealing with its depiction of a young girl seated in a bower of stylized flowers with paired birds overhead. 1804. [Courtesy Jordan Museum of The Twenty]

**107** *Paper Cutwork, Lincoln County.*
An art form closely related to *Fraktur* is paper cutwork. This rare signed Lincoln County example by Abraham Meyer is designed with both vertical and horizontal symmetry, utilizing traditional Pennsylvania-German folk motifs. 1824.

**108** *Spiritual Wonder-Clock, Lincoln County.*
Derived from earlier *Books of Hours*, the spiritual wonder-clock is a meditation upon the symbolic significance of the hours of the day. This piece is signed at the bottom, "Written the 11th day of April in the Year of Christ 1821, this picture belongs to Magdalena Albrecht." 1821.

**109** *Birth Record, Welland County.*
One of numerous similar examples handdrawn by an itinerant Pennsylvania scrivener frequently called the "Ehre Vater Artist." This birth record made for Johannes Seider of Welland County indicates his birth in 1785 in Pennsylvania, "two miles from Meyerstown." Circa 1800.

**110** *Baptismal Record, Welland or Haldimand County.*
Commemorating the baptism of Ludwig Rauch, of the family of Rauch settlers who migrated from Germany to the Cayuga area in Welland and Haldimand counties in the 1840s, this hand-drawn certificate features hearts, tulips, stars and geometric borders. 1868.

106

107

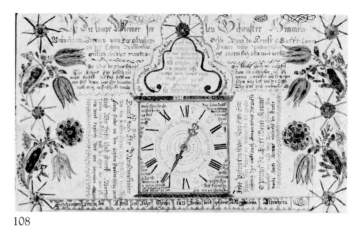

108

110

109

111

112

111 *Birth-and-Baptismal Record, York County.*
An exceptionally skilful artist, who was also
probably a schoolteacher in Vaughan and
Markham townships of York County, executed this and numerous other certificates
and drawings in the first two decades of the
nineteenth century. This "York County
*Taufschein* (baptismal record) Artist" was an
itinerant scrivener who worked in both
Pennsylvania and Ontario. 1809.

112 *Birth-and-Baptismal Record, York County.*
The itinerant artist Joseph Lochbaum was a
schoolteacher in Pennsylvania before swing-
ing through the Markham area in the early
nineteenth century, when he produced
numerous "nine-hearts" certificates for
children of early settlers. This example records the birth of Joseph Burkholder in 1801.
Circa 1830.

113 *Baptismal Record, York County.*
This profusely decorated record made by
Christian L. Hoover (1835-1918) for
Elisabeth Bercki is typical of several made
during the 1854 to 1855 period. Most of his
records are free-spirited adaptations of
printed forms by Heinrich Dulheur or Heinrich Otto. 1854.

113

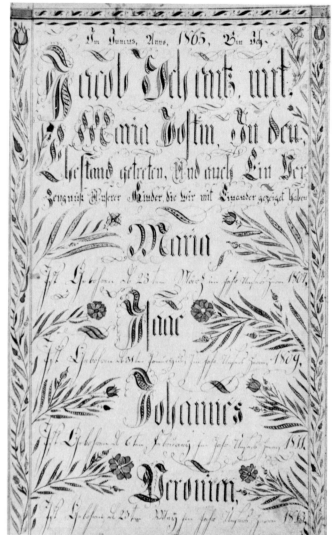

114

Dieses
Neue Testament
Gehöret Mir
Anna Musselman

Soll dieses Buch verloren gehn, so kan man hier mein name fehn:
In Ober Canade wohne ich, Hiernach vornemlich richte dich.

Hier giebt es jetzt beweiß, Daß diese liebe Annah,
Ihr buch gelernt mit fleiß; Von einem Tag zum an-

Nun, hab alle zeit Gott vor augen, So wirst du einst in
Himmel fahren: Wo die Engel sitzen bey Paaren.

Geschrieben in Ober Canada December d28 im Jahr 1835

114 *Family Registers, Eastern Pennsylvania.*
These family registers record the marriages and offspring of two generations of Shantz families who were among Pennsylvania-German pioneers making the trek to Waterloo County in the early nineteenth century. The register at the left for Isaac Shantz, "the old progenitor of the Shantzes that came to Canada," is probably the work of the "Earl Township Artist" who worked in several counties of eastern Pennsylvania. The register for Jacob Shantz is by Jacob Shumacher, a Montgomery County schoolteacher whose work is closely copied from that of the Earl Township Artist. Circa 1790 and 1821.

115 *Bookplate, Waterloo County.*
This hand-lettered bookplate is among the earliest Canadian works by Isaac Z. Hunsicker (1803-1870), schoolteacher and *Fraktur* artist, who migrated to Waterloo Township from Montgomery County, Pennsylvania sometime between 1832 and 1835. This bookplate for Anna Musselman reveals his typical incorporation of Biblical texts, aphorisms and ornamentation. 1835.

116  *Bookplate/Genealogy, Waterloo County.*
Possibly the masterpiece of Ontario *Fraktur* is
this double bookplate and genealogy executed by Abraham Latschaw (1799-1870) for
Bishop Benjamin Eby (1785-1853). Its refined
calligraphy and traditional folk-art motifs are
superbly drawn and indicate the outstanding
artistic skill of this cabinetmaker and *Fraktur*
artist. 1823. [Courtesy Kitchener Public
Library and Waterloo County Historical
Society]

117 *Songbook, Lancaster County,*
*Pennsylvania.*
The *Fraktur* career of Anna Weber (1814-
1888) differed from that of many other artists.
Most produced *Fraktur* as a semi-professional
activity, but the aging Anna Weber busied
herself making pictures for hosts, friends and
children. The earliest known dated piece
from her hand is her 1829 Lancaster songbook. 1866.

118 *Drawing, Waterloo County.*
In contrast to the simplicity of her own
songbook (Plate 117) is the relative complex-
ity of Anna Weber's more detailed pictures.
This example illustrates her typical arrangement of birds and flowers in a symmetrical
composition. The unique charm of this drawing is its fanciful depiction of paired sheep,
bedecked in blue-and-white checkered coats.
1875.

119 *Drawing, Waterloo County.*
The largest and most detailed of all of Anna
Weber's drawings also bears the earliest date.
In this ambitious picture she has arranged
twenty-two birds, in eleven pairs, perched on
three stylized trees. The primitive yet charming border is composed of dots of alternating
colours. 1870.

122

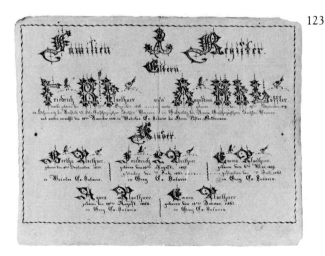

123

120 *Birth Record, Waterloo County.*
One of the last practising *Fraktur* artists in
Ontario was Joseph D. Bauman (1815-1899)
from near St. Jacobs. This birth record was
made on the occasion of the fifth birthday of
Daniel B. Horst (born 1876), a younger
brother of the woodcarver David B. Horst. Its
paired birds and central floral motif are copied
from earlier Pennsylvania printed forms.
1881.

121 *Baptismal Record, York County.*
An itinerant artist utilizing Neoclassical design elements produced several bookplates
and birth-and-baptismal certificates in both
York and Waterloo counties. The example
shown here records the birth of Barbara Risser
in Markham Township on January 22, 1818.
Anticipating that she would be baptized in
the 1830s, the artist left a space on the certificate. Circa 1825 to 1830.

122 *Birth, Baptismal and Confirmation Record.*
Recording the birth of Jacob Sittler on August 2, 1817, the text testifies to the victory
over the grave. This *Fraktur* specimen most
likely comes out of the Lutheran tradition. It
may have been executed either in Ohio
(Jacob's birthplace) or in Ontario, after the
Sittlers moved to Canada. Circa 1830 to
1840.

123 *Family Register, Grey County.*
One of the most widely travelled practitioners in Ontario, Wilhelm Gerhard (1864-
1913) produced *Fraktur* family registers in
nearly every Germanic settlement of southwestern Ontario. This hand-lettered example
was done for the family of Friedrich K.
Ploethner (1826-1883), weaver and cabinetmaker of Normanby Township, Grey
County. Circa 1880.

125

124 *Paper Cutwork, Waterloo County.*
This paper cutout, folded twice before cutting in order to produce biaxial symmetry, records the birth of Lidia Kolb on February 19, 1842. Most known similar pieces are mounted on brightly coloured paper backing, providing strong contrast for the symmetrical arrangement of floral and geometric designs. Mid-nineteenth century.

125 *Paper Cutwork, Waterloo County.*
Cut from ledger paper dated 1851, this design with paired horses was folded twice to produce both horizontal and vertical axial symmetry. Mid-nineteenth century.

126 *Paper Cutwork, Waterloo County.*
While most paper cuttings produced in Waterloo County during the nineteenth century are symmetrically composed like *Fraktur* drawings, this example is of interest because it abandons the rigid harmonic scheme of paired elements. Its wealth of detail includes a central tree, many varieties of fruit, flowers and birds, and a hanging cluster of five hearts. It was preserved for several generations in the Bible of Christian B. Eby (1821-1859), son of Bishop Benjamin Eby and a minister in the Mennonite church for many years. Mid-nineteenth century.

128

127 *Paper Cutwork and Passion-Prayer.*
Bold colour and meticulous cutwork accompany a consoling German text from the hymn, *O Sacred Head Now Wounded.* Found in the village of Conestogo in Waterloo County, the piece was kept in the Bible of Heinrich Rembe (born 1858), who was pastor of St. Matthew's Lutheran Church from 1900 to 1904. Third quarter nineteenth century.

128 *Farm Setting, Waterloo County.*
This primitive water colour gives a valuable insight into the transitional Pennsylvania-German farm in Waterloo County. To the left of a later Ontario Victorian house can be seen the traditional overhanging bank-barn as well as the four-bay garden typical of early nineteenth century Pennsylvania-German homesteads in southern Ontario. Late nineteenth century.

129 *Farm Scene, Waterloo County.*
A charming rendition of a Waterloo County farm, this drawing was done by Orvie Shantz, then a pupil at the Lexington School near Waterloo. It shows the John Wissler house where Orvie Shantz was raised; it was built in 1842 on the banks of the Grand River. Circa 1930.

129

145

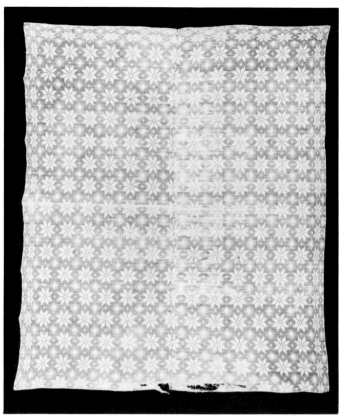

130

131

130 *Blanket, (detail), Lincoln County.*
Woven by Samuel Fry (1812-1881) of Vineland for his personal use, this wool blanket is embroidered with his initials. One of the few Mennonite weavers in Ontario, Fry apprenticed in the profession in Bucks County, Pennsylvania in the 1830s. Circa 1840 to 1860. [Courtesy Royal Ontario Museum]

131 *Coverlet, Waterloo County.*
This pink and white coverlet has a repeating pattern of diamonds and eight-pointed stars, motifs which are found also in needlework and on quilts in Pennsylvania-German areas of Ontario. Circa 1840 to 1860. [Courtesy Royal Ontario Museum]

132

133

132 *Jacquard Coverlet, (detail), Waterloo County.*
Among the many well-executed coverlets woven by the Roman Catholic Nolls family of weavers at Petersburg in Waterloo County is this blue and white example made for Rev. Eugen Funcken (misspelled on the coverlet). Funcken was a poet, writer and the early spiritual leader in nearby St. Agatha. 1869.

133 *Jacquard Coverlet, (detail), Grey County.*
The red and white coverlet shown in detail here has been preserved by descendants of Friedrich K. Ploethner (1826-1883) whose account book indicates that he practised weaving at his home near Neustadt from 1868 to 1883. He was a brother of August Ploethner, a well known weaver at Preston (Cambridge) in Waterloo County around the same time. Circa 1870 to 1880.

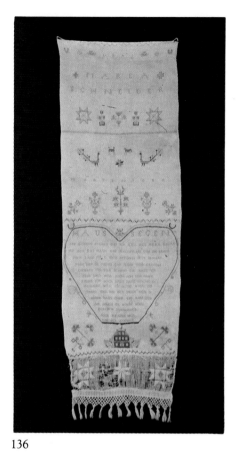

134

135

136

134 *Amish Show Towel, Waterloo County.*
A simple but appealing show towel of Amish workmanship is this 1897 panel worked in continuous chain-stitch by Katie Jantzi from near New Hamburg in Waterloo County. Its focal point is a large basket of flowers and scrolls worked in wool. 1897.

135 *Mennonite Show Towel,*
*Waterloo County.*
Elisabeth Martin decorated this unusually wide towel in 1861 with a range of stylized trees, pots of flowers, peacocks, other birds, eight-pointed stars, lozenge motifs and two large hearts on the lower panel. 1861.

136 *Mennonite Show Towel,*
*Waterloo County.*
This long panel, embroidered in 1841 by Mary Snider (1822-1916) before her 1843 marriage to Rev. Peter Martin (1820-1902), is a rare combination of needlework composition and *Fraktur* design. The inclusion of a house-blessing on a show towel is also rare; the form was taken directly from Pennsylvania printed *Fraktur* forms. 1841.

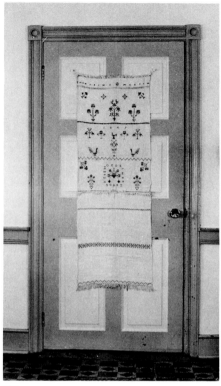

137

137 *Door for Show Towel,*
*Daniel H. Weber Homestead.*
Rare evidence that show towels actually were
hung on doors is this panelled door in the
parlour of the Daniel H. Weber homestead
south of Conestogo in Waterloo County. A
towel would hang from the two clearly visible
brass pegs, which indicates that needlework
was done at least in part "for show." The
profusely decorated towel was made by
Catharina Martin in 1847. 1837.

138 *Mennonite Show Towel,*
*Waterloo County.*
One of the most spectacular Ontario Mennonite show towels is this one done in chain
stitch by Mary Snyder (1832-1916). It is
adorned with boldly coloured flowers, eight-
pointed stars, a tree with nine perched birds
of many varieties, roosters and the rare depiction of confronting horses and riders. 1852.

139

142

140

143

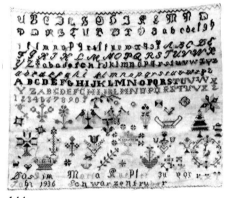

141

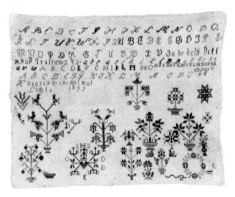

144

---

139 *Miniature Sampler, Lincoln County.*
Several tiny samplers have been handed down through generations of the Fry family of Vineland. This example, with its symmetricaw arrangement of roses, lions, eight-pointed stars and roosters, is worked on a punched-paper backing. 1858. [Courtesy Royal Ontario Museum]

140 *Sampler, York County.*
A nine-year-old girl, Susanna Byer of Markham Township, worked this horizontal panel in 1827 by incorporating a diverse "sample" of motifs. As with most Ontario-German samplers, the letter "J" does not appear in the alphabet. 1827.

141 *Sampler, Waterloo County.*
Fanny Bricker, daughter of the legendary Waterloo County hero Sam Bricker, worked this vertical sampler at the age of twelve. Its text reads in part: "Fanny Bricker is my name. Upper Canada is my station. Waterloo is my dwelling place and Christ is my salvation." 1827.

142 *Sampler/Family Register, Waterloo County.*
A late Pennsylvania-German sampler done in Waterloo County, this needlework family register utilizes traditional motifs from embroidered show towels and the acronym OEHBDDE. It records the births of its maker (Anna Martin) and her two brothers. 1883.

143 *Amish Sampler, Waterloo County.*
A wide range of embroidered articles was made in the Amish-Mennonite areas of Waterloo, Oxford and Perth counties. This sampler was done by "Katarina Lichti in Wilmot 1872."

144 *Amish Sampler, Waterloo County.*
This twentieth-century sampler is a late perpetuation of a traditional craft in the Amish community of southwestern Ontario. Strikingly similar to the samplers and towels made in western Canada's Hutterite communities, it is profusely decorated with folk motifs and the maker's name, Maria Kuepfer Schwartzentruber. 1936.

145

---

145 *Quilt, Waterloo County.*
Passed down through the Snider family, this
appliquéd quilt has bold Pennsylvania-
German folk designs: undulating border of
vines and grapes enclosing four geometric
sunbursts. Circa 1875.

146 *Quilt, Waterloo County.*
Made by Henrietta Einwaechter Goettling
(1880-1961) of New Dundee, this "Sunshine
and Shadow" quilt has particularly deep hues
forming a large eight-pointed star as its
dominant motif.  1918.

147 *Quilt, Bruce County.*
From Bruce County, this "Blazing Star" quilt
makes effective use of primary colours. Its
solid red border, red-and-yellow star and
tulips make it a bold statement of colour and
design. Late nineteenth century.

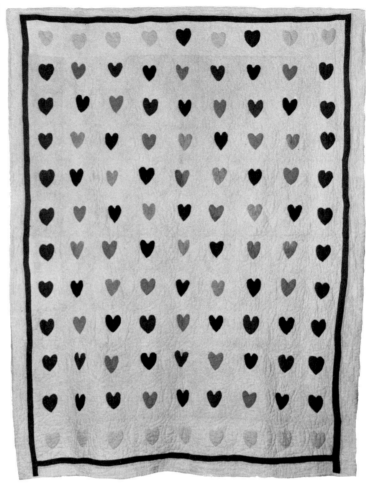

148 *Quilt, Huron County.*
One of the more fanciful deployments of the
heart motif in the decorative arts is this
appliquéd quilt from Zurich in Huron
County. A total of 108 hearts in four colours
are arranged in twelve rows of nine. Late
nineteenth century.

149

150

151

152

149 *Hooked Rug, Waterloo County.*
This hooked rug, from near St. Jacobs in
Waterloo County, makes use of traditional
Pennsylvania-German design elements:
stars, rosettes and geometric patterns. Late
nineteenth century.

150 *Hooked Rug, Waterloo County.*
Descended through one of the Martin
families in the Conestogo-Bloomingdale
area, this rug is dated twice in the centre and
features two eight-pointed stars in red against
a green background. 1896.

151 *Hooked Rug, Waterloo County.*
The colours and manner of graphic repre-
sentation of the folk-art spirit in this rug are
particularly charming. It was made by Re-
becca Schweitzer of New Hamburg. 1886.

152 *Hooked Rug, Perth County.*
One of Ontario's great hooked-rug artists was
Maria Beck Warning (1832-1918), who lived
in the village of Brunner, Perth County. Possibly her finest work is this 1893 rug in which
a central rooster is enclosed within a border of
undulating tulips and hearts. 1893.

153

154

153 *Storage Jar, Niagara Peninsula.*
Found in Welland County, this simple
straight-sided storage jar is given dramatic
visual effect by means of brown slip patches
applied in a rather considered manner over a
buff background. Nineteenth century.

154 *Storage Jar, Lincoln County.*
This jar was recovered along with shards
stamped "B. Lent" during the excavation of a
pottery site near Jordan. It is a remarkable
example of decorated Ontario earthenware
with its tulips and other floral elements incised and painted in imitation of Pennsylvania *sgrafitto* techniques. Circa 1835 to
1840. [Collection of Department of Ar-
chaeology, Brock University]

155 *Storage Jar, York County.*
Made by either Philip Ensminger or Cyrus
Eby who potted at Markham in the early
1860s, this decorated utilitarian jar is glazed
with traditional Pennsylvania-German
motifs. It is inscribed "Markham Pottery
1862."

156

157

158

156 *Flower Pots, York County.*
Found in nearby communities of Markham Township, these two flower pots are undoubtedly the work of a single potter. Refinements include pinch-decorated rims and bases, fine turnings, applied crimp moulding and glazing of green spatter over buff. Second half nineteenth century.

157 *Storage Jars, Waterloo County.*
The earliest dated examples of Ontario pottery are several earthenware pieces made by the Mennonite potter Jacob Bock (1798-1867). Reminiscent of formal prototypes, these jars feature applied faces, figures and the name "S. Ambrosius." The jar on the left has forty-six applied faces; on the bottom is the inscription, "Waterloo September 17, 1825 Upper Canada Jacob Bock." The jar on the right is inscribed, "Waterloo the 4 Jan 1825."

158 *Barrel, Waterloo County.*
Another remarkably early piece of earthenware pottery is this barrel which is inscribed "1827 Waterloo." It is possible that this early redware barrel is the work of Jacob Bock. 1827.

159

160

159 *Large Pitcher and Miniatures,
Waterloo County.*
At least two Waterloo County potters —
William K. Eby and Adam Biernstihl — are
reported by descendants to have made miniatures like these for children, grandchildren
and friends. The large pitcher with heavy
spatter decoration was found in St. Jacobs
and is probably from the Eby pottery at nearby
Conestogo. Second half nineteenth century.

160 *Green-glazed Pottery, Western Ontario.*
A distinctive mark of the pottery of William
K. Eby (1831-1905) is a dark green glaze on
several pieces made specifically for his own
family. Among the specialty pieces shown
here is a covered sugar bowl, a miniature
pitcher and jug, a handle-less cup and saucer,
a spittoon, and a rare *Ringkrug*, or "ring jug,"
sometimes called a "harvest ring." The
green-glazed storage jar was found at Chippawa Hill in Bruce County and may possibly
have been made there by Cyrus Eby, a
younger brother who worked at Markham,
Conestogo and Chippawa Hill. Late
nineteenth century.

161 *Decorated Bowl, Waterloo County.*
One of the most striking expressions of Ontario-German folk-decorated pottery is this large bowl made by Adam Biernstihl for his daughter Emilie. The inscription, "Emilie Biernstihl Bridgeport," the wavy lines and primitively drawn chickens are in green slip over a buff base. Late nineteenth century.

162 *Specialty Pieces, Waterloo County.*
Among a small number of rare specialty pieces made by William Eby are examples with blue and green stick-work decoration against a pinkish clay. Illustrated are a spoon holder, sugar bowl and cup and saucer. The goblet-like piece on the left has the words "spoon holder" worked into the glaze. Late nineteenth century.

163 *Pie Plates, Waterloo County.*
The pie plate at the right, with its brown slip patches over a light base, was found in St. Jacobs. It is very possibly from the Eby pottery. The plate at the left is decorated with the characteristic plum motifs used by Eby on plates and, in rarer instances, pitchers. Late nineteenth century.

162

163

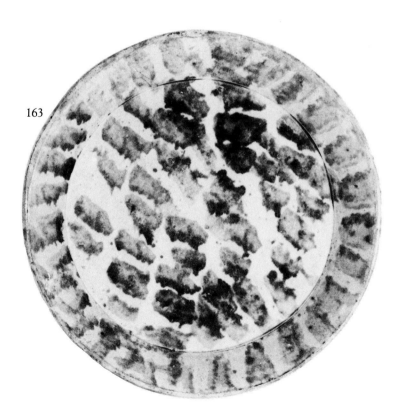

161

164

164 *Storage Jar, Waterloo County.*
Identical in size, form and glaze to another piece signed "Joseph Wagner," this storage jar appears to be unique with its heart motif applied and embossed beneath the lip. Late nineteenth century.

165 *Small Pitcher and Bowl, Waterloo County.*
This pair of pieces features brilliant colouration with blue and green slip spattered and dripped heavily over a brown and beige mottled base. They are most likely from the pottery of Adam Biernstihl (1825-1899) of Lexington and Bridgeport. Late nineteenth century.

166 *Pitcher, Waterloo County.*
This rare signed pitcher features brown slip decoration and finely moulded lip and handle. Stamped beneath the spout and highlighted in green are the words: "Joseph Wagner, Maker Berlin Ont." Late nineteenth century.

167 *Large Flower Pot, Waterloo County.*
This immense decorated flower pot from the Bridgeport area of Waterloo County is embellished with applied motifs made from the impression of a butter print. These motifs and the applied ring handles are highlighted in green. Late nineteenth century.

168 *Bank, Perth County.*
A novelty piece found near Milverton in Perth County, this earthenware bank with its perched birds is reminiscent of Pennsylvania and German examples. Possibly the work of Adam's son, Henry Biernstihl, it is distinguished by marbleized glazing and the inscriptions "HB" and "1876."

165

166

167

168

163

169

171

170

172

**169** *Pitcher and Miniatures, Waterloo County.*
These pieces have been preserved by descendants of the Waterloo potter Daniel Jacobi (1850-1905), indicating that he produced a wide variety of miniature jugs, pitchers and other forms. The large pitcher is marked by brown slip spotting on the pinkish clay background, colours characteristic of several pieces from his pottery. Late nineteenth century.

**170** *Flower Pot and Stand, Waterloo County.*
The Jacobi and Biernstihl potteries appear to have produced some of the largest earthenware objects known in the Ontario-German tradition. Daniel Jacobi fashioned several three-piece flower stands (pot, saucer, cylindrical base), finished in dramatic green and brown slip over a lighter base colour. Late nineteenth century.

**171** *Large Pitcher, Waterloo County.*
This large, bulbous earthenware pitcher found in Waterloo County boasts one of the brightest colour schemes of known examples. The mottled glaze is made up of bright oranges, greens and browns, producing a vivid visual display. Nineteenth century.

**172** *Storage Jars, Huron County.*
From the Huron Pottery at Egmondville have come numerous distinctive pieces, in particular earthenware decorated with blue finger-painted flowers in the manner of stoneware. These examples are particularly refined with their delicately drawn flowers on a yellow background. Late nineteenth century.

**173** *Urn, Huron County.*
Some highly varied pottery forms have been found in the Seaforth-Egmondville area of Huron County, possibly products of the Huron Pottery. This unglazed urn is an unusually refined form, reminiscent of Neoclassical prototypes popular in Europe. Late nineteenth century.

173

174

174 *Springerle Board, Haldimand County.*
An art form associated with the kitchen which had special prominence on festive occasions, the "Springerle" board was used for making fancy cookies. This and other similar boards were made by William Nagel (1871-1938) in the Fisherville-Rainham Centre area around 1895. Late nineteenth century.

175 *Butter Prints, Waterloo and Bruce counties.*
Hand-carved butter prints from Germanic Ontario are relatively uncommon, particularly when compared to the number made in Pennsylvania. The butter print with cross-hatched heart motif (left) was found in Waterloo County, while the one with deeply carved heart and floral decoration (right) was found near Port Elgin. Nineteenth century.

176 *Cabbage Cutters, Waterloo County.*
Even the cabbage cutter was occasionally transformed into an aesthetic object. Sometimes, a heart pierced the board which was used to hang the cutter. These examples from Waterloo County are highly unusual in such relief-carved motifs as a wide heart and an eight-pointed star. Nineteenth century.

177 *Apple Peeler, York County.*
One of the truly outstanding examples of Pennsylvania-German folk-art decoration on a domestic utensil is this apple peeler from Markham Township. Its base is spectacularly decorated and carries the inscription, "David Byer 1843." [Courtesy Black Creek Pioneer Village]

178 *Heckles, Southwestern Ontario.*
A comb used for breaking down the fibre of the flax plant in preparation for weaving, the typical Ontario-German heckle normally has a round cluster of spikes mounted on a slightly scrolled or shaped backboard, unlike the rectangular form of Pennsylvania heckles. The 1825 heckle with six-point compass stars is from Lincoln County, while the 1855 example with its painted folk-art bird motif was found at Zurich in Huron County. Dated 1825 and 1855.

175

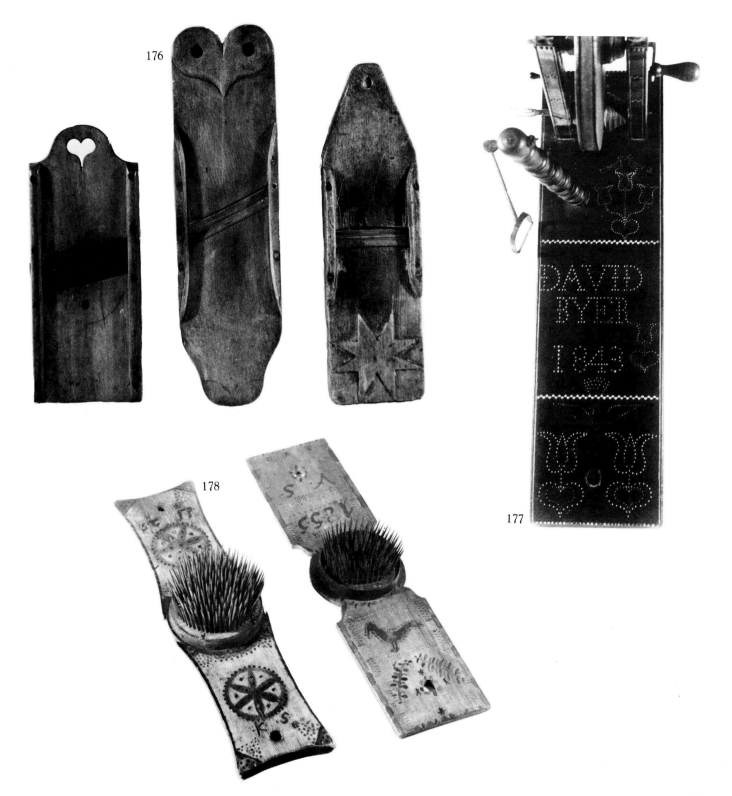

179

180

168

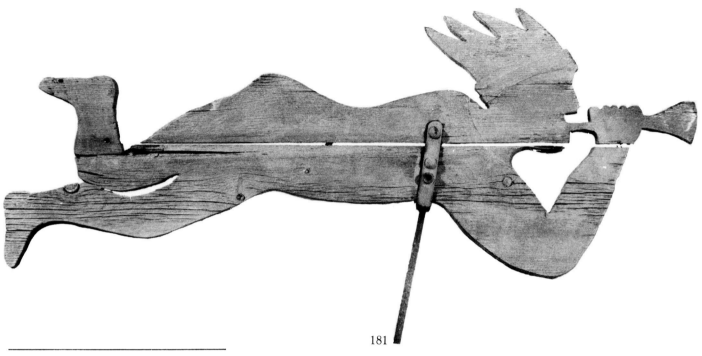

181

179 *Whirligig, Haldimand County.*
This painted whirligig, a classic caricature of
the traffic officer, was made by William
Hartwick (Hartwig), a cabinetmaker near
Fisherville in Haldimand County. Its expressive face and well-shaped arms make it a
strong folk-art expression. Late nineteenth
century.

180 *Whirligig, Bruce or Grey County.*
Made by Justus Dierlamm of near Neustadt,
this piece is a highly imaginative combination of whirligig and weathervane. Late
nineteenth century.

181 *Weathervane, Bruce or Grey County.*
Many weathervanes made in Canada and the
United States are patterned after classic and
popular forms, including the Indian or the
Angel Gabriel. This weathervane from
around Neustadt is a unique variation on
these themes: it combines both the Indian
and Gabriel images into a single figure, complete with trumpet and head-dress. Late
nineteenth or early twentieth century.

169

182

183

182  *David B. Horst, Waterloo County.*
In his later life, the Mennonite woodcarver David B. Horst (1873-1965) of St. Jacobs took to making carved and painted animals for children, friends and personal enjoyment. In this picture, several of his carvings are visible in the windows of his cottage. Horst is pictured on crutches at the left. 1947.

183  *Large Rooster, Waterloo County.*
One of David Horst's most dramatic carvings is this large crowing rooster. Solid colours are used to highlight the comb and upswept tail, while the body is finished with stipple decoration. Circa 1935 to 1943.

184

185

184 *Group of Carvings, Waterloo County.*
In this group of carved and painted pieces can be seen the versatility of the aging David Horst. The large turkey and yellow songbird reflect his fondness for strong colouration. The pair of stippled guinea hens may have been inspired by an Anna Weber drawing of 1874 (see *Ontario Fraktur*, Plate 192). Circa 1935 to 1943.

185 *Carving of King George V, Waterloo County.*
King George V was frequently in the news during the 1930s. He visited Canada in 1935 before his death in 1936. It is reported by descendants that David Horst kept a newspaper picture of the monarch, on which he based this superb woodcarving. Horst's meticulous concern with minute detail extends even to the coat of arms on the uniform. Circa 1938.

186

188

189

190

187

186 *Carved Picture Frame, Waterloo County.*
Made on the occasion of a wedding in 1942,
this folk-art frame is richly embellished with
floral motifs. It and a comb box made for
Amos Martin in 1939 are among the few
wall-pieces David Horst designed for friends
and hosts. The text, composed by Moses G.
Reist in the early twentieth century, records
his unhappy life and confinement in a
sanatorium after being kicked in the head by a
horse. 1942.

187 *Carved Birds, Waterloo County.*
Like David Horst, the carving career of John
Hummel (1892-1970) of Maryhill, Waterloo
County, began late in life. One of his favour-
ite subjects was the bird-tree popular also in
Germany and Pennsylvania. Circa 1965.

188 *Carved Bird, Perth County.*
A retired farmer in the Old Order Amish area
of Millbank, Perth County, Daniel Kuepfer
carved numerous small animals and birds
which he frequently mounted on heart
shaped bases. Circa 1950.

189 *Inlaid Frames, Bruce County.*
Inlaid furniture and accessories are found
abundantly in the Germanic areas of lower
Bruce and Grey counties. The larger frame
shown here is probably the work of the Neustadt cabinetmaker John P. Klempp (1857-
1914), while the smaller one is likely an
attempt by an amateur to copy Klempp's more
refined work. Circa 1880 to 1890.

190 *Stencilled Frame, Waterloo County.*
A distinctive body of furniture exhibiting
Alsatian or south-German characteristics was
made for the Amish population in the
Petersburg-Baden area of Wilmot Township
in Waterloo County. This stencilled pine
frame is possibly a presentation-piece, as were
several *Kleiderschränke* and other pieces bearing names of recipients. 1867.

191 *Wallbox, Waterloo County.*
A large wallbox carved from basswood made
by Fred G. Hoffman (1845-1926) for his host,
David Bender of Punkeydoodles Corners near
the intersection of Waterloo, Oxford and
Perth counties. As with other examples of his
work, chip-carved geometric designs are
further enhanced by red and green paint, a
scheme used by later practitioners in Waterloo County, as well as by David Horst. 1921.

191

192

193

**192** *Wallbox, York County.*
Found at Markham, and nearly identical to another known in the area, this pine wallbox is decorated with incised geometric motifs painted green in contrast to a brown-stained background. Late nineteenth or early twentieth century.

**193** *Wallbox, Bruce or Grey County.*
In the category of what is sometimes called a "spice box" (but probably having a more general function), this pine wallbox with drawer and carved top retains its original black and red painted finish. It was found in the Germanic settlement of Neustadt. Nineteenth century.

**194** *Letter Box, Waterloo County.*
Of simple design, this pine letter tray from Baden in Waterloo County is given strong aesthetic appeal by its heart cut-out and original feather-grained decoration. Second quarter nineteenth century.

**195** *Wallbox, Perth County.*
Decorated wallboxes from Germanic areas of southern Ontario are somewhat of a rarity. This exception, from North Easthope Township in Perth County, is distinguished by tiny flowers delicately painted against a light blue background. Second quarter nineteenth century.

194

195

**196** *Box Lock, Waterloo County.*
Several German locksmiths, notably Peter Wilker and Andrew Wolf of Wilmot and Waterloo townships, respectively, produced heavy box locks of high quality, such as the example shown here. The keyhole plate comes from the Aaron B. Weber house on the Lexington-Conestogo Road, while the door latch with heart motif is from the Joseph Schneider House in Berlin (Kitchener). Early to mid-nineteenth century.

**197** *Iron Utensils, Southwestern Ontario.*
On occasion, the simple utilitarian iron utensil is given some form of decorative appeal. The heart, in particular, has found its way into several pieces illustrated here (left to right): a stove-ring from the Niagara Peninsula, hinges from near Wellesley in Waterloo County, a large spatula from Waterloo County and a small spatula from Haldimand County. Other articles are a "traveler" (used for measuring wheels and other round objects), three meat forks and a combination meat fork/spatula from Waterloo County. Nineteenth century.

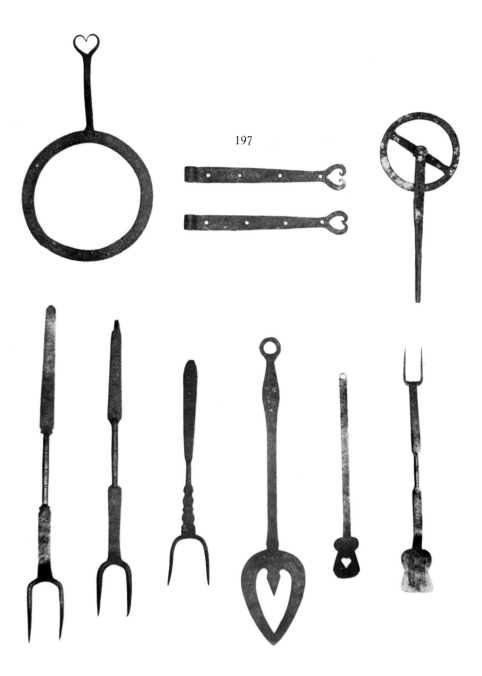

197

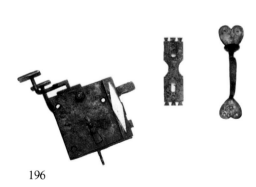

196

175

198 *Powder Horns, Bruce County.*
Found in an area of Continental-German settlement near Chesley in Bruce County, one powder horn is inscribed "C. Faust," while its mate is decorated with incised birds and stylized trees. Late nineteenth century.

199 *Pouch, Waterloo County.*
An outstanding expression of Pennsylvania-German folk art on a functional object is this leather pouch from Waterloo County. Its cut-out six-point compass star in the centre is flanked by undulating tulips. 1836.

200 *Rocking Horse, Waterloo County.*
Similar to other toys made in Berlin (Kitchener) in the late nineteenth century, this rocking horse from the Bearinger family in Waterloo is decorated with sponge and stencil painting. Late nineteenth century.

201 *Stencils, Waterloo County.*
After his return from Europe at the end of the First World War, Emanuel Soehner made a set of stencils which he copied from earlier examples and used to decorate several churches and house interiors in Waterloo County, including the Lutheran church at Floradale. Circa 1918 to 1920.

202 *Wall Stencilling, Waterloo County.*
Only rarely has evidence been found of extensive wall stencilling in Pennsylvania-German houses in southwestern Ontario. A notable exception is the David Eby house at the west end of Waterloo whose parlour once had walls fully decorated with pineapples, flowers, rosettes and other motifs. Second quarter nineteenth century.

203 *Gamesboard, Perth County.*
Among the finest folk-art objects created by Eckhardt Wettlaufer (1845-1919) is this painted crokinole board with stylized tulips which he made for his son Adam (born 1870), reputedly as a fifth-year birthday present. Circa 1875.

203

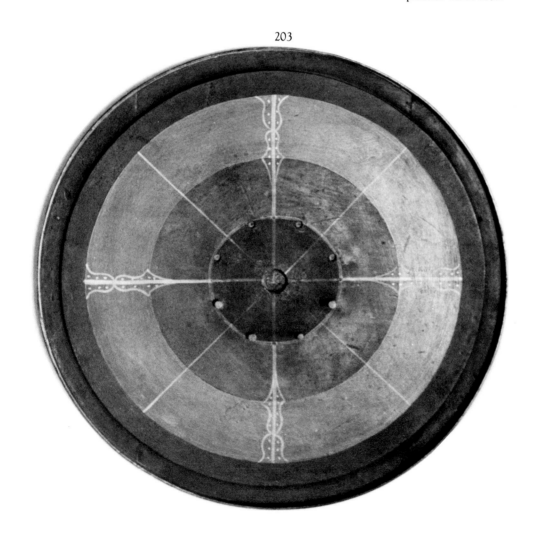

204 *Crucifix, Found in Waterloo County.*
Two similar crucifixes have been found in the Maryhill area of Waterloo County, but they may have been brought from Germany by pioneer immigrants. The base of this example is carved in a Neoclassical style, suggesting a pre-1840 date. Nineteenth century.

205 *Shrine, Renfrew County.*
This household shrine is primitively conceived and executed in its scalloped edges and polychrome design. From the Luloff family of the Augsburg area of Renfrew County, its decorative treatment derives from a Germanic-baroque background. Late nineteenth or early twentieth century.

206 *"P & FR" Marker, Lincoln County.*
This roughly hewn stone slab in the Mennonite Burial Ground at Vineland is appealing in its simplicity. Frequently, pioneer
gravestones have misspelled words, indicating that amateur stone cutters were not
always literate. Here, the word "Dide" suggests a strictly phonetic spelling. The incised
semi-circular enclosure is reminiscent of the
*Urbogen* symbol of the sun's descending arc
seen on markers in eastern Pennsylvania.
1829.

207 *Jacob Berky Marker, York County.*
One of the few decorated Pennsylvania-
German markers in the Wideman Cemetery
just north of Markham in York County, this
stone and several near it are signed "J. Morris,
Toronto." The radiating half-sun cut into the
top may be a more developed form of the
motif seen in Plate 206. 1824.

207

208

209

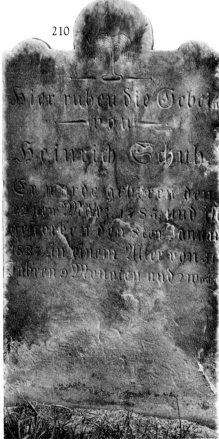

210

211

**208** *Hanna Schantz Marker, Waterloo County.* This stone is decorated with a quatrefoil flower surrounded by a double semi-circle. It commemorates the three-year-old child of Benjamin Schantz (1811-1865) and Lidia Kolb (1814-1862), who later moved to Bruce County, Ontario. 1841.

**209** *Elizabeth Eby Marker, Waterloo County.* Of the few gravemarkers in Waterloo County executed in the Pennsylvania-German style, most are located in the First Mennonite ("East End") Cemetery in Kitchener. This unusually beautiful example has a deeply cut tulip with drooping sepals accompanied by fine lettering in the *Fraktur* manner. 1844.

**210** *Heinrich Schuh Marker, Waterloo County.* The carved weeping willow appears on several markers in the First Mennonite, Hagey and Martin cemeteries in Waterloo County. Heinrich Schuh was a Mennonite minister who came to Waterloo County from York County, Pennsylvania. The family was ill-fated: a daughter was killed by lightning, a son was murdered in a swamp and Heinrich himself was felled by a stroke. 1837.

**211** *Maria Bauman Marker, Waterloo County.* The Pennsylvania-German heart graces this stone marker for the infant Maria Bauman. The third daughter of Benjamin and Susannah (Bechtel) Bauman, she was born September 18, 1831, and died March 17, 1832. This and other decorated gravestones in the First Mennonite Cemetery are the work of a highly competent stonecutter, possibly the cabinetmaker John Hoffman (1808-1878). 1832.

212 *Sarah Bechtel Marker, Waterloo County.*
Some markers indicate a transition between Pennsylvania-German traditions and newer English-urban influences, as does this somewhat formal Blair Cemetery slab erected for Sarah Bechtel. Its Roman lettering and popular aphorism are characteristic of English-speaking Canada at mid-century, while its six-pointed compass star is a familiar Pennsylvania-German device. 1842.

213 *Hiram Thomas Marker, Waterloo County.*
The single eye, possibly suggesting divine wisdom, is a motif which occurs rarely on Ontario-German tombstones. It is more likely to appear along with Masonic symbols than by itself. This unusual example stands in the First Mennonite Cemetery, Kitchener. 1845.

214 *Iron Cross, Waterloo County.*
A form of gravemarker which is almost uniquely Continental-German or Alsatian is the scrolled iron marker found in several Roman Catholic cemeteries of southwestern Ontario. This single-bar example is in the St. Agatha Cemetery. Late nineteenth century.

215 *Iron Cross, Waterloo County.*
In addition to the ornamental scrolls seen in Plate 214, this cross is given further interest by lances or spear-like forms and double vertical and horizontal bars. The iron corpus on the small cross is painted white in contrast to the black-painted wrought-iron. Late nineteenth century.

212

213

214

215

216

218

217

216 *Iron Cross, Waterloo County.*
On some iron crosses, a small stone slab with names of the deceased is attached to the point at which the bars meet. This cross is particularly elaborate with its many C-scrolls and broken pediment. The placement of curves creates a heart motif on either side of the stone slabs. Late nineteenth century.

217 *Iron Cross, Waterloo County.*
This superb Continental-German design iron cross stands in the cemetery of St. Boniface Church in Maryhill. The paired cast-iron angels have delicate ribbing on their wings and charming, smiling faces. Late nineteenth century.

218 *Cemetery Gate, Waterloo County.*
This iron entrance gate to the Maryhill Cemetery was built by J.D. Miller of Bridgeport at a cost of $106. The spears of the finials lead into a *fleur-de-lis* design. The cross at the top begins the spear and cyma-curve motif carried on in the rest of the gate. Late nineteenth century.

219 *Iron Cross, Bruce County.*
Cut into the metal panel at the centre of this iron cross at Immaculate Conception Church in the village of Formosa is information concerning three young Knopfler children (Susan, Anton, Anna), all of whom died between November 11 and 14, 1879.

220 *Iron Cross, Bruce County.*
This wrought-iron cross is of pleasing design with spears, coils, cross-and-orb, and applied heart-shaped panel. Late nineteenth century.

221 *Iron Cross, Bruce County.*
A number of crosses in the cemetery of St. Francis Xavier Church at Carlsruhe are distinguished by unusual, narrow horizontal stone slabs that fill the spaces between the double bars of the cross. This marker for Maria Zettler is enhanced by simple scrolls, spikes and a cross-and-heart motif. Late nineteenth century.

219

220

221

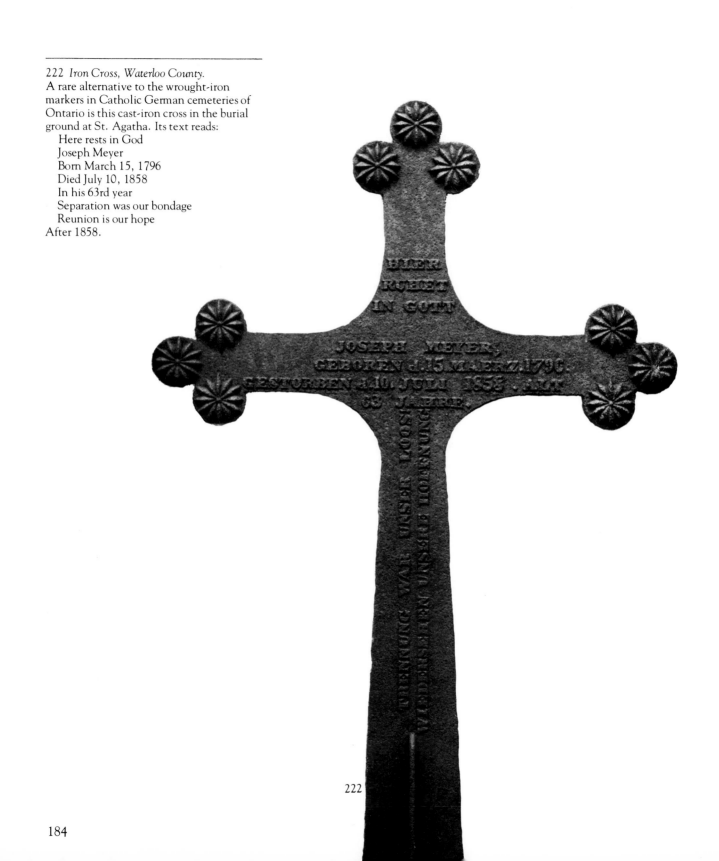

222 *Iron Cross, Waterloo County.*
A rare alternative to the wrought-iron markers in Catholic German cemeteries of Ontario is this cast-iron cross in the burial ground at St. Agatha. Its text reads:

Here rests in God
Joseph Meyer
Born March 15, 1796
Died July 10, 1858
In his 63rd year
Separation was our bondage
Reunion is our hope

After 1858.

222

# 4 The Prairie Provinces

With the opening of the Canadian Prairies in the late nineteenth century, large numbers of German-speaking people and settlers of other ethnic backgrounds migrated to this vast interior region. The majority of Germanic settlers were Mennonites, augmented by a small number of Hutterites. In common speech, these pioneers are often called "Russian Mennonites," alluding to the southern Ukraine which they left in the 1870s to seek a new life in the prairie farmlands of North America. In order to include these settlers, who migrated to areas of Manitoba, Saskatchewan, Alberta and, later, British Columbia, under the general heading of "Germanic settlers," some clarification of terminology is required.

A brief history of these prairie Mennonites indicates something of the continuous Anabaptist migrations brought on by the persecutions of both church and state. Two geographical regions of Europe where the Anabaptist wing of the Reformation flourished were the Swiss-Austrian-German area in the south and the Spanish Netherlands in the north. From this northern Germanic group came the forerunners of those Mennonites who were eventually to establish their homes in western Canada.

Despite certain differences among the various sub-regions of these northern groups (found variously in Flanders, Holland, Zeeland, Groeningen and Friesland), they shared a theological stance whose unity was further strengthened by persecution. They were given a haven in the Danzig area of Prussia's Vistula Delta by landlords who sought them out to farm marsh and swampland,[1] much as Cornwallis did later in Nova Scotia. These people achieved what others had been unable to attain — they drained the marshes and became prosperous farmers and artisans. As had so often been the fate of oppressed groups who eventually came to be feared by aristocrats and merchants in the surrounding culture, they were penalized for their success through legal constraints, prohibition of land expansion, severe taxation and the threat of loss of their long-standing contractual guarantees.

By the last quarter of the eighteenth century, hostility to the Mennonites in the Danzig region had become overwhelmingly detrimental to their economic, cultural and spiritual survival. In what seems to be a familiar historical pattern, they were again favoured by an invitation to become homesteaders in a new land. Once more, the initiative came from the East, this time from Catherine the Great of Russia, to settle new lands claimed by Russia following her victory in wars with Turkey. It is estimated that more than half of the Prussian Mennonites left the Vistula Delta in 1786 and made the long trek to an area along the Chortitza River to its junction with the Dnieper River just north of the Black Sea.[2]

Thus began the period of domicile for these uprooted Anabaptists which caused them in later times to be designated "Russian Mennonites." During the first decade of their life in this area, they established a number of "colonies" comprising several villages. The first of these was the Chortitza Colony (later called the Old Colony), founded at the convergence of the Chortitza and Dnieper Rivers in 1789. With increased numbers due to births and continuing migration from Prussia, it became necessary to establish additional villages. The Molotschna Colony came into being after Czar Paul signed a manifesto in 1800 solidifying rights earlier promised verbally by Catherine.

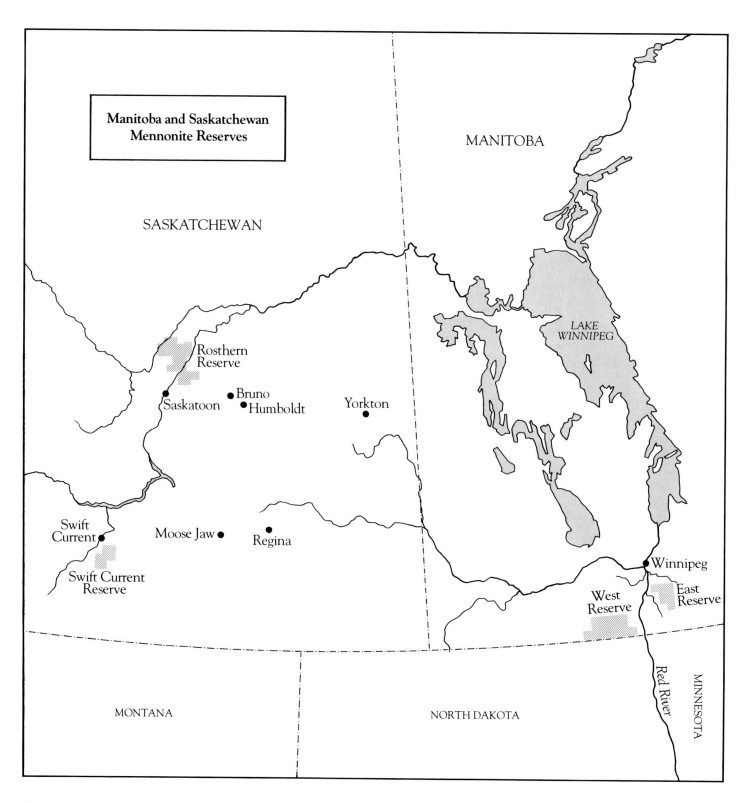

Manitoba and Saskatchewan
Mennonite Reserves

MANITOBA

SASKATCHEWAN

*LAKE WINNIPEG*

Rosthern
Reserve

● Bruno
● Saskatoon  ● Humboldt

Yorkton

Swift
Current

● Moose Jaw  ● Regina

Swift Current
Reserve

● Winnipeg

West
Reserve

East
Reserve

*Red River*

MINNESOTA

MONTANA

NORTH DAKOTA

This assurance gave immediate incentive for several thousand Mennonites to leave their Prussian homeland, arriving in southern Russia after 1804. In later years, several "daughter" colonies sprang up including the Bergthal Settlement (1836) and the Fuerstenland Settlement (1864).[3]

These transplanted Mennonites made their homes in south Russia for less than a century before unforeseen changes in the political climate meant another abrogation of privileges and the exile of thousands of individuals. By the 1870s, the spirit of nationalism that had earlier swept across most of Europe stirred the aspirations of the Russian leadership under Czar Alexander II. An intense programme of Russianization was undertaken which involved the mandatory use of the Russian language for instruction in schools. The many German colonists of western and southern Russia were particularly affected, because they had tenaciously maintained their own language and customs. An additional difficulty for these settlers was an ethical one — the abolition of their right of exemption from military conscription. When various efforts at compromise failed, the mood in the Mennonite colonies returned to the gloomy pessimism which had plagued earlier generations in Europe. The hope for any future would require the abandonment of all that had been built up for nearly a century and the willingness to undertake yet another long trek toward some remote land of promise.

When representatives learned at this time of possibilities of migration to North America with promises of religious liberty, exemption from military service and favourable economic prospects, it was decided by many to leave their homes in Russia. After receiving positive reports from delegates who had gone to inspect farmlands in Manitoba and the United States, a mass migration ensued during the period from 1874 to 1876. It was an enormous movement of a large group of people from a familiar setting to an unfamiliar one. In one case, nearly the entire population of a single colony (Bergthal) was moved intact from south Russia to southern Manitoba. As historian William Schroeder states, reflecting upon the departure of the last eighty families from Bergthal: "With the arrival in Manitoba of this last group, the migration from Bergthal to Manitoba was completed. An entire colony of about three thousand people had been transplanted from one continent to another."[4]

A final comment needs to be made concerning the extent to which these Manitoba Mennonites can be considered "Germanic" in cultural background. Mention has previously been made of their origins in northern Germany, Friesland, Flanders, Belgium and Holland. Under the protection of their Prussian feudal landlords and the group contractual assurances afforded them in the Vistula Delta, they had enjoyed comparative security from cultural absorption. When they moved to southern Russia after 1789, they established colonies and villages that maintained an inner religious and cultural cohesiveness. Their resistance to the customs, language and religious life of their Russian peasant neighbours is witnessed ultimately by their refusal to be assimilated, even when it was demanded by law after 1870. Influences from those living nearby appear to have been minimal, especially in view of the primitive state of their Russian neighbours. In the words of historian Cornelius Krahn: "In truth, the territory of the Ukraine where the Mennonites built their temporary, miserable mud huts, had only recently been acquired by Russia and was a place of exile from Moscow, where wild Nomads pastured their herds. Not a shrub could be seen and never had a plowshare torn the soil."[5]

Each village was given a German name, often in memory of an earlier one left behind in the Danzig region. This pattern of naming by memory was later to be repeated in southern Manitoba and Saskatchewan. Attendance at school in the German language was obligatory in the Mennonite colonies, and numerous intellectual leaders wielded their influence, among them the teacher, Tobias Voth, the evangelist and poet, Bernhard Harder, and the economist and educator, Johann Cornies.[6]

Perhaps nowhere is the preservation of and adherence to a German cultural background by these "Russian Mennonites" more dramatically described than in the account of historian Gerhard Lohrenz:

> . . . to many Mennonites of that time it seemed that their very existence was threatened. They were not willing to render any service and the intellectuals in this group, men such as [Leonard] Suderman, [Cornelius] Jansen, [Jakob] Peters and others, felt that being a Christian and a German was identical. . . . they were neither willing nor able to make the adjustments the Mennonites of Russia would have to make, namely to break out of their complete cultural isolation. Henceforth they would have to reckon themselves with Russian culture and reckon with it. When their petitions presented to the Russian government did not have the desired effect, they decided to leave the country.[7]

Whatever the negative implications of such cultural

conservatism, the historian may be heartened by the consequent possibility of studying the preservation of traditional customs, decorative arts and craftsmanship from an earlier Germanic heritage. While some adaptation to a new environment is evident in the techniques and subjects produced by Mennonite craftsmen in both southern Russia and southern Manitoba, there was a strong tendency to maintain the styles of the northern European ethos from which they had sprung. By contrast, it is interesting to observe a rapidly changing mode of decoration and craftsmanship among those Mennonites who remained in Russia after 1874 and accommodated themselves to the national reforms of that period. When Mennonites again fled Russia after the October Revolution in 1917 and the persecutions of the following decades, they brought with them artifacts which reflect a profound change of content, technique and decorative manner. They reveal a much closer participation in the surrounding Russian milieu.

The large influx of Mennonites from Russia to Manitoba in 1874 followed by a year an exploratory trip to Canada by an initial delegation. This advance group consulted with Mennonites in Berlin (Kitchener), Ontario, inspected farmlands south of Winnipeg and negotiated protections and exemptions from military service with the Minister of Agriculture.[8] After this first-hand inspection of the new land on the eastern edge of the Canadian Prairies and the establishment of contractual guarantees, a massive transmigration began. The Bergthal Colony left Russia in three stages, arriving in 1874, 1875, and 1876.[9] With the immigration of some eighteen thousand Mennonites from the various Russian colonies, a large independent religious community was established south of Winnipeg which was to grow in comparative cultural isolation.

The Manitoba-Mennonite pioneers were quick to create villages patterned after those in Russia, and in many cases they retained the German names of earlier homesteads. These settlers formed their villages in two geographic regions provided by government agreement: in the East Reserve southeast of Winnipeg and the West Reserve to the southwest. Reminiscent of earlier places in both Prussia and Russia are such names as Chortitz, Blumenort, Grunthal, Rosenfeld, Altona, Steinbach, Hochfeld, Gnadental, Schoenfeld and New Bergthal.

As the farmland of southern Manitoba was taken up in its entirety by early settlers and their children, it became necessary for later immigrants to move further north and west. Smaller numbers took up land in Saskatchewan, notably on the Rosthern Reserve and the Swift Current Reserve near the present-day cities of Saskatoon and Swift Current respectively. Some moved from Manitoba to Alberta, settling near Gleichen. Many of these left the harsh and dry Albertan Prairie to join their co-religionists in the Rosthern Reserve of Saskatchewan.[10] This area was to receive immigrants from Russia and Prussia, as well as Manitobans moving west in hope of new economic opportunity. In each Saskatchewan reserve, villages were organized somewhat in the manner of Russian and Manitoban communities, but with minor variations in layout and relationship to open fields. Perhaps due in part to the conservative elements that populated the Saskatchewan communities, as well as to certain administrative and organizational modifications, the Saskatchewan-Mennonite settlements seem to have weathered pressures toward change or destruction much longer than their Manitoba counterparts.[11]

Despite the building of modern roads and communications systems, the Mennonite villages of both Manitoba and Saskatchewan remain today an effective expression of a group's religious and cultural cohesiveness. In spite of the breakdown of the formal village structure with its *Schulz*, or mayor, its administrative levels and arrangements, there is still evident an informal clustering of families of like name in surviving villages or their remnants. In Manitoba, this is particularly true of the West Reserve. In spite of modernization there is still a tangible "we-ness" and a sense of historical importance among the Mennonite settlers and their descendants who have left a strong cultural imprint upon the farmlands and small towns of western Canada.

Small groups of Lutheran and Roman Catholic Germans also moved west to Manitoba, Saskatchewan and Alberta. Many of the places where they settled still retain Germanic names. In Saskatchewan, Benedictine priests established a school and served new parishes. They founded the Catholic Settlement Society of Rosthern at the beginning of this century.[12] The principal villages created in this area, some sixty miles east of Saskatoon, are: Humboldt, Engelfeld, Bruno and Muenster. The people around Muenster still attend and support St. Peter's Cathedral, built by local immigrant carpenters in 1909. It is hailed as a notable tourist attraction, because of its paintings of Count Berthold Imhoff and its remarkable architectural details. The few Catholic-German communities are still cohesive units, although they have not retained the language.

In addition to Mennonites and Old Order Amish, the third Anabaptist group surviving today is that known variously as Hutterian, Hutterian Brethren or Hutterites. Hutterite historians generally regard 1528 as the year in which this religious society was founded. In that year a group of Anabaptist refugees who were travelling to Austerlitz in Moravia, cast their personal possessions upon a cloak which they spread on the ground. In this symbolic act, the doctrine of "all things in common" was entrenched in one branch of the Reformation.[13] To the present day, the Hutterite tradition is distinguished more than anything else by its adherence to the prime importance of the community, or *Bruderhof*.

The persecutions — political, religious, economic — which afflicted their Mennonite and Amish brethren were also visited upon the growing Hutterian communities. The consequences of these hardships and the disastrous impact of the Thirty Years' War was near-annihilation. Small remnants survived by migrating eastward into Slovakia, Transylvania and Wallachia. New hope of religious and economic freedom appeared in 1770, when Hutterites were invited to settle in the Ukraine. Like Mennonites from further to the north, the Hutterites emigrated to Russia in the late eighteenth century anticipating the protection of their rights to abstain from military service and to conduct their own religious and cultural life in relative isolation from the pressures of a surrounding population or central government.

The Hutterites fell victim to the same conditions threatening the Mennonites in south Russia when political realities changed after the middle of the nineteenth century. These people were also vulnerable to the charge of obstructing the national interest as the programme of Russification reached its height. Such "German pockets" were unacceptable to an emerging nationalism which was taking up the predictable policy of eradicating anything "foreign," particularly anything French or German.

It appears that the turning point for the Hutterites in the Ukraine was the Universal Military Training Act of 1872 in which special exemptions earlier granted to the Anabaptist pacifists by Catherine the Great were repealed. As a result, virtually the entire Hutterite population, some 800 persons,[14] left Russia and relocated in South Dakota between 1874 and 1877. Hutterians in North America quickly established themselves in colonies, founded almost exclusively upon agrarian productivity.

The entry of the United States into the First World War brought hardships to the Hutterites of South Dakota similar to those they had fled on earlier occasions. The imprisonment of Hutterite pacifists (and the death of two in army camps) provided incentive for yet another exodus. At the invitation of the Canadian government, most of these settlers migrated north into Manitoba, Saskatchewan and Alberta between 1918 and 1923.[15]

By the middle of the twentieth century, the North American Hutterite population had risen considerably, as had the number of colonies. In 1965, a total of over 15,000 Hutterites were dispersed in 170 colonies. Of these, 120 were located in Canada (63 in Alberta, 42 in Manitoba and 15 in Saskatchewan).[16]

Of all Christian utopian communities, it is the Hutterians who have managed to survive for the greatest length of time. They have sustained a dynamic tension between economic progressivism and religious conservatism. In matters of work and technical skill, they look outward and forward; in matters of faith they look inward and backward.

## Architecture

The very first homes of the Mennonites in Manitoba were "semlins" (simlins) or "soddies," a simple temporary shelter built out of sod, wood, grass and soil. Built two feet into the ground, they provided some measure of protection during bitter winters. Often they provided shelter for livestock as well. A typical model stands today at the Mennonite Village Museum at Steinbach.

Wood was an expensive commodity on the Prairies, but after a time it was possible to afford it, and more permanent log houses and barns were constructed. The roofs were at first thatched but, later, thatching was replaced by shingles. Of particular interest is the house-barn, a style brought along from Russia and earlier farms of northern and eastern Europe. In each location, it proved an ideal means of protection for both man and beast against the severe prairie climate.

Very few house-barns have survived in the East Reserve of Manitoba, but one notable exception is a rapidly deteriorating example at Grunthal. In Steinbach, Manitoba, on the other hand, Mr. and Mrs. Herman Barkman recall with sadness the destruction of the last remaining house-barn in that community some years ago. Its last inhabitants "were moved to tears when the new owner destroyed it as quickly and thoroughly as possible by setting fire to it and then bulldozing the remains into the foundation."[17]

The situation is more fortunate in Manitoba's West Reserve where a considerable number of these buildings remain standing, though many have undergone various degrees of structural alteration. One especially fine house-barn recently moved to the grounds of the Mennonite Village Museum at Steinbach retains the original shutters and typical blue-and-white colour scheme. The placement of the barn in relationship to the house varies; in some cases it is at a right angle to the house. Others have a small connecting section (*Gang*) between house and barn, or house and barn might form a single continuous structure.

The interior of the house is normally divided into eight or more rooms with kitchen, pantry, living room and bedroom all situated on the first floor. At the centre of the house is a large brick hearth (*Ziegelofen*) used for both cooking and heating. The upstairs is usually a long, one-room storage attic.[18] One house-barn that survives in a remarkable state of preservation is presently owned by Frank and John Letkeman near Rosthern, Saskatchewan. The only remaining building in the village of Hochfeld, this 1909 structure still has its original built-in cupboards, desks and wardrobes.

An excellent re-creation of the early *Strassendorfer* (street) type of village used by the western Mennonites was seen by the writers in a Saskatoon garden. Mr. Jake Wall (born 1902), now retired, began to build a model of the home he remembered as a young child. A friend had given him odd bits of plywood, and he thought that it would be an enjoyable pastime. The project grew in the next two years to become a complete miniature of the original Mennonite village of Neuhorst, Saskatchewan (Plate 226). Working from his keen memory, he reconstructed the entire village — all seventeen buildings — complete with fences and trees as he recalled it from his childhood. The model is large enough that one can actually walk down the main street to the centre where the church and school were located. Jake remembers that his house was across from the school; his father rebuilt it in 1908 when he was six years old. One of the houses had a thatched roof (Jake thinks it was Herman Peter's), and

this too is faithfully shown. The typical colour scheme for these houses was white with blue or green trim on the doors, windows and shutters, while the barns were left unpainted. When questioned about the bright red barns on his model, Jake admitted this to be a departure — for obvious aesthetic reasons. Although he receives many requests to exhibit his village at local fairs and parades, Jake prefers to keep it intact in his own garden. Every winter he carefully dismantles it, and makes minor repairs so that it can be viewed each summer by passers-by in Saskatoon.

The first Hutterite settlers in South Dakota built fieldstone houses closely related to the structures they had known in Europe. After the migration to Canada, however, the Hutterite residences, schools, dining halls, workshops and other buildings lost any distinctiveness, except for the spatial arrangement to serve community needs. If architectural expression no longer maintained tangible ties to the past, matters of custom, dress and language did. English is learned and used today, but it is German that prevails at their religious services and events. As one writer has put it, "German is to the Hutterite a sacred language. As in the way of dressing, it is symbolic of belonging."[19]

## Furniture

The furnishings of early Mennonite houses in Manitoba and Saskatchewan are fascinating statements of a strong ethnic tradition. It is likely that the very first furniture was extremely crude and makeshift,[20] but the pieces subsequently made by local craftsmen reveal excellent workmanship and design. Most of the furniture produced during the late nineteenth and early twentieth century exhibits careful attention to fine craftsmanship, with mortise-and-tenon construction, dovetailing and the use of wooden pegs to strengthen joinery.

In general, the domestic furniture made in these Mennonite villages uses some kind of soft wood (pine, spruce, fir), often enlivened by vibrant painted colours. Many of the large case-pieces are in bright yellow or red with green or black on mouldings and feet. In a few rare cases, decorative motifs may ornament a piece, as in the painted tulip and birds on the pediment of a Manitoba wardrobe (Plate 229). Occasionally, painted facades are grained, for example on the large storage chest illustrated in Plate 233; here paint is also used to create the impression of architectural columns at the corners.

Manitoba and Saskatchewan furniture is distinguished by simplified baroque tendencies, such as scrollwork on backboards and skirts. These are elements faintly reminiscent of other ethnically determined furniture, like that made in the Polish settlements of Renfrew County, Ontario, although much simplified and formalized in comparison with the latter. The Mennonite pieces are charming, simple descendants of the more sophisticated baroque forms known to the German ancestors of these pioneers. The forms were undoubtedly perpetuated as the craft was taken eastward with them through Prussia and southern Russia.

Among some of the most intriguing pieces of furniture are the small corner cupboards which were mounted on a triangular shelf supported at the corner of the wainscotting of two adjoining walls. Most of them are comparatively plain. However, they usually sit on an independent bracket base and have a removable cornice, frequently enhanced by scrolled shaping and painting. Variations on the cornice include pediment effects, cutouts and turnings.

It has been suggested that in Catholic homes in south Germany, small corner cupboards formed part of the corner "shrine," the so-called *Herr Gott's Winkel* (Lord God's Corner). In Protestant homes, such a cupboard was situated above the householder's chair and contained a Bible and hymnals for daily devotions.[21]

Another characteristic form is the sleeping bench, called a *Schlafbank* (or its dialect variant, *Schlopbank*), found in most Manitoba and Saskatchewan Mennonite homes. Like the French-Canadian *banc-lit*, it served a dual purpose, as a bench and for storage underneath or, by pulling its box seat forward, as a bed. Most of these sleeping benches are of very simple design with a flat seat, straight panelled backs and curved arms. Some, however, received more decorative treatment with shaped backboards, splats or gracefully shaped stiles. One such bench had the extraordinary detail of an incised eagle surmounting the backboard. It was seen by the authors on its way to an antique dealer in North Dakota — the fate of many fine pieces. Contrasting two-colour paint schemes were popularly used; some have mustard yellow and brilliant vermillion along with black. Many of the benches seen in museums have unfortunately been stripped or "skinned." As a result they have lost their intended vibrant quality.

The typical western Mennonite table is usually of nearly square proportions. It can be recognized by the cleated top, applied horizontal mouldings and shaped angle brackets at the juncture of the skirt and tapered legs. Most are painted bright yellow and are sometimes given further appeal by the use of mouldings around the base of the skirt.

It is not surprising that in all the Germanic settlements the cradle received some kind of decoration. The high rate of infant mortality in pioneer communities added poignant and immediate concern for the care of the young, reflected in these carefully made cradles. The rockers of the western cradle are different from the eastern types; wide cyma-curved pieces of wrought-iron attach the rocker to the base. The tops of the ends sometimes are pediment-shaped with a cut-out.

Among the most distinctive of forms found in both the Mennonite and Hutterite settlements is the massive storage chest (*Kiste*), almost always mounted on a removable bracket base. Their very size suggests that they were probably intended to replace chests of drawers (of which comparatively few examples are known), wardrobes or linen presses for storing blankets and other bedding. Most of these chests are enhanced with elaborate iron hinges, locks and handles. Peculiar features are the large brass bosses mounted on the top of the lids secured by screws from underneath. The custom of pasting drawings, water-colours, even *Fraktur* under the lid was common. These chests are virtually identical to those brought to Canada by immigrants during the nineteenth century, indicating how closely the indigenous craftsmen of Manitoba and Saskatchewan observed long-established design traditions.

Popular in the West were "wag-on-wall" or "Kroeger"-type clocks that had decorated faces and exposed pendulum and weights. The prevailing view has been that these clocks were made by German craftsmen in Russia, adhering to prototypes remembered from Prussia or northern Germany. Yet the substantial number found in Manitoba poses the intriguing question whether a local craftsman, using works imported from Europe, may have decorated faces on request. In fact, we were surprised to discover evidence of such clocks having been made in Saskatchewan by Cornelius Ens (1884-1960), who was born in Edenburg not far from Rosthern. A niece remembers that he worked in the nearby town of Aberdeen and that as late as the 1950s he made nine clocks, all for his children. She recalls the cacophony in the room where they were stored, especially at 12 o'clock. Cornelius was evidently self-taught and enjoyed fiddling with time-pieces. He improvised with old pieces, even using old pitchfork tines for the sound mechanisms. While he may have painted some of the clock faces himself, the only one remaining in the family sports decals in the corners. The fate of the other clocks he made is not known for they, along with Cornelius' property, were auctioned off after his death.

From the finely crafted corner cupboards and *Kisten* to the more rustic forms used in the kitchen or even the barn, the furniture of western Canada's Mennonite settlements demonstrates vitality and strength. The bold colours and forms rank these pieces among the more distinctive of ethnic furniture in Canada. They are evidence of the rapid adaptation of settlers to pioneer conditions and their capacity to advance quickly from a preoccupation with fundamental survival to the development of competent craftsmanship with undoubted aesthetic appeal.

## Fraktur

The art of *Fraktur*, or text illumination, was practised to a rather limited extent among the first two generations of Mennonites in southern Manitoba and less frequently among the pioneers who arrived in Saskatchewan some twenty years later. In western Canada, it was a survival of the tradition developed in northern Germany and, later, in nineteenth-century Russia.

The Germans of Nova Scotia brought little of a *Fraktur* tradition with them, while in Ontario the Swiss-German decorative tradition flourished in the highly diverse *Fraktur* forms created in the Pennsylvania-German regions of that province. In Manitoba, which was settled at a much later date than either of these provinces, *Fraktur* seems to have arisen out of a narrower context. In Pennsylvania and Ontario, *Fraktur* was done at home by amateurs, at school by teachers and pupils and in far-flung regions by itinerant professional scriveners, but in Manitoba the tradition was for the most part restricted to the school. There are comparatively few instances of birth records, family registers and other types done outside this rather structured atmosphere.

*Fraktur* found in Manitoba fall into two categories, "Russian" and indigenous. The former, of course, is not Russian at all but was produced by north-German Men-

nonite settlers in south Russia. The schools impressed German culture and language on the minds of students while at the same time providing both the verbal and written reinforcement of these values.

In the inventories of settlers' effects brought from Russia to Manitoba and Saskatchewan are listed small libraries of religious books in German. As well, several families have preserved a particular form of non-religious book used in the colony schools of southern Russia. The *Rechenbuch*, or arithmetic book, was divided into four major sections corresponding to mathematical functions: addition, subtraction, multiplication and division. Interspersed among handwritten exercises are various *Fraktur* motifs and designs. Each section features a boldly decorated title page on which appears colourful drawings of urns, tulips, roses, stylized trees, animals, buildings, houses and even views of cities. Some elements of the surrounding Russian culture, normally kept at considerable distance, are occasionally visible in the form of the onion-domes of Russian Orthodox churches. One page in the 1832 arithmetic book of Bernhard Rempel lists mathematical equivalents between German and Russian currencies and other measurements. That the lavish decoration of arithmetic books was standard practice in the schools of the various Mennonite colonies in Russia is attested to by the sizeable number of examples belonging to descendants of pioneer immigrants.

Imported *Fraktur* illuminated texts are also encountered frequently, sometimes in the form of birthday wishes but more commonly as Christmas and New Year's wishes. Russian specimens reflecting the work of professionals and amateurs are known. Such texts generally have strong religious overtones coupled with greetings of the season or event. These imported *Fraktur* served as prototypes for later examples done on this side of the Atlantic. According to various accounts, it was customary in prairie schools for the teacher to have each student write a New Year's wish in the finest possible hand as a gift for the pupil's parents. It was introduced by a large *Fraktur* title, done with pen and brush in two or three colours, and signed at the end with a statement of filial affection. The number of surviving examples indicates that this custom was practised in western schools from the 1880s into the early twentieth century.

The most characteristic type of indigenous *Fraktur* known in the Manitoba-Mennonite settlements also originated in the schools. Many school copybooks from approximately 1880 to 1920 contain an eclectic mixture of Spenserian penmanship, drawings based upon alphabets, and texts or titles of texts printed by hand in *Fraktur* form. An example is the copybook worked by the young Cornelius Klippenstein in 1918 (Plate 250). That *Fraktur* was taught in the Mennonite schools in the manner used at an earlier date in the German schools of Pennsylvania is suggested in the personal recollection of Peter T. Wiebe. Describing a typical school day in the village of Friedenstal, Manitoba, he gives the following account:

> This very important part [of the programme] consisted of what was usually referred to as *Schoenschreiben* [penmanship, literally, beautiful writing]. The tools for this art consisted of *Schreibenhefte* [notebooks], made by the teacher, a penholder, and a bottle of ink, sunk into the top of the desk. The writing books were made of foolscap sewn along the fold, and then cut into two little ruled booklets. Across the top of each page of this booklet the teacher wrote one sample line in his near-perfect hand. This piece of art was called *Vorschrift* [sample writing], and was set there for us to imitate, though without hope to equal.[22]

*Fraktur* bookplates are also commonly found, both of the imported and indigenous variety. In a few cases, a separate piece of paper was decorated and inscribed with the owner's name, much as we think of a bookplate today. The more usual practice, however, was to sign the inside front cover and then give the name or short inscription some decorative flourishes.

Some miscellaneous *Fraktur* drawings suggest that even within the comparative isolation of these settlements the eventual dilution of folk-art tradition was inevitable. One indication is in a drawing that appears to perpetuate conventional *Fraktur* elements, but contains the unusual and non-traditional addition of beagle dogs.

Due to a unique and fortunate motivation, the practise of *Fraktur* has been sustained to the present day. It has been a long-established custom in Hutterian society to hand-copy sermons, religious histories and hymns. Sermons are normally read, not preached, and are ordinarily copied from earlier Hutterite works. In every age, there have been persons who regarded themselves as called to the task of perpetuating awareness of Anabaptist history through the copying of chronicles. Such a man was David Hofer. He transcribed Hutterite texts in South Dakota in 1912, and they were brought to Canada when the colony relocated to the northwest of Winnipeg.

As in the Maritimes and Ontario, Germanic settlers in the West seemed compelled to decorate to the furthest extreme the smallest and simplest objects. The desire to transform function into beauty is seen in all aspects of domestic life. Decorated tools, pencil boxes, utensils, hinges, pouches and wallboxes all reflect the impulse to embellish what would otherwise be plain.

## Textiles

Although even today acres of brilliant blue flax fields can be seen during the summer in southern Manitoba, no implements used in early linen-making have been found. Looms, too, seem not to have figured prominently in the home textile traditions of the Mennonites and Hutterites in the western provinces. This is readily explained: by the time Germanic immigrants settled this region, factory-made linens, coverlets, bedding and clothing were all readily available.

Needlework, on the other hand, was considered an essential part of every young girl's domestic education, and it took the form of embroidery and cross-stitching. In addition to the decoration of clothing and bedding, more elaborate examples of Mennonite embroidery are seen in the samplers done both in Russia and Manitoba. As in non-German traditions, these contain alphabets, numerals and an array of motifs often designed as challenges to the skill of the young maker. Even though Mennonite samplers are similar to their English and Scottish counterparts, they differ in their use of the German alphabet and their symmetrical arrangement of elements.

More common than traditional samplers in Mennonite settlements are the various forms of Berlin-work that became popular in the late nineteenth century. Aphorisms, house blessings, religious verses (together with *trompe l'oeil* effects achieved by glueing on commercial embossments), shells, flower petals and the like were all cross-stitched in brilliantly coloured wool. The background for this type of work was usually an inexpensive, punched-paper card which eliminated the need for thread counting normally required in such a process. As backings with printed designs became available, this type of work was reduced to something like the stitchery kits available today.

It is in the Hutterite colonies that the most conservative and dramatic German decorative textile traditions were sustained until close to the present day. Of all Germanic groups, the Hutterites produced the greatest volume of needlework in Canada in the late nineteenth and early twentieth centuries. Their embroidered handkerchiefs, towels and samplers are among the most lavishly decorated textiles made in this country.

Commercially produced men's white linen or cotton handkerchiefs of all varieties provided a convenient surface for a special form of embroidery among Hutterite girls. These decorated pieces appear in a considerable variety of designs and stitches. They were clearly intended to be shown off, not used; and as remarkably explicit tokens of love, they served something like valentines. The name of the maker and the recipient are often accompanied by mawkish sentiments, frequently rhymed and accompanied by needlework motifs. Made for special occasions, these handkerchiefs are highly varied in colour, design, text and choice of motifs. Many read horizontally, while others employ a diagonal format with the text turned at right angles. Often, extremely fine cross-stitching is used for the whole piece; others utilize the satin stitch, the stem stitch or the blanket stitch, all in brilliant embroidery floss.

Decorated Hutterite towels were expressions of skills developed and mastered. One girl could produce several embroidered towels or samplers, not necessarily all intended for the dower chest. Factory-made silk embroidery floss of all colours was used on utilitarian linen cut from lengths of commercial issue purchased by the bolt. Many have the typical red and blue striping along the selvages. Lengths varied with the individual's intentions. Some towels are known to be as long as seven feet.

Unlike Pennsylvania-German show towels, which were usually cross-stitched in red and blue against a white homespun ground, the Hutterite towel is, in effect, an elongated sampler of variegated colours. Both could have served the purpose of covering the towel actually in use and therefore be for "show" only. The Hutterite towel was neither pierced nor drawn with any lace-like effects. One is immediately struck by the profusion of motifs. Many styles of alphabets, most incomplete, start large in the top row and become progressively smaller as variations are worked in both upper and lower case toward the bottom third. It seems almost as if a girl took pride in attempting to stitch the greatest number of alphabets possible; one towel we examined had twenty-six. Although the letters normally occupy more than two-thirds of the surface,

numerals and folk-art motifs of every conceivable description would be tightly compressed within the remaining space. These motifs appear to be squeezed in randomly as space dictated, without regard for symmetry. The lively hues of commercial embroidery floss often make these towels a blazing riot of colour.

A few samplers follow the conventional English square or rectangular format. The maker's name is embroidered along with the date, but there are no sentimental or lugubrious verses. These are strictly renderings of various alphabets, numerals and motifs, which range from an ordinary window or a ribbon tied in a bow, to the Germanic confrontal birds and trees of life.

Open weave canvas was a popular support for samplers. The mesh count of approximately ten pairs of threads per inch made it fairly easy to work out a cross-stitch pattern, even for an inexperienced girl. These canvas samplers are stylistically similar to those done on linen, but wool was used in place of silk floss. One woman recalls from her youth that when wool was not to be had, it was necessary to carefully pull the weft threads from discarded fabrics for the specific colours desired.

Some years ago, it was popular to use cross-stitch embroidery on the large heavy black shawls worn by women. On one corner above or inside the trim the first name and the number 19 were stitched; directly in the corner was some kind of motif, perhaps an eight-pointed star or multiples and variations thereof. Turning the corner to the right, the surname appeared and the last two numbers of the year of completion. Today, a similar format is followed but liquid embroidery is often used instead.

Contemporary Hutterian needlework has shifted to quicker methods, sometimes utilizing "jumbo" knits in synthetic fibres which can be machine washed. Women interviewed in the colonies emphatically stated that the cross-stitched samplers and handkerchiefs were really the old-fashioned things — things of the past. They were more anxious to display their recent handiwork, including placemats, coasters, appliance covers and crocheted slippers. These products are consistent with the Hutterites' modern farm machinery, woodworking and machine shops and sophisticated electrical appliances that attest to a highly productive society. This is a culture that retains its conservative religious beliefs and customs within a framework of twentieth-century technology.

# Gravemarkers

The relatively late date of settlement in the western provinces was a factor in the rapid assimilation of customs, even among conservative German-speaking immigrants. If it was the retention of their language that maintained the distinctiveness of Mennonites and other settlers of Germanic background, then it was in their gravemarkers that this emphasis on language is most visible.

It is a rare occurrence to find stone markers in the burial grounds of Mennonite villages in Manitoba and Saskatchewan. Unlike the slate or sandstone markers used at a much earlier time in the Maritimes and Ontario, the Germanic tombstones of the Prairie Provinces are usually made of cement — the customary practice among most peoples there. A few early examples of simple wooden slabs are still to be found, such as those for the Klippenstein settlers at New Bergthal, Manitoba. In other cases, rough stones were scratched with initials and a death date as in those at Grunthal, near Steinbach, Manitoba.

Interestingly enough, the use of cement for slab markers makes it possible to create some calligraphic designs not easily achieved in stone. Nevertheless, relatively little decoration of this kind was attempted, although intaglio lettering was frequently inscribed while the cement was in the process of hardening, allowing for considerable flexibility in letter shape. Some cement markers have names and epitaphs which appear to have been imprinted with wooden blocks. In some instances the cement is painted white with letters outlined in black for contrast. The fact that very few gravemarkers exhibit any imaginative or folk-art designs may also be a reflection of the rigours encountered by the early settlers. They were less affluent than the Ontario-Germans, and their winters were considerably more severe.

There are some gravemarkers in Manitoba of more historical interest than decorative value. Two have been transplanted from Russia to the Mennonite Village Museum, Steinbach. One is an obelisk commemorating Johann Bartsche, a Mennonite who led a migration from Prussia to Russia, which was originally erected in Rosenthal, Russia, in 1890. Among its incidental historical features are the bullet holes from the guns of the Russian Revolution of 1916 to 1919. This large stone was sent to Canada in 1968. Another obelisk memorializes Jacob Hoeppner, who had consulted with Catherine the Great regarding religious freedom. This monument, together with an accompanying flat tombstone decorated with an anchor, were moved from Chortitza, Russia, in 1973.

On a smaller scale, indigenous Manitoba gravemarkers are simply inscribed in German, at least in the East and West reserves. Only a few have modest decorations in the form of simple floral accents, vine designs or incised scrolls. This is particularly true in the cemeteries at Rosenfeld and Winkler. Popular Neoclassical devices, like garlands, trees and roses, appear on later stones that still have German inscriptions.

In the tiny Saskatchewan village of Blumenthal, not far from Rosthern, is a cemetery where a few markers were given a modest decorative treatment. Headstones for several Berg settlers bear German epitaphs, and the stone for Peter Berg (1858-1938) is enhanced with a simple quatrefoil design similar to some motifs used on Ontario stones. Surprisingly, the sun motif appears here, too, on the marker for Lena Berg (1935-1953).

In the town of Bruno, located in the Catholic-German area east of Saskatoon, is an attractive and well-maintained cemetery. Here are to be found many wrought-iron gravemarkers almost identical in size and construction to those in the Catholic cemeteries of Waterloo County, Ontario. The Bruno crosses appear to have been erected principally in the 1920s and 1930s, and as a result they are still set well above ground in their rectangular concrete bases. A dramatic feature of one example is a large cast-iron heart attached at the crossing of the base. Simply inscribed in white are the name and dates of the deceased, and below is a smaller Latin cross. Neither the Corpus nor surmounting cross seen in Ontario is used here. All the crosses bear identical scroll decoration within the double bars and at the base where it is flanked by flaring cyma-curve bars on either side.

Such prominent Roman Catholic pioneer names as Brockmann, Pulvermacher and Hergott are recorded in the Germanic cemeteries of the Prairie Provinces. Other cemeteries draw attention to a great diversity of Mennonite names: Dyck, Klippenstein, Harder, Banman, Giesbrecht, Isaac, Reimer, Friesen, Penner, Barkman, Enns, Wiebe, Tiessen, Toews, Esau, Fehr, Rempel and Sawatsky. These, along with Hutterite names such as Hofer, Gross, Wipf, Waldner, Tschetter and Stahl, are indicative of a diversity of places of origin, but with commonalities of language, culture and decorative traditions.

223 *Jonas Dyck House, Manitoba.*
One of the earliest surviving Manitoba
Mennonite homes is this log house with its
steep thatched roof. Built by the pioneer
settler Jonas Dyck at the village of Waldheim,
near Morden, it has since been moved to the
grounds of the Mennonite Village Museum of
Steinbach. 1876.

224 *Johann Fehrs House, Manitoba.*
The Mennonites settling in western Canada
built a distinctive type of structure found also
in northern and eastern Europe, the house-
barn. Frequently, the house and barn are continuous. In other cases, the house is set at
right angles to the barn (as in this example),
joined by an enclosed section, or *Gang*. Late
nineteenth century.

224

225

226

225 *Letkeman House, Saskatchewan.*
Like the settlers of southern Manitoba,
Mennonite pioneers in Saskatchewan's
Moose Jaw and Rosthern reserves retained
the house-barn of their ancestors. This
example at Hochfield, northwest of Hague,
Saskatchewan, is unusual in that it survives
almost unchanged since it was built, even
retaining the original furnishings. In this
interior view can be seen the kitchen door
opening directly into the stock barn. 1908.

226 *Miniature Mennonite Village,
Saskatchewan.*
This elaborate replica of the Mennonite
village of Neuhorst, Saskatchewan, includes
among its seventeen structures a school, a
church and house-barns arranged along a
wide street. Engaged in conversation with
one of the authors is the builder, Mr. Jake
Wall (born 1902) of Saskatoon who built the
village from memory of his childhood in
Neuhorst. 1977.

227 *Corner Cupboard, Saskatchewan.*
A typical furnishing of the Mennonite home
of western Canada was the small corner cupboard. Most have removable bracket bases,
while this one has simple turned feet. Its
decorative interest consists of striping and
grain-painted finish. It was passed down
through the Friesen family in Saskatchewan.
Late nineteenth century. [Courtesy National
Museum of Man]

227

228 *Table, Manitoba.*
A typical Manitoba-Mennonite form, this table has a removable top with dovetailed cleats. Its decorative elements include scrolled corner brackets, applied mouldings and a two-colour scheme of yellow with green trim. Late nineteenth century.

229 *Storage Cupboard, Manitoba.*
This pine storage cupboard, from near Winkler, Manitoba, has a characteristic scrolled bracket base and is painted in yellow and black, with panels carved in the doors. A rare example of folk-decorated furniture, its pediment is flanked by carved eagles' heads with a central tulip, as well as carved and painted confronting birds. Late nineteenth century.

230 *Bookcase, Manitoba.*
A tall pine shelving unit from southern Manitoba, which has pegs in the back to secure it to a wall, is joined using mortise-and-tenon construction. It is accentuated by baroque shaping of its upper sides and retains its original red paint. Late nineteenth century.

228

200

229

230

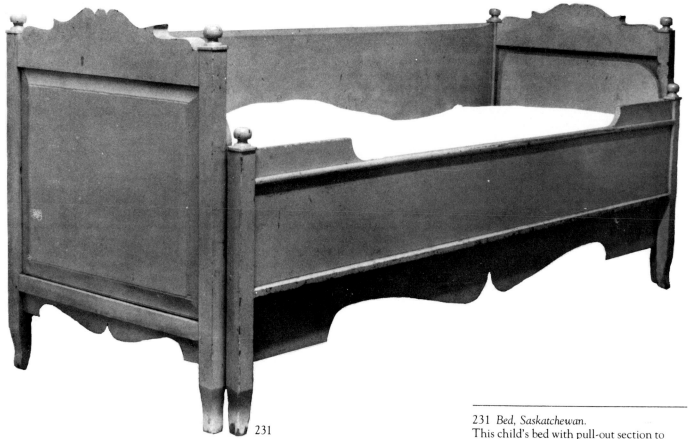

231

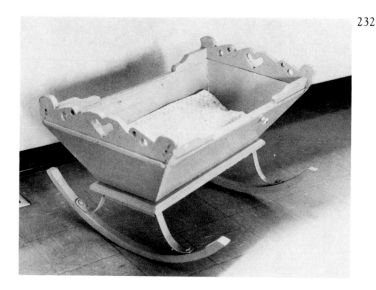

232

231 *Bed, Saskatchewan.*
This child's bed with pull-out section to enlarge its capacity exhibits strong Germanic features in the scrolled ends and base. Late nineteenth or early twentieth century. [Courtesy Rosthern Junior College Museum]

232 *Cradle, Manitoba.*
Cradles in Mennonite settlements of both Manitoba and Saskatchewan frequently feature wrought-iron rockers, shaped ends and cut-outs, in this case in the form of a heart. Late nineteenth century. [Courtesy Steinbach Mennonite Village Museum]

233 *Storage Chest, probably south Russia.*
Chests used for the storage of bedding and other articles of the Mennonite settlers who migrated from southern Russia to western Canada are normally of immense size and mounted on detachable scrolled bracket bases. This chest is particularly refined in its construction, simulated painted columns and feather-grained decoration. Nineteenth century.

202

233

234

234 *Sleeping-Bench, Manitoba.*
The *Schlafbank* or bench-bed, popular in eastern Europe, was made in western Canada by Mennonite and Hutterite settlers into the twentieth century. This example from southern Manitoba retains the original bright orange-red colour, ivory trim around the raised panels and black striping on its vertical splats. Late nineteenth century.

235

235 *Sleeping-Bench, Saskatchewan.*
This bench from the Rosthern Reserve of
Saskatchewan, made somewhat later than
the example in Plate 234, retains the basic
form but has the variation of solid back and
arms. It is finished with excellent grain-
painted decoration. Late nineteenth or early
twentieth century.

236

237

238

206

**236  Bench, Saskatchewan.**
This Saskatchewan Hutterite bench displays characteristics similar to those used by Mennonite makers. The piece is boldly designed with heavy scalloping and raised panels. Early twentieth century. [Courtesy National Museum of Man]

**237  Trinket Box, Saskatchewan.**
Reputedly made by Susanna Tschetter of the Riverview Hutterite Colony near Saskatoon, this pine box is delightfully decorated. Twentieth century.

**238  Clocks, Saskatchewan.**
While many "Kroeger" clocks found in the Mennonite villages of western Canada were made earlier in Europe, an interesting exception to the rule is a group of such clocks made as recently as the mid-twentieth century by Cornelius Ens (1884-1960) of Edenburg, Saskatchewan, shown in this photograph taken about 1960. Mid-twentieth century.

**239  Pencil Box, Manitoba.**
A simple utilitarian object which has aesthetic appeal is this pencil box with painted floral motifs. The base is initialled "ESP." Late nineteenth century. [Courtesy Steinbach Mennonite Village Museum]

**240  Trinket Boxes, Manitoba.**
Found near Winkler in Manitoba's West Reserve, these cardboard boxes are boldly decorated with applied rye straw designs from the Germanic vocabulary. Late nineteenth century.

**241  Pouch, Saskatchewan.**
This leather pouch from an area of Germanic settlement near Riverton, Saskatchewan, features incised and stained decoration, including floral motifs, initials and the date 1882. [Courtesy National Museum of Man]

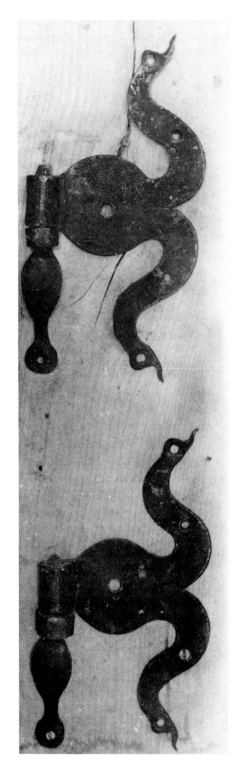

242

243

**242** *Hinges, North Dakota.*
Brought from North Dakota by Hutterites to the Rock Lake Colony northwest of Winnipeg, these iron hinges are in the style of prototypes made a full two centuries earlier. Early twentieth century.

**243** *Cookie Cutter, Saskatchewan.*
This tin cookie cutter with horse and rider is mounted on a wooden base. It must have made highly desirable Christmas cookies, and was reputedly created by one J. B. Guenther from near Hague, Saskatchewan. Late nineteenth or early twentieth century.

**244** *New Year's Wish, South Russia.*
The tradition of making hand-lettered and decorated New Year's wishes, a rarity in Pennsylvania-German folk art, was brought to Canada by descendants of east-European Mennonites who had lived in Russia, where this example was made. 1808. [Courtesy Steinbach Mennonite Village Museum]

**245** *Birthday Wish, South Russia.*
A presentation-piece from teacher to student, this birthday wish calls attention to God's Providence and the new year just beginning. Its hand-written text is augmented by stylized tulips, other floral elements and a geometric border. It is inscribed "Gerhard Dyck 1868."

244

245

246

246 *Hutterite History Book, North Dakota.*
The tradition of hand-lettering and binding
historical and religious books has been maintained in North American Hutterite communities. This volume of Hutterite history
was handwritten by David Hofer in 1912 and
brought to Manitoba shortly afterwards.
1912.

247 *Hutterite History Book.*
Introducing David Hofer's history of the
Hutterian Brethren is this elaborate title page
with *Fraktur* lettering in red and blue inks.
1912.

# Das andre Theil der Regiſter von

den Geſchichten deren ſie in Gefängniß gelegen, und als
Chriſtliche Helden den Glauben Göttlicher Wahrheit
mit ihrem Blut bezeugt haben durch
Feuer Waſſer und Schmerz.

**248** *Reckoning Book, South Russia.*
Among articles brought from Russia by Mennonite settlers in western Canada were arithmetic or "reckoning" books used in colony schools there. This illuminated page introduces the addition section of Bernhard Rempel's arithmetic book used when he was a student at Schoenhorst in south Russia. 1832.

**249** *Reckoning Book, Russia.*
Like school arithmetic books used by other groups, particularly the Schwenkfelders in eastern Pennsylvania, this child's reckoning book is profusely embellished with *Fraktur* lettering. The page introduces the subtraction section of Bernhard Rempel's book with a scene from a town in Russia. 1832.

**250** *School Copybook, Manitoba.*
This colourfully decorated "scribbler" by Cornelius Klippenstein was used when he was a pupil at Old Bergthal in southern Manitoba. The title page is beautifully lettered in *Fraktur* style, using contrasting colours and with dotted lines highlighting individual letters. Early nineteenth century. [Courtesy Canadian Mennonite Bible College Archives]

250

249

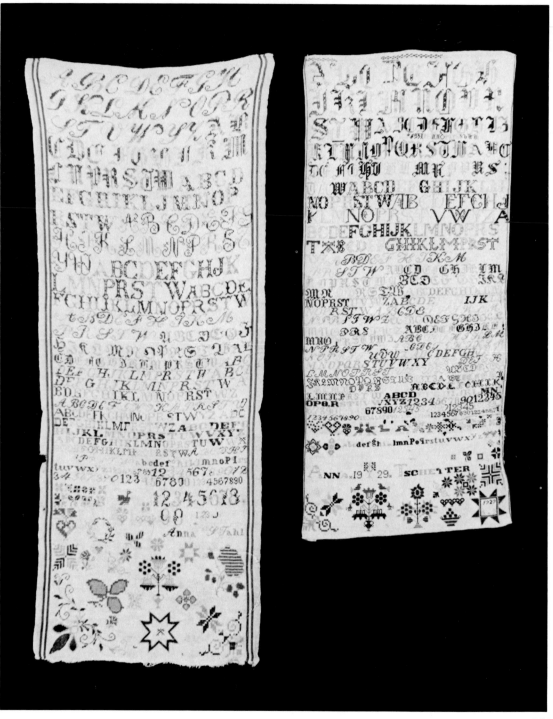

251 *Hutterite Towels, Saskatchewan.*
Embroidered towels from Hutterite colonies frequently depict several alphabets in varied scripts followed by an array of traditional folk motifs, the name of the maker and date of completion. These towels by Anna Stahl (left) and Anna Tschetter (right) show the typical high concentration of design elements. Undated and 1929.

252 *Hutterite Towel, Saskatchewan.*
This long towel worked by the thirteen-year-old Anna Wipf is profusely decorated with stylized birds, trees, hearts and other motifs, as well as twenty-seven alphabets.
[Courtesy National Museum of Man]

252

**253** *Handkerchiefs.*
Given by Hutterite girls as love tokens during courtship, embroidered handkerchiefs often were very sentimental. The lines were worked in one or two directions, along with varied motifs and the names of both maker and recipient. The paired birds on the Sarah Cross handkerchief are virtually identical to those on the decorated box in Plate 237. Twentieth century.

**254** *Sampler, Western United States.*
One of the most detailed Hutterite samplers known is this large panel embroidered by the fifteen-year-old Sadie Kleinsasser. It was brought from the United States to Canada during Hutterite migrations. 1911. [Courtesy National Museum of Man]

253

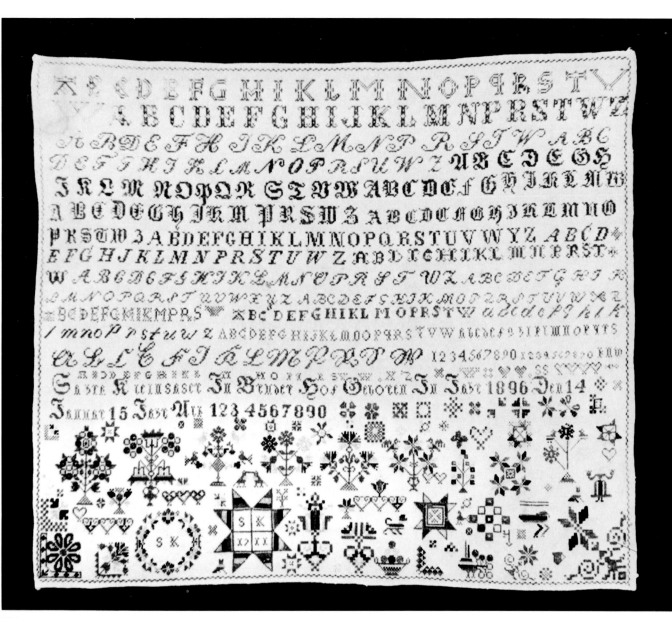

254

217

255

255 *Jacob Hoeppner Marker, Manitoba.*
This tall stone marker commemorates the pioneer Jacob Hoeppner (1797-1883) who led early settlers from south Russia to Manitoba. Moved from its original location on the island of Chortitza on the Dnieper River in southern Russia, it now stands on the grounds of the Steinbach Mennonite Village Museum. Its focal point is an anchor, a traditional symbol of spiritual refuge. 1883.

256 *Barbara Sawatzky Marker, Manitoba.*
Like many gravemarkers in the Mennonite villages of southern Manitoba, this monument for Barbara Sawatzky (1880-1925) at Grunthal in the East Reserve is made of cement, with letters or designs formed by imprinting during the drying stage. 1925.

257 *Sara Hoeppner Marker, Manitoba.*
Moved to the Steinbach Mennonite Village Museum from southern Russia in 1973, this stone marker records the birth and death of Sara Hoeppner (1733-1826). This and other markers provide evidence of the maintenance of German language and customs in both Russia and Canada. 1826.

256

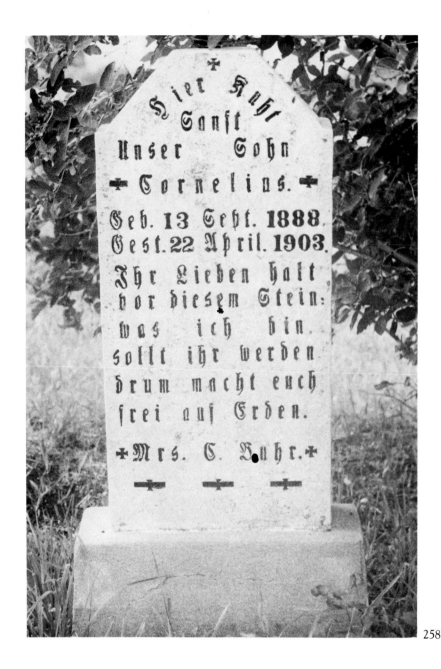

258

259

258 *Cornelius Buhr Marker, Manitoba.*
This cement marker for Cornelius Buhr in the Steinbach Cemetery has imprinted lettering and is decorated with cross motifs. The epitaph, requested by the mother of this fifteen-year-old child reads: "What I am, you will become. To that end, make yourself free on earth." 1903.

259 *Lena Berg Marker, Saskatchewan.*
A modest but rare example of a decorated gravemarker among the Mennonite cemeteries of Saskatchewan is this stone for Lena Berg (1935-1953) at Blumenthal in the Rosthern Reserve. The setting half-sun is reminiscent of designs on the Mennonite gravestones in the Vineland and Wideman cemeteries in Ontario (Plates 206 and 207).

260 *Leo Pulvermacher, Iron Marker, Saskatchewan.*
In the Roman Catholic cemetery of Bruno, Saskatchewan, are several beautifully scrolled wrought-iron gravemarkers. This example uses a central heart to commemorate an infant who was born and died on the same day. Its design is similar to examples in Alsatian and German cemeteries in southern Ontario. 1920.

# Alles Het en End

Perhaps it is a peculiar consequence of the geographical vastness of the Canadian Prairies that distinct cultural groupings will be able to maintain their identity long into the future. That endless horizon which measures the loneliness of distances also serves to deflect the outward gaze back again toward the village or community. The solitude of the modern individual — can he really expect to survive outside Winnipeg, Regina and Saskatoon? Here is a land that has defeated many a single opportunist, yet at the same time nourished strong communities, societies and colonies that share cultural, linguistic and spiritual commonalities. From Hochfeld to Riverview to Engelfeld — in each and through each a distinctive strand of Germanic fabric is visible to the historian, the anthropologist or anyone who respects cultural heritage. These people, who came to Canada at such late date, have already shaped much of the character of this country's uplands, meeting the harshness of latitude and climate with the life-imbuing quality of able craftsmanship and artistic ingenuity. The flat line and brown earth of the Prairies are dramatically qualified by the undulating line of furniture, the broken calligraphy of *Fraktur* and the vivid colours of decorated textiles. When it comes time in the late summer for harvesting the fruits of the land, one seems to find here a people who have been practising for the event by the continual reaping of beauty throughout the year.

In the 1750s the Germanic settlers of Lunenburg County, Nova Scotia, sought to look beyond mere survival and to alleviate their crude beginnings by creating furnishings of real aesthetic appeal. They were successful in spite of their lowly status in the eyes of some of their neighbours. Half a century later, Pennsylvania Germans in Ontario quickly proved that things utilitarian could also be beautiful. They, together with the Continental Germans, established both creative and productive communities. Unfortunately, they seem never to have enjoyed proper cultural prominence, in part because they were under the constant shadow of the politically and culturally dominant English-speaking majority. The western provinces, on the other hand, have been a colourful mosaic of many ethnic groups with the result that specifically Germanic artifacts have previously been difficult to identify. However, among these western groups of Mennonites and Hutterites, there has been a sustained tradition of folk-art expression that has survived into this century.

Together, Canada's widely scattered Germanic settlers have displayed a vibrant, even exuberant decorative approach to life in the new land. They have persistently cleared the wilderness with a vigour and joy that comes from the heart, one of their beloved symbols. This spirit, though it has been modified in the face of urbanization, cross-cultural influences and assimilation into a broader society, has never fully ceased to be expressed in visible forms of all sorts.

For the most part, the need for village craftsmen to produce ethnically distinctive wares has largely disappeared. But it is a testimony to the strength of Germanic traditions that the impulse to repeat long-remembered decorative techniques continues as an animating force within this vaguely felt cultural framework.

Part of Canada's Germanic heritage is the implicit view that to see beauty in the particular is to know beauty in the universal. The decorated utensils, furniture, textiles and artifacts of all kinds pictured here participate strongly in this continuing spirit. It has been an impressive two centuries, a magnificent creative outpouring and a truly splendid harvest.

# Notes

**A Germanic Plenitude** (pages 13 to 16)

[1]Anna K. Hess, "Remarks on Historical Research with Special Consideration of the History of German Settlers in Canada," *German-Canadian Yearbook* (1973), p. 26.

[2]Excerpts from "The History and Description of the Southern and Western Townships of Nova Scotia in 1795," by Rev. James Munro (Public Archives of Nova Scotia, Vol. 1941-49), quoted in Ruth E. Kaulback, *Historic Saga of Lehève* (Halifax: Private Printing, 1970), p. 49. Authors' italics.

[3]"Strachan Papers, Letter Book, 1839-1866," (MS 35), Ontario Archives.

[4]William Winthrop Kent, *The Hooked Rug* (New York: Tudor Publishing Company, 1930), p. 144. This account was written in 1930. It is interesting that the events it records are already considerably in the past tense.

[5]Earl F. Robacker, *Pennsylvania Dutch Stuff* (Philadelphia: University of Pennsylvania Press, 1944), p. 50.

[6]G. Elmore Reaman, *The Trail of the Black Walnut* (Toronto: McClelland and Stewart, 1957), p. 180.

[7]Georg K. Weissenborn, "The Germans in Canada: A Chronological Survey," *German-Canadian Yearbook* (1978), p. 23.

[8]Will 71, probated 1855, Waterloo County Surrogate Court, Kitchener, Ontario.

[9]Will 1436, probated 1882, Waterloo County Surrogate Court, Kitchener, Ontario.

**Nova Scotia and the East** (pages 17 to 52)

[1]Account given in Winthrop Bell, *The 'Foreign Protestants' and the Settlement of Nova Scotia* (Toronto: University of Toronto Press, 1961), pp. 9-12.

[2]Quoted in Ruth E. Kaulback, *Historic Saga of Lehève* (Halifax: Private Printing, 1970), p. 35.

[3]Bell, p. 9.

[4]*Ibid.*, p. 99.

[5]*Ibid.*, pp. 405-407. Particularly conclusive on the date and origin of the name is an excerpt from Council Minutes of May 10, 1763: "resolved that the settlement to be made at Merlegash be called the township of Lunenburg."

[6]According to Sigfrid Taubert, by the late 1780s there were two to three thousand Germans in Lunenburg, thus inspiring this Halifax printer to publish a German-Canadian calendar in 1787. See "The First German Printers in Canada," *German-Canadian Yearbook* (1973), p. 72.

[7]Bell, pp. 625-626.

[8]*Ibid.*, p. 628.

[9]*Ibid.*, p. 85.

[10]*Ibid.*, pp. 287-291.

[11]Kaulback, p. 290.

[12]For a detailed study of the life and work of Schumacher, see Frederick S. Weiser, "Daniel Schumacher's Baptismal Register," *Pennsylvania German Society Annual Volume* (1968), pp. 185-407.

[13]Bell, p. 290.

[14]Harold B. Burnham and Dorothy K. Burnham, *'Keep Me Warm One Night': Early Handweaving in Eastern Canada* (Toronto: University of Toronto Press, 1972), p. 10.

[15]Quoted from Norman Creighton, "Land of the Jolly Ox," *Sun Life Review* (April 2, 1964), in Kaulbach, p. 47.

[16]See Klaus Wust, *Folk Art in Stone* (Edinburgh, Virginia: Shenandoah History, 1970). For a general overview of Nova Scotia gravemarkers, see Deborah Trask, *Life How Short, Eternity How Long: Gravestone Carving and Carvers in Nova Scotia* (Halifax: Nova Scotia Museum, 1978). Also of related interest are Preston A. Barba, *Pennsylvania German Tombstones* (Pennsylvania German Society, 1954), and Frederick S. Weiser, "Baptismal Certificate and Gravemarker; Pennsylvania German Folk Art at the Beginning and the End of Life," in Jan M. G. Quimby and Scott T. Swank, ed. *Perspectives on American Folk Art* (New York: W. W. Norton & Co., 1980), pp. 134-151.

**Ontario** (pages 53 to 184)

[1]George K. Weissenborn, "The Germans in Canada: A Chronological Survey," *German-Canadian Yearbook* (1978), p. 26.

[2]John Andre, "William Bent Berczy (1791-1873)," *German-Canadian Yearbook* (1975), p. 167.

[3]G. Elmore Reaman, *The Trail of the Black Walnut* (Toronto: McClelland and Stewart, 1957), p. 96.

[4]The difficult financial situation of this group is borne out in an 1837 letter written by John S. Cooper to William H. Merritt in which he requests employment for the German settlers as road-builders in areas along the shores of Lake Erie: "The enclosed petition will show that there are a number of German settlers in the Township of Rainham that are likely to suffer from want of bread. . . . They are industrious hard-working people but they are very poor and will see hard times before next harvest if they can get no help" (Merritt Papers, Pkg. 31, Archives of Ontario).

[5]Albert Hess, "Deutsche Bräuche and Volkslieder in Maryhill (Waterloo County)," German-Canadian Yearbook (1976), p. 222.

[6]Dr. Gottlieb Leibrandt, "Deutsche Ortsgründungen und Ortsnamen in der Grafschaft Waterloo," German-Canadian Yearbook (1973), p. 124.

[7]This story of a nineteenth-century spiritual friendship was brought to our attention by a twentieth-century friend, Orland Gingerich of Baden, Ontario.

[8]Gerhard P. Bassler, "The 'Inundation' of British North America with 'the Refuse of Foreign Pauperism': Assisted Emigration from Southern Germany in the Mid-19th Century," German-Canadian Yearbook (1978), p. 96.

[9]Ibid., p. 101.

[10]Information on this and other houses in the area was generously provided by residents and owners of early homes in the Vineland region, including Barbara Coffman, Barclay Holmes and Rick and Holly Henemader.

[11]Information from Barclay Holmes, who now lives in the High home. May 26, 1979.

[12]Mr. Edgar Bundscho of Tavistock remembers that the spire of St. Anthony's was damaged by lightning around 1915, resulting in alterations which shortened the original pinnacle to the present cupola.

[13]See the booklet, "Immaculate Conception Church," a souvenir publication brought out on the occasion of the church's redecoration in 1975.

[14]A tall chest of drawers with the initials "MM" and dated 1821 is illustrated in Donald B. Webster, English-Canadian Furniture of the Georgian Period (Toronto: McGraw-Hill Ryerson, 1979), p. 190. This piece is claimed by the author of that study to have been made for the wife of Samuel T. Moyer. This thesis falters under closer scrutiny: the initials "MM" do not match any of the names of Moyer's three wives.

[15]Among the few known exceptions are two examples illustrated in Howard Pain, The Heritage of Upper Canadian Furniture (Toronto: Van Nostrand Reinhold, Ltd., 1978), Plates 939 and 955.

[16]Pain, Plate 1024.

[17]For further information concerning the Doan cabinetmakers, see John McIntyre, "John and Ebenezer Doan: Builders and Furniture Craftsmen," Canadian Collector (July/August 1979), pp. 27-31.

[18]Lynda M. Nykor and Patricia D. Musson, Mennonite Furniture: The Ontario Tradition in York County (Toronto: Lorimer, 1977), pp. 46-48. Illustrations of Snider furniture appear in Ann Crawford, ed., Henry Snider: His Ancestors and Descendants (Toronto: Private Printing, 1976), pp. 218-225. For additional examples, see Pain, Plates 989, 1052, 1067 and 1118.

[19]See Pain, Plates 985-87 and 994. See also Philip Shackleton, The Furniture of Old Ontario (Toronto: Macmillan of Canada, 1973), Plate 366.

[20]Der Deutsche Canadier (January 2, 1845), p. 4.

[21]For an excellent interpretive study of a body of furniture that was possibly made in the workshop of Abraham Latschaw, see Stanley Johannesen, "The Unknown Furniture Master of Waterloo County," Canadian Collector (July/August 1977), pp. 18-23.

[22]Henry and Barbara Dobson, The Early Furniture of Ontario and the Atlantic Provinces (Toronto: M. F. Feheley Publishers, Ltd., 1974), p. 191.

[23]Pain, Plate 1031.

[24]The authors are grateful for having had the opportunity to consult research material compiled on Johann Adam Eyer by Pastor Frederick S. Weiser.

[25]Joseph Lochbaum's name was discovered almost simultaneously on two certificates, one by Pastor Frederick S. Weiser in Pennsylvania, the other shown to the authors by John Lunau of the Markham District Historical Museum. The certificates were made and signed in Pennsylvania and Ontario, respectively, indicating the itinerant pattern of this schoolteacher-cum-Fraktur artist.

[26]As narrated by grandchildren, Mrs. Edwin Byer of Markham and Mrs. Vera Reesor Taylor of Utica, Ontario. For further information and for a survey of Fraktur artists in Ontario, see Michael S. Bird, Ontario Fraktur: A Pennsylvania-German Folk Art Tradition in Early Canada (Toronto: M. F. Feheley Publishers, Ltd., 1977).

[27]This process is described in detail by Harold and Dorothy Burnham in their definitive study, *'Keep Me Warm One Night': Early Handweaving in Eastern Canada* (Toronto: University of Toronto Press, 1972), pp. 15-25. Another illuminating account is given in Ellen J. Gehret and Alan G. Keyser, *The Homespun Textile Tradition of the Pennsylvania Germans* (Harrisburg: Pennsylvania Historical and Museum Commission, 1976), pp. 2-5.

[28]Burnham and Burnham, p. 329.

[29]*Ibid.*, p. 330.

[30]*Ibid.*, p. 318.

[31]A coverlet with this "trademark," woven for Mary A. Horning in 1841, is illustrated in Burnham, p. 334, Plate 433.

[32]See Burnham, pp. 172-73.

[33]Illustrated in Burnham, p. 69, Plate 85.

[34]Burnham, p. 13.

[35]*Ibid.*, p. 320.

[36]*Ibid.*, p. 377.

[37]An earlier account of the life and work of this weaver is to be found in Michael S. Bird, "Friedrich K. Ploethner (1826-1883): Cabinetmaker and Weaver," *Canadian Collector* (May/June 1980), pp. 28-31.

[38]This information was obtained in an interview on August 10, 1979, with Mrs. Aaron B. Weber of RR1, Waterloo, Ontario.

[39]David L. Newlands, *Early Ontario Potters: Their Craft and Trade* (Toronto: McGraw-Hill Ryerson, 1979), p. 165.

[40]*Ibid.*, pp. 165-66.

[41]Information obtained in correspondence (February 27, 1980) with Barbara Coffman of Vineland, Ontario.

[42]See David W. Rupp, "The B. Lent Pottery, c. 1836-1841," *Canadian Collector* (May/June 1980), pp. 39-43.

[43]Newlands, pp. 76, 98.

[44]*Ibid.*, p. 79.

[45]Ezra E. Eby, *A Biographical History of Early Settlers and Their Descendants in Waterloo Township* (reprinted by Eldon D. Weber, 1975), p. 69 (no. 1130).

[46]Newlands, pp. 75-76.

[47]Interview with Simeon Martin, grandson of William K. Eby, January 5, 1979.

[48]According to Simeon Martin, there were three sizes of pie plates, including large for pork-sausage pie, middle size for fruit pies, and small for young girls using dough left over from mother's baking. The use of these plates may have been broader in actuality, but this is an interesting recollection of usage in one household.

[49]Newlands, p. 104.

[50]*Ibid.*, pp. 103, 105, 109.

[51]*Ibid.*, p. 109.

[52]Interview with Simeon Martin, January 5, 1979.

[53]Potters of Continental or Pennsylvania-German background in Brant County include John Yeigh of Burford, Henry Schuler and Jacob Henry Ahrens of Paris.

[54]Newlands, p. 113.

[55]*Ibid.*, p. 114.

[56]*Ibid.*, p. 91.

[57]*Ibid.*, pp. 98-99.

[58]Interviews with Viola Waddel, September 8 and October 11, 1978.

[59]A more detailed account of the life and work of Fred Hoffman appears in Terry Kobayashi, "Fred G. Hoffman (1845-1926): Itinerant Woodcarver of Waterloo and Oxford Counties," *Canadian Antiques and Art Review* (Spring, 1981).

[60]For further information concerning the life and work of this Mennonite artist, see Terry Kobayashi, "David B. Horst (1873-1965): St. Jacobs Woodcarver," *Waterloo Historical Society* (1977), pp. 78-92 and "Folk Art in Wood," *Canadian Antiques and Art Review* (March, 1980), pp. 26-30.

[61]Isaac R. Horst, *Up The Conestogo* (Mount Forest, Ontario: Private Printing, 1979), pp. 329-354.

[62]Toronto: McClelland and Stewart, 1941.

[63]Mabel Dunham, *Grand River* (Toronto: McClelland and Stewart, 1945), p. 103.

[64]See Ezra E. Eby *A Biographical History*, p. 63 (no. 995).

[65]For information on and discussion of iron gravemarkers in Ontario, see Nancy-Lou Patterson, "The Iron Cross and the Tree of Life," *Ontario History* (March, 1976), pp. 1-16; and also Camilla C. Coumans, "Ornamental Iron Grave Markers," *Waterloo Historical Society* (1962), pp. 72-75.

**The Prairie Provinces** (pages 185 to 222)

[1]Frank Harder, "Who Am I?," in Lawrence Klippenstein and Julius G. Toews, eds., *Mennonite Memories: Settling in Western Canada* (Winnipeg: Centennial Publications, 1979), p. 5.

[2]*Ibid.*, p. 7.

[3]Gerhard Lohrenz, *The Mennonites of Western Canada* (Steinbach, Manitoba: Private Printing, 1974), p. 11.

[4]William Schroeder, *The Bergthal Colony* (Winnipeg: Canadian Mennonite Bible College Publications, 1974), p. 57.

[5]Lohrenz, p. 9.

[6]*Ibid.*, p. 13.

[7]*Ibid.*, p. 15.

[8]*Ibid.*, p. 20.

[9]*Ibid.*, p. 22.

[10]Anonymous, "Homesteading at Rosthern," in Klippenstein and Toews, p. 164.

[11]According to Richard J. Friesen, "The stability of the modified Saskatchewan system is reflected in the survival rate of the Saskatchewan villages as compared to those of Manitoba. There, of the 120 villages established, only seventeen still existed in 1960, while in the two Saskatchewan reserves, twenty-one of the original fifty-two villages survived in some form and many still function as they once did." ("Villages in Saskatchewan," in Klippenstein and Toews, p. 189.)

[12]Historical plaque, village of Engelfeld, Saskatchewan, commemorating the arrival of German Catholic settlers in the area.

[13]John W. Bennett, *Hutterite Brethren* (Stanford: Stanford University Press, 1967), p. 27.

[14]John A. Hostetler and Gertrude E. Huntington, *The Hutterites in North America* (New York: Holt, Rinehart and Winston, 1967), p. 3.

[15]John A. Hostetler, *Hutterite Life* (Scottdale, Pennsylvania: Herald Press, 1965), p. 12.

[16]*Ibid.*, p. 12.

[17]Interview with Mr. and Mrs. Herman Barkman, July 23, 1979.

[18]See John C. Reimer and Julius G. Toews, "Mennonite Buildings," in Klippenstein and Toews, pp. 114-118.

[19]*Ibid.*, p. 17.

[20]The primitive nature of pioneer furniture of the Mennonite settlers is suggested by William Schroeder's description: "The furniture was almost exclusively make-shift in character. The boxes in which their freight had been packed became their tables, beds, benches and cupboards." (*The Bergthal Colony*, p. 54.)

[21]These insights concerning corner cupboards in south German homes were generously shared by Pastor Frederick S. Weiser.

[22]Peter T. Wiebe, "Learning Was Hard," in Klippenstein and Toews, p. 136.

# Glossary

**American Empire** In furniture design, the heavy style developed in France during the Napoleonic period. Popular in the United States until the middle of the nineteenth century, it emphasized columns, pediments and other Neoclassical elements.

**Ashlar Masonry** Squared building stones permitting thin mortar joints.

**Baroque** Elaborate ornamentation of architecture or furniture characterized by continually flowing curves, scrolls and carved details.

**Berlin-work** Late nineteenth-century embroidery work, utilized commercial patterns for designs and mottoes, frequently worked on punched-paper backing sheets.

**Biedermeier** The simplification of the French Empire style by German cabinetmakers in the early and mid-nineteenth century, utilizing matched veneers, inlay, ebonized accents and architectural motifs.

**Bruderhof** Literally "brotherhood," referring to the colony within which Hutterite life is given religious, social and economic organization. There are today approximately 180 Hutterite colonies in North America, of which two-thirds are located in western Canada.

**Bucherzeichen** A bookplate in the *Fraktur* style.

**Cabriole** In furniture, a leg which curves outward at the top and inward further down to produce a reversing curve.

**Chip-carving** A manner of carving in which a knife, chisel or other sharp instrument is used to chip out gouges or indentations from an edge or surface.

**Chippendale** Furniture derived from Thomas Chippendale's design book, *The Director*, first published in 1754. Such furniture was given simplified or provincialized interpretation by American and Canadian cabinetmakers from the late eighteenth to mid-nineteenth century.

**Cornice** Uppermost horizontal section of an architectural or furniture entablature.

**Cyma** In architecture or furniture, an outline formed by mouldings or members which are shaped; having a partly convex and partly concave curve.

**Dentil** In architecture or furniture, a series of spaced rectangular blocks ("teeth") running the length of a cornice.

**Draw Table** A table having a top made in three sections which allows the table to be extended by drawing the ends out from beneath the centre section.

**Earthenware** Pottery of baked or hardened clay, capable of firing at low temperature.

**Entablature** The horizontal upper part of an architectural structure or piece of furniture supported by columns.

**Ethnocentric** The tendency to look inward to race, culture or group for values, beliefs and practices. The term is used in this study to denote a culture's conserving role in maintaining traditional design and subject matter in the decorative arts.

**Familien-Register** A *Fraktur* family register.

**Fenestration** In architecture, the design and arrangement of windows and other exterior openings of a building.

**Fluting** Carved or gouged channels or grooves to produce a decorative rhythmic effect on a column or surface.

**Forebay** The side of a barn with entrances to the stock floor.

**"Foreign Protestants"** German-speaking persons from Protestant areas of the German states, France and Switzerland recruited in 1749 by Colonel Edward Cornwallis to establish a settlement in Nova Scotia.

**Fraktur** Ornamental calligraphy derived from medieval "Gothic" form. Developed in areas of Switzerland and Germany, it attained its greatest flowering in Pennsylvania. The tradition of hand-lettered texts, augmented by stylized birds, hearts, tulips and geometric designs was brought to Ontario by Swiss-German pioneers from Pennsylvania and to the Prairie Provinces by east and north European Mennonites and Hutterites.

**Geburtschein** A *Fraktur* birth record.

**Georgian** In architecture, the term denotes a style developed in England between 1714-1830 (during the reigns of George I through George IV). Houses and other structures in this style are characterized by simple elegance, harmonious lines, symmetrical arrangement of exterior features and modest utilization of Neoclassical elements.

**Gothic** In architecture, the utilization of features of a style originating in the twelfth century, including the pointed arch and the ribbed vault.

**Graining** A manner of painted decoration, either to simulate formal hardwoods such as mahogany, maple and rosewood, or to create an abstract effect.

**Heckle** Known variously as heckle, hackel or hatchel (hetchel). A comb consisting of a board with a central cluster of spikes used to break down flax fibres to prepare them for spinning. Some were decorated by makers or owners with painted or incised folk-art motifs.

**Heiratschein** Marriage certificate done in *Fraktur*.

**Hepplewhite** Furniture based on George Hepplewhite's *Guide*, in the classic tradition, with square tapered legs and sweeping curves.

**Itinerant Artists** Craftspersons whose artistic activity carried them on long journeys in search of patrons. Notable examples include *Fraktur* practitioners who travelled widely across Pennsylvania and Ontario offering to inscribe family Bibles or certificates for a small fee.

**Kiste** A box, trunk or chest used for storage purposes. The plural is *Kisten.*

**Kleiderschrank** German term for a clothes cupboard or wardrobe. Often erroneously called simply a *Schrank,* a general term which refers to any kind of cupboard. The plural is *Kleiderschränke.*

**Linen Press** An English form of clothes cupboard comprised of two sections of nearly equal size, the bottom of which has several drawers, with doors on the upper portion. This form, made in the Niagara Peninsula, is distinct from the wardrobe form made in Waterloo County and in the Huron area, with a shallow lower section and tall upper section for hanging of clothes.

**Lintel** A horizontal architectural member supporting weight above a door or window.

**Lozenge** A diamond-shaped figure, notably in the form of panels found on architecture and furniture.

**Marbleizing** Also called marbleing, a decorative technique in which a surface is painted to simulate variegated marble.

**Mennonite Village** A distinctive community form, arranged as a *Strassdorf,* or street village, with surrounding farmlands. This plan was brought to Manitoba and Saskatchewan by Friesian, Dutch and Prussian Mennonite settlers who had used it previously in southern Russia.

**Montbéliard** A countship which, although virtually surrounded by France, was administered by the ducal house of Württemberg. This small principality, "French in language and Protestant in religion" (Bell), was the native home of numerous families who settled at Lunenburg, Nova Scotia.

**Mullion** In furniture or architecture the wooden dividers between glass window panes.

**Neoclassical** In decorative arts, the revival of elements of the classic architectural style of ancient Greece and Rome.

**Neogothic** The late perpetuation or revival of Gothic themes and design features in late nineteenth and early twentieth century furniture and architecture.

**Ogee** A double curve, resembling the letter S.

**Pediment** An architectural feature, frequently carried over to furniture, amounting to a gable-like feature, typically triangular and outlined with cornices. Variations include broken, curved or scrolled forms.

**Pilaster** An applied detail simulating a column, with base and capital, used in architecture and furniture. .

**Provincial** In architecture, furniture and decorative arts, the term normally suggests a somewhat naïve, primitive, unsophisticated interpretation of formal style by rural craftspersons.

**Quarter Column** The portion of a column or dowel formed by lengthwise cutting into four sections, used frequently as a refinement in architecture and furniture.

**Queen Anne** Architecture and furniture style prevailing in England in the early eighteenth century, using among other elements the cabriole leg, arched panels and panes. The Queen Anne style was retained and adapted widely in North America, including by Pennsylvania-German cabinetmakers who used several dominant English styles in conjunction with Germanic design and construction features.

**Quoin** In architecture, corner stones, often larger than other stones or bricks, intended to enhance the design and strength of buildings.

**Redware** *See* earthenware.

**Reeding** Decorative work in architecture and furniture consisting of raised moulding (vertical, horizontal or diagonal), which is cut in a convex manner so as to produce the reverse effect of fluting.

**Relief-carving** Any carved detail in which a design or figure is rendered in raised contrast to its background.

**Reserves** Lands in western Canada offered to various groups willing to settle large blocks or areas. Mennonites arriving in the late nineteenth century established themselves at the East and West Reserves in Manitoba and at the Rosthern and Swift Current Reserves in Saskatchewan.

**Retardataire** Referring to the phenomenon by which styles are perpetuated in rural or ethnically defined areas long after they have gone out of vogue in urban centres.

**"Russian" Mennonites** A phrase used frequently — and incorrectly — to describe Mennonites of Friesian, Dutch or Prussian origin who had settled in southern Russia for approximately a century before migrating to Canada in the late nineteenth and early twentieth centuries.

**Sailcloth Mats** Canvas mats cut from sailcloth and given decorative treatment. Examples of this rare art form have been found in Lunenburg County, Nova Scotia, with painted Maritime subjects and traditional geometric and folk-art motifs.

**Schlafbank** A Germanic sleeping bench found in the western provinces.

**Sheraton** Furniture deriving from Thomas Sheraton's *Drawing Book* of 1792-95. In contrast to the tapered square leg of

Hepplewhite furniture, Sheraton pieces normally feature finely turned legs. Sheraton styles were probably the most popular among furniture forms made in Canada during the first half of the nineteenth century.

**Show Towel**  A popular name given to embroidered hand towels worked in cross or chain-stitch by Mennonite girls in Pennsylvania and Ontario. Like *Fraktur*, they are normally symmetrical arrangements of traditional folk-art designs and usually feature the name of their maker and date of completion.

**South Shore**  The lower coastal area of Nova Scotia, generally extending from Halifax in a southwesterly direction to a point below Yarmouth.

**Spatter-decorated**  Pottery on which the decoration is applied randomly.

**Sponge Painting**  A manner of decorative painting in which one or more colours were applied by means of a sponge, potato, fingers, crumpled paper or other objects against a contrasting colour to produce a mottled effect.

**Springerle Board**  A wooden board with carved motifs on which the dough was rolled to imprint designs on Springerle cookies.

**Stoneware**  A hard, opaque, vitrified ceramic ware, fired at high temperature.

**Tauf-und-Geburtschein**  Combined *Fraktur* baptismal and birth record.

**Trompe l'oeil**  A visual deception used frequently in paintings, to create illusions of tactile and spatial qualities.

**Umbrage**  In architecture, a recessed sheltered space.

**Ur-bogen**  In decorative arts, a semi-circular arc, considered by some to be symbolic of the sun as it approaches the winter solstice. This sun motif is occasionally found on furniture, architecture, *Fraktur,* and decorated gravemarkers.

**Vernacular**  A local interpretation of a generalized design principle, frequently dictated by the ethos of a larger religious or ethnic group.

**Versammlungshaus**  A meeting house, particularly among Mennonites, Amish or Hutterites. Although serving religious purposes, it is not given the sacramental importance assigned to the church in magisterial Protestantism or Roman Catholicism.

**Vorschrift**  A writing specimen in *Fraktur* lettering, usually done under a teacher's supervision. The plural is Vorschriften.

**Wainscotting**  Woodwork, including paneling and moulding, lining the lower portion of an interior wall.

**Wall Cupboard**  Any cupboard, whether open or enclosed with solid or glazed doors, situated against the wall and used for storage of dishes and utensils. Popular names for this form include "flatwall cupboard" (Canada) and "Dutch cupboard" (Pennsylvania).

**Weltanschauung**  Literally "world view," the term refers to the outlook of a particular group, whether cultured or religious.

**Whirligig**  Originally meaning anything that whirls, the term has come in North America to designate handcarved figures with flat arms, often mounted outdoors and set in motion by wind. Like weathervanes, they are sometimes given considerable artistic enhancement by their makers.

# Acknowledgments

Looking back over a research adventure which has covered a time period of more than four years and an expanse of geography three thousand miles wide, the challenge of enumerating those persons who have assisted us along the way is a staggering one, indeed. Even the broad categories of individuals who have been so generous in their support are several in number. In particular we are indebted to five groups — historians and other scholars, institutional personnel (museums, libraries, archives), dealers, private collectors and "people in the countryside."

Among scholars in the field who have provided immense assistance, we are especially grateful to Pastor Frederick S. Weiser of Hanover, Pennsylvania, for his profound insights and brutally candid criticism along the way. Other persons in the United States who have provided much assistance include Clair Conway, Ellen Gehret, Jan Gleysteen, Frank Halpern, Don and Patricia Herr, Alan Keyser, Clarence Kulp, Jr., Larry Neff, John Ruth, Bruce Shoemaker, Richard and Joan Flanders Smith, and Mary Hammond Sullivan.

In Canada, we are grateful for the enthusiastic support of Professor Nancy-Lou Patterson, whose love of Mennonite decorative arts and her research on this subject span fifteen years. As the pioneer in this field, she has opened a rich field of study to us all. Professor Peter C. Erb has been an invaluable source of critical insight, as have been also J. Winfield Fretz, Orland Gingerich and Stanley Johannesen. Other scholars and writers who have graciously shared their research and views include Lorna Bergey, Ruth Dwyer, Frank Epp, Gary Esser, Harold Funk, J. Russell Harper, Lawrence Klippenstein, Katherine Lamb, Rev. Gerhard Lohrenz, Lynn McMurray, Steve Prystupa, Ted Regehr, John Rempel, Scott Robson, Grace Schmidt, Sam Steiner, Bernard Thiessen, Deborah Trask, and William Waiser.

A special word of gratitude needs to be voiced with respect to several dealers in art and antiques. It is a sad pitfall that so much research overlooks the contributions of dealers, whether from oversight or distrust. Our personal experience has been that dealers are often not only generous in their assistance but are, in many cases, the only source of precious historical information concerning artifacts. Among dealers who have gone out of their way to retain and share historical background to objects under study, we are particularly appreciative of the conscientious efforts of, among others, Lindsay Anderson, Jim and Teresa Barker, James Bisback and Johnny Kalisch, Henry and Barbara Dobson, Leslie and Nell Donaldson, John and Vicki Forbes, Rick and Holly Henemader, Leslie Langille, Ron and Rose O'Hara and Michael Rowan. The thread of cultural continuity between artifact and the setting in which it was created is extremely delicate, and without the dedication of these dealers to find and record this connection, we would on many occasions have come sadly upon dead ends in our research.

Persons associated with institutions who allowed us to examine documents, artifacts and pertinent materials include Susan Burke, Dorothy Burnham, Mary Champion, Barbara Coffman, Russell Cooper, Harry Crowfoot, Eleanor Currie, Magnus Einarrson, Lou Feindl, Bruce Ferguson, Tom Lackey, John Lunau, Wesley Mattie, David L. Newlands, Steve Prystupa, Scott Robson, David Rupp, Alf Schenk, Phil Tilney, John Vollmer and many part-time staff who gave hours and even full days of their time to make us at home.

We also wish to express our profound gratitude to the many collectors, relatives and descendants of artists and craftspersons and other individuals "in the countryside". Among these many supporters and enablers are Art and Mary Armstrong, Jean Armstrong, Mr. and Mrs. William Baker, Jake Baetz, Darrol Barkman, Mr. and Mrs. Herman Barkman, Lovina Bauman, Dr. and Mrs. Peter Bell, Alice Bender, Matilda Bender, Clay and Carole Benson, Dan and Melba Bingeman, Mr. and Mrs. Fred Blayney, Louis Bodnar, Ed Boyagen, Klaus Breed, Mr. and Mrs. John Butler, Mr. and Mrs. Edwin Byer, Bill and Caroline Byfield, Nick and Carole Cameron, Mr. and Mrs. Eric Carter, Ron Cascaden and Wendy Wright, Don and Jane Caskenette, Mr. and Mrs. Robert Christie, Carole Collins, Dorothy Cox, Dr. and Mrs. Lawrence Cummings, Jim and Penny Curtiss, Katherine Daley, Art and Mary Dawson, Alf and Irene Dernesch, Bing and Henrietta Dobson, Mr. and Mrs. Verne Drexler, Howard and Maggie Dyck, Isaac Dyck, Mr. and Mrs. Gordon Eby, Mr. and Mrs. Jake Enns, Gerald and Marlene Fagan, Richard Field, Cora Fischer, Mr. and Mrs. Peter Follett, Dr. and Mrs. Claude Forler, Hyla Fox, Jake Friessen, Doug Gemeinhard, Phil Gemeinhard, Rev. Cyril Gingerich, Mr. and Mrs. Milton Good, Tom and Martha Graham, John and Heather Harbinson, Ross Hirtle, Joshua Hofer, Katrina Hofer, Barclay Holmes, Mr. and Mrs. David

Horst, Charles and Gay Humber, Chris Huntington, Bill and Sue Hyslop, Dave Jacobi, Dave and Judy Kergin, Jake Kleinsasser, Ethel Knight, Jonathan Kormos, Mr. and Mrs. Herbert Kuntz, John and Frank Letkeman, Mr. and Mrs. Gerald Levitt, Mr. and Mrs. David Lichti, Mr. and Mrs. Ed Lock, Mrs. Evan MacDonald, Mr. and Mrs. Kenneth MacDonald, John MacGowan, Mathias Martin, Nancy Martin, Simeon Martin, Bill McDonald, Jim McDougal, Blake and Ruth McKendry, Lynn and Merla McMurray, Ralph Meyer, Hank and Carole Milberg, Mr. and Mrs. Jim Miller, Dave and Sandy Moore, Mr. and Mrs. George Murray, Robert and June O'Neill, Gwen Pemberton, Mr. and Mrs. Henry Peters, Harry and Tillie Porter, Ethel Poth, Ralph and Patricia Price, Mr. and Mrs. Gary Reed, Mary Reimer, Rev. and Mrs. James Reusser, Mr. and Mrs. John Rock, Robert and Marg Rowell, George Sawatsky, Wolfgang and Carole Schlombs, the late William Schmalz, Milo and Laura Shantz, Mr. and Mrs. Robin Simpson, Mark and Wendy Smallecombe, Verne and Maggie Smart, Dick Spafford, Mike Stahl, Murray Stewart, Evelyn Sturgeon, Dennis and Diane Teakle, Paul and Hildy Tiessen, Deborah Trask, Nick and Maggie Treanor, Viola Waddel, Jake Wall, John and Pat Weber, Dale Wilson, Ross and Hajra Wilson, John Wine and Anne Peters, Rev. George Youmatoff, Joe and Marjorie Zinger, John and Vicki Zinszer, Sherman Zwicker and others who have preferred to remain anonymous. To all of these, *Danke Schön.*

Finally, we would like to thank our editor, James T. Wills, the book's designer, Howard Pain, and the staff at Van Nostrand Reinhold for their help.

Photography
The following have generously provided photographs:
Henry and Barbara Dobson #8, 14, 60, 73, 85, 97
Maurice Green #69, 71
Tom Lackey #27
National Museum of Man #92
Howard Pain #64, 66, 67, 68, 75, 79, 82, 102, 103
Scott Robson (Nova Scotia Museum) #32, 35
Royal Ontario Museum #130, 131, 139
David Rupp #154
Waddington's #62
All other photographs are by the authors.

# Bibliography

AMES, KENNETH L. *Beyond Necessity: Art in the Folk Tradition.* Winterthur, Delaware: The Henry Francis du Pont Winterthur Museum, 1977.

ANDRE, JOHN. "William Bent Berczy (1791-1873)," *German-Canadian Yearbook* (1975), pp. 167-180.

ARTHUR, ERIC and DUDLEY WITNEY. *The Barn: A Vanishing Landmark in North America.* Toronto: McClelland and Stewart, 1972.

BARBA, PRESTON A. *Pennsylvania German Tombstones.* Pennsylvania German Society, 1954.

BASSLER, GERHARD P. "The 'Inundation' of British North America with 'the Refuse of Foreign Pauperism': Assisted Emigration from Southern Germany in the Mid-19th Century," *German-Canadian Yearbook* (1978), pp. 93-113.

BELL, WINTHROP. *The 'Foreign Protestants' and the Settlement of Nova Scotia.* Toronto: University of Toronto Press, 1961.

BENNETT, JOHN W. *Hutterite Brethren.* Stanford: Stanford University Press, 1967.

BIRD, MICHAEL S. *Beyond Survival: Ontario-German Decorative Arts in the Queen's Bush.* Bruce County Museum and Ontario Heritage Foundation, 1980.

————. "Christian L. Hoover (1835-1918): Markham Township Fraktur Artist," *Canadian Collector* (July/August 1977), pp. 28-31.

————. "Fraktur in the Niagara Peninsula," *Circa 76* (June, 1977).

————. "Friedrich K. Ploethner (1826-1883): Cabinetmaker and Weaver," *Canadian Collector* (May/June 1980), pp. 28-32.

————. "Jacob Bock (1798-1867): Early Germanic Potter of Waterloo County," *The Upper Canadian* (November/December 1980), pp. 30-31.

————. *Ontario Fraktur: A Pennsylvania German Folk Art Tradition in Early Canada.* Toronto: M.F. Feheley Publishers, Ltd., 1977.

————. "Pennsylvania-German Parallels: Decorative Arts of Lancaster County and Ontario," *Canadian Antiques and Art Review* (October, 1979), pp. 20-27.

————. "Perpetuation and Adaptation: The Furniture and Craftsmanship of John Gemeinhardt (1826-1912)," *Canadian Antiques and Art Review* (March, 1981), pp 19-34.

————. "A Spirit of Exuberance: Germanic Decorative Arts in Nova Scotia and Ontario," *Canadian Antiques and Art Review* (September, 1979), pp. 16-23.

————. "Three Waterloo County Fraktur Artists," *Waterloo County Historical Society* (1976), pp. 78-89.

BISHOP, ROBERT. *American Folk Sculpture.* New York: E. P. Dutton, 1974.

BORNEMAN, HENRY S. *Pennsylvania German Illuminated Manuscripts.* New York: Dover Publications, 1964.

BURKHOLDER, LEWIS J. *A Brief History of the Mennonites in Ontario.* Toronto: Livingstone Press, 1935.

BURNHAM, DOROTHY K. *Pieced Quilts of Ontario.* Toronto: Royal Ontario Museum, 1971.

BURNHAM, HAROLD B. and DOROTHY K. BURNHAM. *'Keep Me Warm One Night': Early Handweaving in Eastern Canada.* Toronto: University of Toronto Press, 1972.

CARPENTER, CAROLE HENDERSON. *Many Voices: A Study of Folklore Activities in Canadian Culture.* Ottawa: National Museum of Man, 1979.

CHAMPION, ISABEL, ed. *Markham: 1793-1900.* Markham, Ontario: Markham Historical Society, 1979.

CHRISTENSEN, ERWIN O. *Early American Wood Carving.* New York: Dover Publications, 1972.

————. *The Index of American Design.* New York: Macmillan Co., 1950.

CONKLIN, PAUL K. *Two Paths to Utopia: The Hutterites and the Llano Colony.* Lincoln, Nebraska: University of Nebraska Press, 1964.

CONROY, MARY. *Canada's Quilts.* Toronto: Griffen House Press, 1976.

COUMANS, CAMILLA C. "Ornamental Iron Grave Markers," *Waterloo County Historical Society* (1962), pp. 72-75.

CRAWFORD, ANN, ed. *Henry Snider: His Ancestors and Descendants.* Toronto: Private Printing, 1976.

CREIGHTON, HELEN. *Folklore of Lunenburg County, Nova Scotia.* Toronto: McGraw-Hill Ryerson, 1976.

DEBOR, HERBERT WILHELM, "Early German Immigration in Nova Scotia," *German-Canadian Yearbook* (1973), pp. 67-70.

de JOUVANCOURT, HUGUES. *Cornelius Krieghoff.* Toronto: Musson Book Company 1971.

DESBRISAY, M. B. *History of the County of Lunenburg.* Bridgewater, Nova Scotia: The Bridgewater Bulletin (reprint), 1967.

DOBSON, HENRY and BARBARA DOBSON. *The Early Furniture of Ontario and the Atlantic Provinces.* Toronto: M. F. Feheley Publishers, Ltd., 1974.

DUNHAM, MABEL. *Grand River.* Toronto: McClelland and Stewart, 1945.

————. *The Trail of the Conestoga.* Toronto: McClelland and Stewart, 1942.

DWYER, RUTH, *Mennonite Decorative Arts.* Catalogue for Exhibition at McMaster University Art Gallery, February 1-22, 1981. Hamilton, Ontario: McMaster University, 1981.

EBY, EZRA E. *A Biographical History of Early Settlers and their Descendants in Waterloo Township.* Berlin: Private Printing, 1894 (reprinted 1975).

EPP, FRANK H. *Mennonites in Canada, 1786-1920: The History of a Separate People.* Toronto: Macmillan of Canada, 1974.

ERB, PETER C. "The Canadian Poems of Eugen Funcken, C.R.," *German-Canadian Yearbook* (1978), pp. 225-233.

FABIAN, MONROE H. *The Pennsylvania-German Decorated Chest.* New York: Universe Books, 1978.

FALES, DEAN A., JR. *American Painted Furniture: 1660-1880.* New York: E. P. Dutton, 1972.

FERGUSON, BRUCE W. *Decorated Nova Scotia Furnishings.* Halifax: Dalhousie Art Gallery, 1978.

FRETZ, J. WINFIELD. *The Mennonites in Ontario.* Waterloo: The Mennonite Historical Society of Ontario, 1967.

FRIESEN, RICHARD J. "Villages in Saskatchewan," in Klippenstein, Lawrence and Julius G. Toews. *Mennonite Memories: Settling in Western Canada.* Winnipeg: Centennial Publications, 1977, pp. 187-194.

FRIESEN, WILLIAM, "A Mennonite Community in the East Reserve, Its Origin and Growth," in Swainson, Donald, *Historical Essays on the Prairie Provinces.* Toronto: McClelland and Stewart, 1970, pp. 99-119.

GEHRET, ELLEN J. "'O Noble Heart': An Examination of a Motif of Design from Pennsylvania German Embroidered Hand Towels," *Quarterly of the Pennsylvania German Society* (July, 1980), pp. 1-14.

GEHRET, ELLEN J. and ALAN G. KEYSER. *The Homespun Textile Tradition of the Pennsylvania Germans.* Harrisburg: Pennsylvania Historical and Museum Commission, 1976.

GINGERICH, ORLAND. *The Amish of Canada.* Scottdale and Kitchener: Herald Press, 1972.

GLASSIE, HENRY. *Pattern in the Material Folk Culture of the Eastern United States.* Philadelphia: University of Pennsylvania Press, 1968.

GOOD, E. REGINALD. *Anna's Art.* Kitchener, Ontario: Private Printing, 1976.

GREENSPAN, SHEILA. "Pennsylvania German Frakturs in Canada". Toronto, M.A. Thesis, 1968.

GROSS, PAUL S. *The Hutterite Way.* Saskatoon: Freeman Publishing Company, 1965.

GUNNION, VERNON S., and CARROLL J. HOPF. *Pennsylvania German Fraktur.* Lancaster, Pennsylvania: Pennsylvania Farm Museum of Landis Valley, 1967.

HANKS, CAROLE. *Early Ontario Gravestones.* Toronto: McGraw-Hill Ryerson, 1974.

HANSEN, H. J. *European Folk Art.* New York: McGraw Hill, 1968.

HARDER, FRANK. "Who Am I?", in Klippenstein, Lawrence and Julius G. Toews. *Mennonite Memories: Settling in Western Canada.* Winnipeg: Centennial Publications, 1967, pp. 1-10.

HARPER, J. RUSSELL. *A People's Art.* Toronto: University of Toronto Press, 1974.

_____ . *Krieghoff.* Toronto: University of Toronto Press, 1979.

HESS, ALBERT. "Deutsche Bräuche und Volkslieder in Maryhill (Waterloo County)," *German-Canadian Yearbook* (1976), pp. 221-225.

HESS, ANNA K. "Remarks on Historical Research With Special Consideration of the History of German Settlers in Canada," *German-Canadian Yearbook* (1973), pp. 25-29.

HOLSTEIN, JONATHAN. *The Pieced Quilt: A North American Tradition.* Toronto: McClelland and Stewart, 1973.

HORSCH, JOHN. *The Hutterian Brethren, 1528-1931.* Goshen, Indiana: Mennonite Historical Society, 1931.

HORST, ISAAC R. *Up the Conestoga.* Mount Forest, Ontario: Private Printing, 1979.

HOSTETLER, JOHN A. *Amish Society.* Baltimore: Johns Hopkins Press, 1965.

_____ . *Hutterite Life.* Scottdale, Pennsylvania: Herald Press, 1965.

HOSTETLER, JOHN A. and GERTRUDE E. HUNTINGTON. *The Hutterites in North America.* New York: Holt, Rinehart and Winston, 1967.

IMMACULATE CONCEPTION CHURCH. (Souvenir Booklet). Formosa, Ontario: Private Printing, 1975.

JOHANNESEN, STANLEY. "The Unknown Furniture Master of Waterloo County," *Canadian Collector* (July/August 1977), pp. 18-23.

JOHANNESEN, STANLEY and MICHAEL S. BIRD. *"Furniture and Fraktur: An Exhibition of Artifacts from Waterloo County and Germanic Ontario"* (Sept. 18-Oct. 16, 1977). Waterloo: University of Waterloo Art Gallery, 1977.

JUBILÄUMS-BÜCHLEIN: *Der evangelische lutherische Synode von Canada, 1911.*

KALBFLEISCH, HERBERT KARL. *The History of the Pioneer German Language Press of Ontario, 1835-1918.* Toronto: University of Toronto Press, 1968.

KALLMAN, HELMUT, "The German Contribution to Music in Canada," *German-Canadian Yearbook* (1975), pp. 152-166.

KAUFFMAN, HENRY J. *Early American Ironware.* New York: Charles E. Tuttle, 1966.

_____ . *Pennsylvania Dutch American Folk Art.* New York: Dover Publications, 1964.

KAULBACH, RUTH E. *Historic Saga of Lehève.* Halifax: Private Printing, 1970.

KENT, WILLIAM WINTHROP. *The Hooked Rug.* New York: Tudor Publishing Company, 1930.

KLIPPENSTEIN, LAWRENCE and JULIUS G. TOEWS. *Mennonite Memories: Settling in Western Canada.* Winnipeg: Centennial Publications, 1977.

KOBAYASHI, TERRY. "David B. Horst (1873-1975): St. Jacobs Woodcarver," *Waterloo County Historical Society* (1977), pp. 78-92.

_____ . "Folk Art in Wood," *Canadian Antiques and Art Review* (March, 1980), pp. 26-30.

_____ . "Fred G. Hoffman (1845-1926): Itinerant Woodcarver in Waterloo and Oxford Counties," *Canadian Antiques and Art Review*.

LEIBRANDT, DR. GOTTLIEB. "Deutsche Ortsgrundungen und Ortsnamen in der Grafschaft Waterloo," *German-Canadian Yearbook* (1973), pp. 119-129.

LICHTEN, FRANCES. *Folk Art Motifs of Pennsylvania.* New York: Dover Publications, 1954.

_____ . *Fraktur: The Illuminated Manuscripts of the Pennsylvania Dutch.* Philadelphia: The Free Library of Philadelphia, 1958.

LIPMAN, JEAN and ALICE WINCHESTER. *The Flowering of American Folk Art, 1776-1876.* New York: Viking Press, 1974.

LOHRENZ, GERHARD. *The Mennonites of Western Canada.* Steinbach, Manitoba: Private Printing, 1974.

LONG, AMOS. *The Pennsylvania German Family Farm.* Breinigsville: The Pennsylvania German Society, 1972.

_____ . "Bakeovens in the Pennsylvania Folk-Culture," *Pennsylvania Folklife* (December, 1964), pp. 16-29.

MARTIN, VIRGIL EMERSON. *The Early History of Jakobstellel.* St. Jacobs, Ontario: Private Printing, 1979.

McINTYRE, JOHN, "John and Ebenezer Doan: Builders and Furniture Craftsmen," *Canadian Collector* (July/August 1979), pp. 27-31.

_____ . "Niagara Furniture Makers — I," *Canadian Collector* (May/June 1977), pp. 50-53.

_____ . "Niagara Furniture Makers — II," *Canadian Collector* (Sept/Oct. 1977), pp. 50-53.

_____ . "Niagara Furniture Makers — III," *Canadian Collector* (March/April 1978), pp. 24-28.

_____ . "Niagara Furniture Makers — IV," *Canadian Collector* (July/August 1978), pp. 37-40.

McKENDRY, RUTH. *Quilts and Other Bed Coverings in the Canadian Tradition.* Toronto: Van Nostrand Reinhold Ltd., 1979.

McMURRAY, A. LYNN. "Ontario-German Decorative Arts," in Donald B. Webster, *The Book of Canadian Antiques.* Toronto: McGraw-Hill Ryerson (1974), pp. 128-142.

MEULENBELT-NIEUWBURG, ALBARTA. *Embroidery Motifs from Old Dutch Samplers.* New York: Charles Scribner's Sons, 1974.

NEWLANDS, DAVID L. *Early Ontario Potters: Their Craft and Their Trade.* Toronto: McGraw-Hill Ryerson, 1979.

NYKOR, LYNDA M. and PATRICIA D. MUSSON. *Mennonite Furniture: The Ontario Tradition in York County.* Toronto: Lorimer, 1977.

PAIN, HOWARD. *The Heritage of Upper Canadian Furniture.* Toronto: Van Nostrand Reinhold, 1978.

PATTERSON, NANCY-LOU. "Anna Weber (1814-1888): Waterloo County Fraktur Artist," *Mennonite Life* (December, 1975), pp. 15-19.

_____ . "The Iron Cross and the Tree of Life," *Ontario History* (March, 1976), pp. 1-16.

_____ . "Mennonite Folk Art of Waterloo County," *Ontario History* (September, 1968), pp. 86-90.

_____ . "Mennonite Traditional Arts," *Canadian Antiques Collector* (May, 1971), pp. 78-79.

_____ . *Mennonite Traditional Arts of the Waterloo Region and Southern Ontario.* Kitchener: Kitchener-Waterloo Art Gallery, 1974.

_____ . *Swiss-German and Dutch-German Mennonite Traditional Arts in the Waterloo Region, Ontario.* Ottawa: National Museum of Man, 1979.

_____ . "The Traditional Arts of Mennonite Women," *Art Magazine* (December/January, 1975), pp. 34-37.

PATTERSON, NANCY-LOU and MICHAEL S. BIRD. *A Germanic Flavour: Folk Art of the Region and Other Germanic Settlements of Canada.* Kitchener: Kitchener-Waterloo Art Gallery, 1979.

PETERS, VICTOR. *All Things Common: The Hutterian Way of Life.* Minneapolis: University of Minnesota Press, 1965.

PRICE, ELIZABETH. *Exploring the Bruce: A Driving Tour.* Bruce County Historical Society and Ontario Heritage Foundation, 1980.

QUIMBY, JAN M. G. and SCOTT T. SWANK, *Perspectives on American Folk Art.* New York: W. W. Norton & Co., 1980.

QUIRING, WALTER and HELEN BARTEL. *In the Fullness of Time: 150 Years of Mennonite Sojourn in Russia.* Kitchener, Ontario: Private Printing, 1974.

RAVENSWAAY, CHARLES VAN. *The Arts and Architecture of German Settlements in Missouri.* Columbia, Missouri: University of Missouri Press, 1977.

REAMAN, G. ELMORE. *The Trail of the Black Walnut.* Toronto: McClelland and Stewart, 1974.

REIMER, JOHN C. and JULIUS G. TOEWS. "Mennonite Buildings," in Klippenstein, Lawrence and Julius G. Toews. *Mennonite Memories: Settling in Western Canada.* Winnipeg: Centennial Publications, 1977, pp. 114-118.

REIMER, PETER J. B. "The Church School," in Klippenstein, Lawrence and Julius G. Toews. *Mennonite Memories: Settling in Western Canada.* Winnipeg: Centennial Publications, 1977, pp. 125-127.

REMPEL, JOHN. *Building With Wood.* Toronto: University of Toronto Press, 1968.

ROBACKER, EARL F. *Pennsylvania Dutch Stuff.* Philadelphia: University of Pennsylvania Press, 1944.

ROGER, DIETER. "From German Pioneer Building to 'Bauhaus' and Beyond," *German-Canadian Yearbook* (1978), pp. 135-167.

ROTH, LORRAINE. *Sesquicentennial of the Amish Mennonites of Ontario.* Kitchener, Ontario: Mennonite Historical Society, 1972.

RUPP, DAVID W. "The B. Lent Pottery c. 1836-1841," *Canadian Collector* (May/June 1980), pp. 39-43.

SCHIFFER, HERBERT. *Early Pennsylvania Hardware.* Whitfield, Pennsylvania: Whitfield Press, 1966.

SCHROEDER, WILLIAM. *The Bergthal Colony.* Winnipeg: Canadian Mennonite Bible College Publications, 1974.

SCHUMILAS, CATHERINE and JOAN WILLIAMS. *St. Agatha, 1867-1967.* St. Agatha, Ontario: Private Printing, 1967.

SHACKLETON, PHILIP. *The Furniture of Old Ontario.* Toronto: Macmillan of Canada, 1973.

SHELLEY, DONALD. *The Fraktur-Writings or Illuminated Manuscripts of the Pennsylvania Germans.* Lancaster: The Pennsylvania German Society, 1961.

SPETZ, REV. THEOBALD. *The Catholic Church in Waterloo County.* Hamilton, Ontario: The Catholic Register and Extension, 1916.

STOUDT, JOHN JOSEPH. *Early Pennsylvania Arts and Crafts.* New York: A. S. Barnes, 1964.

STRACHAN, BISHOP JOHN. *Letterbook, 1839-1866.* Ontario Archives, n.d.

SWAINSON, DONALD. *Historical Essays on the Prairie Provinces.* Toronto: McClelland and Stewart, 1970.

TAUBERT, SIEGFRID. "The First German Printers in Canada," *German-Canadian Yearbook* (1973), pp. 71-80.

THIESSEN, HAROLD B. *The Molotschna Colony: A Heritage Remembered.* Kitchener, Ontario: Private Printing, 1979.

TRASK, DEBORAH. *Life How Short, Eternity How Long: Gravestone Carving and Carvers in Nova Scotia.* Halifax: Nova Scotia Museum, 1978.

UTTLEY, V. W. *A History of Kitchener, Ontario.* Waterloo: Wilfrid Laurier University Press (reprint), 1975.

WARKENTIN, JOHN H. *"The Mennonite Settlements of Southern Manitoba."* Toronto, Ph.D. thesis, 1960.

WEBSTER, DONALD B. *The Book of Canadian Antiques.* Toronto: McGraw-Hill Ryerson, 1974.

_____ . *English-Canadian Furniture of the Georgian Period.* Toronto: McGraw-Hill Ryerson, 1979.

_____ . *The William Eby Pottery: Conestogo, Ontario: 1855-1907.* Toronto: Royal Ontario Museum, 1971.

WEISER, FREDERICK S. "Baptismal certificate and gravemarker; Pennsylvania German folk art at the beginning and the end of life," in Quimby, Jan M. G. and Scott T. Swank, *Perspectives on American Folk Art.* New York: W. W. Norton & Co., 1980.

_____ . "Daniel Schumacher's Baptismal Record," *Pennsylvania German Society* (1968), pp. 185-407.

_____ . "IAE SD The Story of Johann Adam Eyer (1755-1837), Schoolmaster and Fraktur Artist, with a Translation of His Roster Book, 1779-1787," *Pennsylvania German Society* (1980), pp. 437-506.

_____ . "Piety and Protocol in Folk Art: Pennsylvania German Fraktur and Baptismal Certificates," *Winterthur Portfolio 8* (1973), pp. 19-43.

_____ . "The Place of Fraktur Among the Mennonites: An Introduction to the Fraktur Collection of the Lancaster Mennonite Historical Society," in *Pennsylvania Mennonite Heritage* (January 1981), pp. 2-9.

WEISER, FREDERICK S. and HOWELL J. HEANEY. *The Pennsylvania German Fraktur of the Free Library of Philadelphia.* 2 vols. Breinigsville: The Pennsylvania German Society, 1977.

WEISER, FREDERICK S. and MARY HAMMOND SULLIVAN. "Decorated Furniture of the Mahantango Valley," *Antiques* (May, 1973), pp. 932-939.

WEISSENBORN, GEORG K. "The Germans in Canada: A Chronological Survey," *German-Canadian Yearbook* (1978), pp. 22-56.

WHITEHEAD, RUTH HOLMES. *Elitekey: Micmac Material Culture from 1600 A.D. to the Present.* Halifax: Nova Scotia Museum, 1980.

WIEBE, PETER T. "Learning Was Hard," in Klippenstein, Lawrence and Julius G. Toews. *Mennonite Memories: Settling in Western Canada.* Winnipeg: Centennial Publications, 1977, pp. 128-150.

WINTEMBERG, W. J. *Folklore of Waterloo County, Ontario.* Ottawa: National Museum of Canada, 1950.

WUST, KLAUS. *Folk Art in Stone.* Edinburgh, Virginia: Shenandoah History, 1970.

ZINGER, JOSEPH A. et al. *New Germany: Maryhill, 1867-1967.* Maryhill, Ontario: Private Printing, 1967.

ZINGER, JOSEPH A. *St. Boniface, Maryhill: 1877-1977.* Maryhill, Ontario: Private Printing, 1977.

# Index

Numbers in ordinary type refer to the text. Those that are italicized refer to plates.